50% OFF Online EMT Prep Course!

Dear Customer,

We consider it an honor and a privilege that you chose our EMT Study Guide. As a way of showing our appreciation and to help us better serve you, we have partnered with Mometrix Test Preparation to offer you **50% off their online EMT Prep Course**. Many EMT courses are needlessly expensive and don't deliver enough value. With their course, you get access to the best EMT prep material, and **you only pay half price**.

Mometrix has structured their online course to perfectly complement your printed study guide. The EMT Prep Course contains **in-depth lessons** that cover all the most important topics, **20+ video reviews** that explain difficult concepts, over **450 practice questions** to ensure you feel prepared, and more than **300 digital flashcards**, so you can study while you're on the go.

Online EMT Prep Course

Topics Included:	*Course Features:*
Preparatory	EMT Study Guide
o EMS Systems o Research	o Get content that complements our best-selling study guide.
Medical Terminology	Full-Length Practice Tests
o Life Span Development o Public Health	o With over 450 practice questions, you can test yourself again and again.
Pharmacology	Mobile Friendly
o Principles of Pharmacology o Medication Administration	o If you need to study on the go, the course is easily accessible from your mobile device.
Assessment	EMT Flashcards
o Primary Assessment o History Taking	o Their course includes a flashcard mode with over 300 content cards to help you study.

To receive this discount, visit them at mometrix.com/university/emt or simply scan this QR code with your smartphone. At the checkout page, enter the discount code: **EMTTPB50**

If you have any questions or concerns, please contact them at support@mometrix.com.

SCAN HERE

FREE Test Taking Tips DVD Offer

To help us better serve you, we have developed a Test Taking Tips DVD that we would like to give you for FREE. **This DVD covers world-class test taking tips that you can use to be even more successful when you are taking your test.**

All that we ask is that you email us your feedback about your study guide. Please let us know what you thought about it – whether that is good, bad or indifferent.

To get your **FREE Test Taking Tips DVD**, email freedvd@studyguideteam.com with "FREE DVD" in the subject line and the following information in the body of the email:

    a. The title of your study guide.

    b. Your product rating on a scale of 1-5, with 5 being the highest rating.

    c. Your feedback about the study guide. What did you think of it?

    d. Your full name and shipping address to send your free DVD.

If you have any questions or concerns, please don't hesitate to contact us at freedvd@studyguideteam.com.

Thanks again!

EMT Prep Book

NREMT Study Guide Exam Review with Practice Test Questions [6th Edition]

Joshua Rueda

Written and edited by TPB Publishing.

TPB Publishing is not associated with or endorsed by any official testing organization. TPB Publishing is a publisher of unofficial educational products. All test and organization names are trademarks of their respective owners. Content in this book is included for utilitarian purposes only and does not constitute an endorsement by TPB Publishing of any particular point of view.

Interested in buying more than 10 copies of our product? Contact us about bulk discounts:
bulkorders@studyguideteam.com

ISBN 13: 9781637756591
ISBN 10: 1637756593

Table of Contents

Welcome

Dear Reader,

Welcome to your new Test Prep Books study guide! We are pleased that you chose us to help you prepare for your exam. There are many study options to choose from, and we appreciate you choosing us. Studying can be a daunting task, but we have designed a smart, effective study guide to help prepare you for what lies ahead.

Whether you're a parent helping your child learn and grow, a high school student working hard to get into your dream college, or a nursing student studying for a complex exam, we want to help give you the tools you need to succeed. We hope this study guide gives you the skills and the confidence to thrive, and we can't thank you enough for allowing us to be part of your journey.

In an effort to continue to improve our products, we welcome feedback from our customers. We look forward to hearing from you. Suggestions, success stories, and criticisms can all be communicated by emailing us at info@studyguideteam.com.

Sincerely,
Test Prep Books Team

FREE Videos/DVD OFFER

Doing well on your exam requires both knowing the test content and understanding how to use that knowledge to do well on the test. We offer completely FREE test taking tip videos. **These videos cover world-class tips that you can use to succeed on your test.**

To get your **FREE videos**, you can use the QR code below or email freevideos@studyguideteam.com with "Free Videos" in the subject line and the following information in the body of the email:

   a. The title of your product
   b. Your product rating on a scale of 1-5, with 5 being the highest
   c. Your feedback about the product

If you have any questions or concerns, please don't hesitate to contact us at info@studyguideteam.com.

1

Quick Overview

As you draw closer to taking your exam, effective preparation becomes more and more important. Thankfully, you have this study guide to help you get ready. Use this guide to help keep your studying on track and refer to it often.

This study guide contains several key sections that will help you be successful on your exam. The guide contains tips for what you should do the night before and the day of the test. Also included are test-taking tips. Knowing the right information is not always enough. Many well-prepared test takers struggle with exams. These tips will help equip you to accurately read, assess, and answer test questions.

A large part of the guide is devoted to showing you what content to expect on the exam and to helping you better understand that content. In this guide are practice test questions so that you can see how well you have grasped the content. Then, answer explanations are provided so that you can understand why you missed certain questions.

Don't try to cram the night before you take your exam. This is not a wise strategy for a few reasons. First, your retention of the information will be low. Your time would be better used by reviewing information you already know rather than trying to learn a lot of new information. Second, you will likely become stressed as you try to gain a large amount of knowledge in a short amount of time. Third, you will be depriving yourself of sleep. So be sure to go to bed at a reasonable time the night before. Being well-rested helps you focus and remain calm.

Be sure to eat a substantial breakfast the morning of the exam. If you are taking the exam in the afternoon, be sure to have a good lunch as well. Being hungry is distracting and can make it difficult to focus. You have hopefully spent lots of time preparing for the exam. Don't let an empty stomach get in the way of success!

When travelling to the testing center, leave earlier than needed. That way, you have a buffer in case you experience any delays. This will help you remain calm and will keep you from missing your appointment time at the testing center.

Be sure to pace yourself during the exam. Don't try to rush through the exam. There is no need to risk performing poorly on the exam just so you can leave the testing center early. Allow yourself to use all of the allotted time if needed.

Remain positive while taking the exam even if you feel like you are performing poorly. Thinking about the content you should have mastered will not help you perform better on the exam.

Once the exam is complete, take some time to relax. Even if you feel that you need to take the exam again, you will be well served by some down time before you begin studying again. It's often easier to convince yourself to study if you know that it will come with a reward!

Test-Taking Strategies

1. Predicting the Answer

When you feel confident in your preparation for a multiple-choice test, try predicting the answer before reading the answer choices. This is especially useful on questions that test objective factual knowledge. By predicting the answer before reading the available choices, you eliminate the possibility that you will be distracted or led astray by an incorrect answer choice. You will feel more confident in your selection if you read the question, predict the answer, and then find your prediction among the answer choices. After using this strategy, be sure to still read all of the answer choices carefully and completely. If you feel unprepared, you should not attempt to predict the answers. This would be a waste of time and an opportunity for your mind to wander in the wrong direction.

2. Reading the Whole Question

Too often, test takers scan a multiple-choice question, recognize a few familiar words, and immediately jump to the answer choices. Test authors are aware of this common impatience, and they will sometimes prey upon it. For instance, a test author might subtly turn the question into a negative, or he or she might redirect the focus of the question right at the end. The only way to avoid falling into these traps is to read the entirety of the question carefully before reading the answer choices.

3. Looking for Wrong Answers

Long and complicated multiple-choice questions can be intimidating. One way to simplify a difficult multiple-choice question is to eliminate all of the answer choices that are clearly wrong. In most sets of answers, there will be at least one selection that can be dismissed right away. If the test is administered on paper, the test taker could draw a line through it to indicate that it may be ignored; otherwise, the test taker will have to perform this operation mentally or on scratch paper. In either case, once the obviously incorrect answers have been eliminated, the remaining choices may be considered. Sometimes identifying the clearly wrong answers will give the test taker some information about the correct answer. For instance, if one of the remaining answer choices is a direct opposite of one of the eliminated answer choices, it may well be the correct answer. The opposite of obviously wrong is obviously right! Of course, this is not always the case. Some answers are obviously incorrect simply because they are irrelevant to the question being asked. Still, identifying and eliminating some incorrect answer choices is a good way to simplify a multiple-choice question.

4. Don't Overanalyze

Anxious test takers often overanalyze questions. When you are nervous, your brain will often run wild, causing you to make associations and discover clues that don't actually exist. If you feel that this may be a problem for you, do whatever you can to slow down during the test. Try taking a deep breath or counting to ten. As you read and consider the question, restrict yourself to the particular words used by the author. Avoid thought tangents about what the author *really* meant, or what he or she was *trying* to say. The only things that matter on a multiple-choice test are the words that are actually in the question. You must avoid reading too much into a multiple-choice question, or supposing that the writer meant something other than what he or she wrote.

5. No Need for Panic

It is wise to learn as many strategies as possible before taking a multiple-choice test, but it is likely that you will come across a few questions for which you simply don't know the answer. In this situation, avoid panicking. Because most multiple-choice tests include dozens of questions, the relative value of a single wrong answer is small. As much as possible, you should compartmentalize each question on a multiple-choice test. In other words, you should not allow your feelings about one question to affect your success on the others. When you find a question that you either don't understand or don't know how to answer, just take a deep breath and do your best. Read the entire question slowly and carefully. Try rephrasing the question a couple of different ways. Then, read all of the answer choices carefully. After eliminating obviously wrong answers, make a selection and move on to the next question.

6. Confusing Answer Choices

When working on a difficult multiple-choice question, there may be a tendency to focus on the answer choices that are the easiest to understand. Many people, whether consciously or not, gravitate to the answer choices that require the least concentration, knowledge, and memory. This is a mistake. When you come across an answer choice that is confusing, you should give it extra attention. A question might be confusing because you do not know the subject matter to which it refers. If this is the case, don't eliminate the answer before you have affirmatively settled on another. When you come across an answer choice of this type, set it aside as you look at the remaining choices. If you can confidently assert that one of the other choices is correct, you can leave the confusing answer aside. Otherwise, you will need to take a moment to try to better understand the confusing answer choice. Rephrasing is one way to tease out the sense of a confusing answer choice.

7. Your First Instinct

Many people struggle with multiple-choice tests because they overthink the questions. If you have studied sufficiently for the test, you should be prepared to trust your first instinct once you have carefully and completely read the question and all of the answer choices. There is a great deal of research suggesting that the mind can come to the correct conclusion very quickly once it has obtained all of the relevant information. At times, it may seem to you as if your intuition is working faster even than your reasoning mind. This may in fact be true. The knowledge you obtain while studying may be retrieved from your subconscious before you have a chance to work out the associations that support it. Verify your instinct by working out the reasons that it should be trusted.

8. Key Words

Many test takers struggle with multiple-choice questions because they have poor reading comprehension skills. Quickly reading and understanding a multiple-choice question requires a mixture of skill and experience. To help with this, try jotting down a few key words and phrases on a piece of scrap paper. Doing this concentrates the process of reading and forces the mind to weigh the relative importance of the question's parts. In selecting words and phrases to write down, the test taker thinks about the question more deeply and carefully. This is especially true for multiple-choice questions that are preceded by a long prompt.

9. Subtle Negatives

One of the oldest tricks in the multiple-choice test writer's book is to subtly reverse the meaning of a question with a word like *not* or *except*. If you are not paying attention to each word in the question, you can easily be led astray by this trick. For instance, a common question format is, "Which of the following is...?" Obviously, if the question instead is, "Which of the following is not...?," then the answer will be quite different. Even worse, the test makers are aware of the potential for this mistake and will include one answer choice that would be correct if the question were not negated or reversed. A test taker who misses the reversal will find what he or she believes to be a correct answer and will be so confident that he or she will fail to reread the question and discover the original error. The only way to avoid this is to practice a wide variety of multiple-choice questions and to pay close attention to each and every word.

10. Reading Every Answer Choice

It may seem obvious, but you should always read every one of the answer choices! Too many test takers fall into the habit of scanning the question and assuming that they understand the question because they recognize a few key words. From there, they pick the first answer choice that answers the question they believe they have read. Test takers who read all of the answer choices might discover that one of the latter answer choices is actually *more* correct. Moreover, reading all of the answer choices can remind you of facts related to the question that can help you arrive at the correct answer. Sometimes, a misstatement or incorrect detail in one of the latter answer choices will trigger your memory of the subject and will enable you to find the right answer. Failing to read all of the answer choices is like not reading all of the items on a restaurant menu: you might miss out on the perfect choice.

11. Spot the Hedges

One of the keys to success on multiple-choice tests is paying close attention to every word. This is never truer than with words like almost, most, some, and sometimes. These words are called "hedges" because they indicate that a statement is not totally true or not true in every place and time. An absolute statement will contain no hedges, but in many subjects, the answers are not always straightforward or absolute. There are always exceptions to the rules in these subjects. For this reason, you should favor those multiple-choice questions that contain hedging language. The presence of qualifying words indicates that the author is taking special care with their words, which is certainly important when composing the right answer. After all, there are many ways to be wrong, but there is only one way to be right! For this reason, it is wise to avoid answers that are absolute when taking a multiple-choice test. An absolute answer is one that says things are either all one way or all another. They often include words like *every, always, best,* and *never*. If you are taking a multiple-choice test in a subject that doesn't lend itself to absolute answers, be on your guard if you see any of these words.

12. Long Answers

In many subject areas, the answers are not simple. As already mentioned, the right answer often requires hedges. Another common feature of the answers to a complex or subjective question are qualifying clauses, which are groups of words that subtly modify the meaning of the sentence. If the question or answer choice describes a rule to which there are exceptions or the subject matter is complicated, ambiguous, or confusing, the correct answer will require many words in order to be expressed clearly and accurately. In essence, you should not be deterred by answer choices that seem

excessively long. Oftentimes, the author of the text will not be able to write the correct answer without offering some qualifications and modifications. Your job is to read the answer choices thoroughly and completely and to select the one that most accurately and precisely answers the question.

13. Restating to Understand

Sometimes, a question on a multiple-choice test is difficult not because of what it asks but because of how it is written. If this is the case, restate the question or answer choice in different words. This process serves a couple of important purposes. First, it forces you to concentrate on the core of the question. In order to rephrase the question accurately, you have to understand it well. Rephrasing the question will concentrate your mind on the key words and ideas. Second, it will present the information to your mind in a fresh way. This process may trigger your memory and render some useful scrap of information picked up while studying.

14. True Statements

Sometimes an answer choice will be true in itself, but it does not answer the question. This is one of the main reasons why it is essential to read the question carefully and completely before proceeding to the answer choices. Too often, test takers skip ahead to the answer choices and look for true statements. Having found one of these, they are content to select it without reference to the question above. Obviously, this provides an easy way for test makers to play tricks. The savvy test taker will always read the entire question before turning to the answer choices. Then, having settled on a correct answer choice, he or she will refer to the original question and ensure that the selected answer is relevant. The mistake of choosing a correct-but-irrelevant answer choice is especially common on questions related to specific pieces of objective knowledge. A prepared test taker will have a wealth of factual knowledge at their disposal, and should not be careless in its application.

15. No Patterns

One of the more dangerous ideas that circulates about multiple-choice tests is that the correct answers tend to fall into patterns. These erroneous ideas range from a belief that B and C are the most common right answers, to the idea that an unprepared test-taker should answer "A-B-A-C-A-D-A-B-A." It cannot be emphasized enough that pattern-seeking of this type is exactly the WRONG way to approach a multiple-choice test. To begin with, it is highly unlikely that the test maker will plot the correct answers according to some predetermined pattern. The questions are scrambled and delivered in a random order. Furthermore, even if the test maker was following a pattern in the assignation of correct answers, there is no reason why the test taker would know which pattern he or she was using. Any attempt to discern a pattern in the answer choices is a waste of time and a distraction from the real work of taking the test. A test taker would be much better served by extra preparation before the test than by reliance on a pattern in the answers.

Introduction to the EMT Exam

Function of the Test

The National Registry of Emergency Medical Technicians (NREMT) certifies EMTs that meet certain requirements. Among these requirements is that the candidate must pass the NREMT Cognitive Exam. Accordingly, the exam is typically taken by adults who wish to gain NREMT certification, and who have already completed a state-approved EMT course and a psychomotor exam.

EMT Cognitive Exam scores typically are only used as part of the NREMT certification process and not by employers or schools (other than the indirect use of considering the individual's certification status). The exam is used throughout the United States and across all jurisdictions therein.

Test Administration

All EMT Cognitive Exams are administered at Pearson VUE testing centers. The test may be taken at any Pearson VUE center at a date, time, and location convenient to the test taker.

Upon completing an approved EMS education program and meeting the other application requirements, individuals seeking certification are given three chances to pass the EMT Cognitive Exam. If the candidate does not pass on an attempt, he or she may apply to retest fifteen days after the failed attempt. If the candidate does not pass on any of the three attempts, he or she must complete an official remedial training program before applying to take the test again. If the individual completes the remedial training program but fails three more attempts, he or she must complete a state-approved education program all over in its entirety before applying for additional retesting attempts.

In compliance with the Americans with Disabilities Act, reasonable accommodations for individuals with documented disabilities are available for the EMT Cognitive Exam administration. Also, the Pearson VUE test centers at which the test is administered are ADA-compliant.

Test Format

The EMT Cognitive Exam is a Computer Adaptive Test, meaning that the computer program used for the test administration adjusts the difficulty of questions based on the test taker's performance up to that point on the test. On the EMT Cognitive Exam, once the testing software determines with 95% confidence that the test taker either does or does not meet the required standard, the test will end and the test taker will have passed or not passed, respectively. The maximum time allowed for the test is two hours, and the number of questions typically ranges between 70 and 120, depending on how quickly the algorithm reaches a result.

The exam is intended to cover the knowledge needed in all facets of work as an EMT. It is designed based on the National EMS Educational Standards, and not on any state-specific curriculum or material. A specific summary of test content follows:

Topic	Share of Exam	Adult / Pediatric Mix
Airway, Respiration, & Ventilation	18%-22%	85% Adult; 15% Pediatric
Cardiology & Resuscitation	20%-24%	85% Adult; 15% Pediatric
Trauma	14%-18%	85% Adult; 15% Pediatric
Medical; Obstetrics & Gynecology	27%-31%	85% Adult; 15% Pediatric
EMS Operations	10%-14%	N/A

Scoring

The test taker is not given a score, per se, but rather simply reaches a point where algorithms in the testing software determine with sufficient confidence that the test taker does or does not meet the required standard. Each question answered correctly adds to the algorithm's confidence that the test taker is qualified, while each incorrect response does the opposite.

Exam results are not available on the day of the test; instead, they are posted to the test taker's NREMT account about two business days after the exam is completed. Individuals may challenge the results of their EMT Cognitive Exam by requesting a manual exam review in writing within 30 days of completion of the exam and submitting a review fee.

Recent/Future Developments

Beginning in 2015, individuals whose applications are approved must complete the EMT Cognitive Exam within 90 days of receipt of the Authorization to Test. No other recent changes have been announced.

Study Prep Plan for the EMT Exam

1   **Schedule -** Use one of our study schedules below or come up with one of your own.

2   **Relax -** Test anxiety can hurt even the best students. There are many ways to reduce stress. Find the one that works best for you.

3   **Execute -** Once you have a good plan in place, be sure to stick to it.

One Week Study Schedule

Day 1	Airway, Respiration, and Ventilation
Day 2	Cardiology and Resuscitation
Day 3	Trauma
Day 4	Medical, Obstetrics, and Gynecology
Day 5	Operations
Day 6	Practice Questions
Day 7	Take Your Exam!

Two Week Study Schedule

Day 1	Airway, Respiration, and Ventilation	Day 8	Practice Questions
Day 2	Practice Questions	Day 9	Operations
Day 3	Cardiology and Resuscitation	Day 10	Practice Questions
Day 4	Practice Questions	Day 11	(Study Break)
Day 5	Trauma	Day 12	Review Practice Questions
Day 6	Practice Questions	Day 13	Review Answer Explanations
Day 7	Medical, Obstetrics, and Gynecology	Day 14	Take Your Exam!

9

One Month Study Schedule						
Day 1	Airway Management	Day 11	Multisystem Trauma	Day 21	Communication Readiness
Day 2	Ventilation	Day 12	Environmental Emergencies	Day 22	Equipment Readiness
Day 3	Respiratory	Day 13	Emergency Trauma Care	Day 23	Zones of Operations for EMTs
Day 4	Practice Questions	Day 14	Practice Questions	Day 24	Maintaining Medical/ Legal Standards
Day 5	Answer Explanations	Day 15	Answer Explanations	Day 25	Good Samaritan Laws
Day 6	Adult and Pediatric Cardiology and Resuscitation	Day 16	Neurological Emergencies	Day 26	Practice Questions
Day 7	Cardiac System	Day 17	Endocrine Disorders	Day 27	Answer Explanations
Day 8	Cardiac Rhythm Disturbances	Day 18	Toxicology	Day 28	(Study Break)
Day 9	Practice Questions	Day 19	Practice Questions	Day 29	Review Answer Explanations
Day 10	Answer Explanations	Day 20	Answer Explanations	Day 30	Take Your Exam!

Airway, Respiration, and Ventilation

Airway Management

Checking and managing a patient's airway to ensure adequate respiration is the first step in almost all medical emergencies. Without adequate respiration, brain damage or death can occur in under ten minutes. Respiratory distress can quickly escalate to respiratory failure. When oxygen cannot reach the heart, the entire cardiopulmonary system can fail, leading to cardiac arrest. The *"ABCs"* of first-responder treatment consist of *A: A*irway management (ensure the physical air passage is clear enough to allow for oxygenation and ventilation), *B: B*reathing (ensure the patient is breathing autonomously or with the help of oxygen therapy), and *C: C*irculation (ensure adequate blood circulation by monitoring the pulse, controlling bleeding, or performing CPR). Airway management consists of patient positioning, provider positioning, opening the airway, and suctioning.

Before beginning this process in either adult or pediatric patients, a physical assessment should be completed as time allows. This assessment may occur by the EMT, visually and by sound, without the patient even realizing it. The EMT should note the patient's work of breath (i.e. is the patient's breathing shallow or labored, is the patient grunting, wheezing, etc.), skin color and condition (i.e. pale, flushed, clammy, gray), and level of alertness. A patient that is overly lethargic and slow to respond likely is in serious danger. Obtaining respiratory rate, pulse rate, blood pressure, and blood oxygen levels is preferred. The Glasgow Coma Scale (GCS) provides EMTs with an indicator for how aggressive they should be in their interventions.

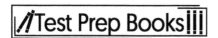

Glasgow Coma Scale

Behavior	Response	Score
Eye opening response	Spontaneously	4
	To speech	3
	To pain	2
	No response	1
Best verbal response	Oriented to time, place and person	5
	Confused	4
	Inappropriate words	3
	Incomprehensible sounds	2
	No response	1
Best motor response	Obeys commands	6
	Moves to localized pain	5
	Flexion withdrawal from pain	4
	Abnormal flexion (decorticate)	3
	Abnormal extension (decerebrate)	2
	No response	1
Total score	**Best response**	**15**
	Comatose client	**8 or less**
	Totally unresponsive	**3**

Adult Patients

Respiratory emergencies in adults are often due to an underlying chronic condition, such as heart disease, nerve disorders, or lung-specific pathologies. Acute conditions that cause respiratory injuries in adults include drug and/or alcohol overdose or lung trauma. While adult respiratory systems are fully developed, health factors such as obesity can affect how the steps of airway management are addressed and other disease conditions can alter the system's functioning capacity.

In the case of respiratory distress in an adult patient, airway management should proceed as follows:

1. Patient Positioning (assuming there is no risk to the patient's cervical spine)

Adult patients should be placed in the supine position with the oral, pharyngeal, and laryngeal axes aligned. To create this alignment, it is likely that padding will be needed under the back of the patient's head; the head needs to be approximately four inches off the ground. Obese patients will likely need a makeshift ramp under their shoulders that is high enough to align the patient's ear canal with their sternum. This type of neutral alignment is referred to as **sniffing position**; it increases air flow by decreasing resistance, and allows for ease of intubation, if needed. A 180-degree supine position can actually hinder airway management success. **Utilizing the Semi-Fowler's position**—a supine position of 30 to 45 degrees—is optimal with adult patients.

2. Provider Positioning

Ideally, at least three providers should be available to support the adult patient. One provider should be positioned at the top of the patient's head, while an assisting provider should be at the right side of the

12

supine patient. The provider at the top of the patient's head maintains the patient's sniffing position, delivers bag valve mask (BVM) ventilation, and assists with CPR/AED processes, if needed. The provider at the right side of the supine patient assists with maintaining patient positioning, relaying any tubing material, and keeping an eye on the airway. The third provider is available for instances where extra handling may be needed, such as in transporting an obese patient, handling side effects of drug or alcohol use (such as loss of motor control or acts of violence) exhibited by the patient, or for rapidly deteriorating patients.

3. Opening the Airway

There are multiple ways to open the airway. The **head-tilt/chin-lift** method tips the head backward by placing one hand near the hairline and using the other hand to leverage the chin distally from the throat. This method is quick, reliable, and especially useful if an object is blocking the throat. This method should not be used if cervical spine injury is suspected.

The **jaw-thrust** method is an alternative, where the EMT places a hand on either side of the patient's face and cups the patient's jaws. The thumbs are placed on the patient's chin while the index and middle fingers are placed just below the temporal bone on the lower jaw. As the thumbs push the chin away, opening the mouth, the four fingers on the lower jaw push upward. This repositions the lower jaw so that the tongue is moved away from the opening of the throat. The EMT will need to hold the jaw in this position while any necessary intubation and/or ventilation occurs. The jaw-thrust was recommended as an alternative to the head-tilt/chin-lift method in instances where cervical spine injury was a concern, but recent studies show that it provides no benefit in this context and should not be considered a viable alternative. Rather, it is recommended to place the patient in the recovery position or use intubation if the cervical spine is at risk.

4. Suctioning

Suctioning refers to clearing any debris from the airway. It can be achieved by log-rolling the patient if vomiting or otherwise turning their head to the side, sweeping the patient's oral cavity with gloved fingers and removing any tangible debris, and through manual or motorized suction techniques. Patients with facial trauma, bleeding, the presence of mucus, or a gurgling sound in the throat will likely need tubal suctioning. Nasal suctioning is usually performed with a soft-tip catheter. For adult patients, suction pressure should be applied for no more than fifteen seconds at a time.

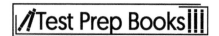
Adult vs. Pediatric Airway

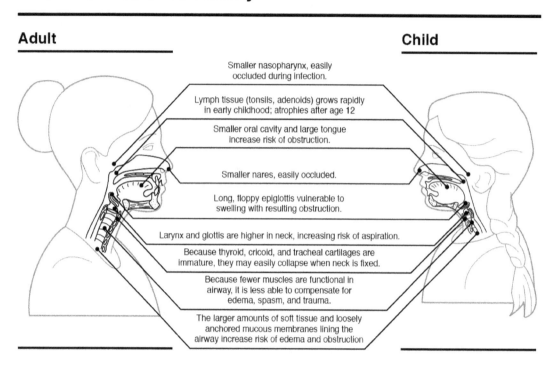

Adult   **Child**

Smaller nasopharynx, easily
occluded during infection.

Lymph tissue (tonsils, adenoids) grows rapidly
in early childhood; atrophies after age 12

Smaller oral cavity and large tongue
increase risk of obstruction.

Smaller nares, easily occluded.

Long, floppy epiglottis vulnerable to
swelling with resulting obstruction.

Larynx and glottis are higher in neck, increasing risk of aspiration.

Because thyroid, cricoid, and tracheal cartilages are
immature, they may easily collapse when neck is fixed.

Because fewer muscles are functional in
airway, it is less able to compensate for
edema, spasm, and trauma.

The larger amounts of soft tissue and loosely
anchored mucous membranes lining the
airway increase risk of edema and obstruction

Pediatric Patients

Respiratory emergencies are the primary reason for pediatric hospital visits and the leading cause of non-congenital death in infants. They are the primary cause for cardiac arrest in children. Pediatric respiratory systems are in a rapid state of development from birth to age two, and many components remain much smaller in size until the child goes through puberty and reaches their full stature in early adulthood. For example, infants and young children primarily respire through the nose, yet the nostrils have a small circumference and are vulnerable to occlusion. The ratio of tongue size to the subglottic region is much smaller in children than in adults; this creates a narrower pathway in the anterior airway, which is also smaller and closer to the tongue. The anterior airway is also cone-shaped; the trachea is short. The physical nature of the oropharyngeal pathway makes it easier for children to choke on larger pieces of food, such as grapes, nuts, or sliced hot dogs, which is why healthcare providers recommend dicing such foods.

Pediatric patients also have less alveoli (the air sacs in the lungs in which the exchange of oxygen and carbon dioxide occurs). They also have less cartilage in the airway and softer rib cages, both contributing to a reduced mechanical ability for lung and chest expansion; breathing primarily occurs via the diaphragm. Finally, children have higher metabolic and oxygen consumption rates. Simply put, this means children require almost double the oxygen consumption of adults, yet the structures and components of the vascular system that assist in pulmonary processes are not yet fully developed. This makes pediatric patients especially vulnerable to respiratory obstructions or distress, and also requires a more detailed level of emergency care.

In the case of respiratory distress in a pediatric patient, airway management would differ from the adult patient as follows:

Patient Positioning (assuming there is no risk to the patient's cervical spine)
In young pediatric patients (three years old and younger), the child should be placed in a supine position with padding under their shoulders to create the sniffing position. In pediatric patients older than three, padding may also be needed under the back of the skull. Proper sniffing position is especially important in pediatric patients due to the large size of their heads, which remains disproportionally larger than their body size through a considerable part of childhood. In the supine position, the chin may be in a closer angle to the chest, effectively obstructing the airway further.

Provider Positioning
Ideally, at least two providers would be available to help the pediatric patient; compared to adult patients, it is unlikely that a pediatric patient would be too large or unruly that three EMTs would be absolutely necessary.

Opening the Airway
The airway can be opened through any method, but jaw-thrust and modified jaw-thrust are often most effective with pediatric patients. Especially with younger pediatric patients, it is important to minimize excessive head and neck movement. However, the pediatric patient's larger tongue size can cause an obstruction; this can be modified by the head-tilt/chin-lift process.

Suctioning
In pediatric patients, the placement and size of tubing (whether it is for suctioning or to provide ventilation) is important. The airway begins between the C3 and C4 vertebrae, so tubing does not need to be inserted as far as is necessary in an adult patient. The pediatric patient's epiglottis is larger and may cause obstruction, and the narrower airway makes it easier to irritate the vagal nerve, which can be innervated through the pharyngeal airway. This can result in bradycardia. Should any of these outcomes occur, they can usually be corrected with BVM ventilation or the use of atropine sulfate. In pediatric patients, suction pressure should be applied for no more than five seconds at a time.

Ventilation

In a medical context, **ventilation** is a component of the cardiopulmonary system. It refers to an inhalation of enough oxygenated air to support metabolic processes at the cellular level, and an exhalation complete enough to remove excessive carbon dioxide from cells and tissues. In a healthy person who is in a relaxed state, the diaphragm manages contractions responsible for the expansion and relaxation of the lungs. In a healthy person who requires more oxygen for functioning (such as in higher altitudes or during vigorous exercise), a number of chest, neck, abdominal, and pelvic muscles contract and relax to increase the rate of ventilation. Artificial ventilation may be required in cardiopulmonary emergencies when airway management techniques are unable to produce sufficient, autonomous breathing in the patient. Adequate artificial ventilation should deliver full or partial tidal volume. Tidal volume should be approximately 10 milliliters of oxygen per kilogram of the patient's body mass.

Adult Patients
Artificial ventilation is commonly utilized in adult patients with a sudden lung injury; however, it is also a common intervention when the patient has a chronic underlying disease to which the acute respiratory event is secondary. For example, an adult patient with sleep apnea may experience a severe cardiovascular event, or a patient with alcoholism may experience apnea when intoxicated. Artificial ventilation can be created through positive pressure or negative pressure. Positive pressure ventilation is the most common type used in emergency settings; it involves creating pressure at the patient's

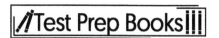

airway to push air into the lungs. Negative pressure ventilation is virtually obsolete, but was commonly used before positive pressure ventilation was introduced in the 1950s.

Common methods of artificial ventilation all require a clear airway utilizing good airway management techniques to ensure successful ventilation. Placing the patient in a supine sniffing position is preferred. Common methods include:

Mouth-to-Mouth and Cardiopulmonary Resuscitation (CPR)

Most commonly recognized as a component of **CPR**, mouth-to-mouth resuscitation involves pressing one's mouth to the patient's mouth, forming a seal, and blowing air directly into the patient's mouth and lungs. It is the first line of defense for non-medical first responders or in instances where ventilation devices are not available. However, non-medical first responders are advised to perform mouth-to-mouth resuscitation with chest compressions. EMTs can deliver mouth-to-mouth resuscitation without chest compressions in cases where chest compressions are not needed. In general, high quality ventilation alone is preferred over CPR unless the patient is in cardiac arrest. If the patient is in cardiac arrest, chest compressions can help the heart deliver partially oxygenated blood to the brain and prevent brain damage or death until the heart can be restarted.

If the practitioner is unable to form a seal with the mouth, a seal can also be made with the nose. Referred to as mouth-to-nose resuscitation, this method can be used if the patient has lower facial injuries, if the patient has vomited, or if the rescuer does not have a barrier available. However, most EMTs will have some sort of barrier available to them. The simplest form is a plain pocket mask that covers the mouth and/or nose, which allows a rescuer to manually blow air in from their own mouth. More commonly utilized mask ventilators employ a bag that sources pressurized oxygen into the patient's lungs.

Finally, if the patient needs CPR, chest compressions are performed alongside ventilation at a rate of 100 to 120 compressions per minute. The area directly under the sternum is depressed approximately five to six centimeters by the heels of the rescuer's hands; this event equals one compression. If providing manual breathing, it should be performed in cycles as follows: 30 compressions are performed, then compressions stop while the rescuer delivers two breaths, and then another 30 compressions are performed.

Bag valve mask (BVM)

Also known as a manual resuscitator, the BVM is the most common ventilation method used in emergency airway management. It is an excellent intermediary ventilation technique when an advanced or long-term ventilation option is not yet available. It is preferable to any type of mouth-to-mouth, mouth-to-nose, or mouth-to-mask method. As its name states, the unit consists of a bag that is attached to an oxygen source on one end, and a pressure valve that connects to a mask for the patient on the other end. BVMs can be used when the airway is open and clear (normally referred to as a "patent airway"), in the instances of respiratory failure, and in instances where intubation is not possible.

The patient should be appropriately positioned; the patient's airway should be opened with an adjunct or laryngoscope, if necessary. The mask should be positioned over the patients nose and mouth; the rescuer should ensure that the mask is the appropriate size to create an adequate seal. The E-C technique should be utilized to hold the mask firmly in place: the thumbs are placed above the lips and the index finger over the chin, creating a C-shape; the remaining fingers are placed under the jaw in an E-shape. If another provide is unable to assist with the BVM, the E-C technique should be performed with just one hand while the other hand is used to compress the bag.

Adults should be ventilated at approximately eight to 12 breaths per minute, receiving approximately seven milliliters of oxygen per breath. This will result in a rate of approximately one bag squeeze every five seconds. Ventilation should be monitored with a pulse oximetry assessment due to higher risk of accidental hyperventilation with this method. The rescuer should note any abdominal distention, which indicates that air is flowing into the stomach. BVM ventilation will be more difficult in patients who are missing teeth, are over 57 years old, have jaw abnormalities, have thick facial hair, or are chronic snorers. BVMs should not be used for exceedingly prolonged periods of time.

Laryngeal Mask Airway (LMA)
The LMA is often an alternative to BVM ventilation, and is becoming more common in emergency settings when a more complicated airway issue is present, such as in cases where patients are unable to be positioned properly. It should not be used in patients with an upper airway obstruction. It should be avoided in patients who have already been on BVM ventilation, are in later stages of pregnancy, who have recently eaten, or who are obese. This ventilation technique greatly reduces the risk for gastric distention. These are best used in contexts where the patient is unconscious, as the device is relatively invasive; in operating rooms, this method requires anesthesia. The LMA is inserted into the patient's oral cavity along the palate into the hypopharynx, which isolates the trachea for concentrated air flow. These devices are often used in conjunction with tracheal tubes.

Demand Valves
These are able to provide 100% of oxygen and use high air pressure and high air flow rates. They are normally used with tracheal tubes.

Tracheal Tubes
This form of ventilating involves placing catheter tubing directly into the trachea that not only maintains the airway, but also ventilates. Endotracheal tubes are most common in emergency and critical care contexts. These thin tubes are inserted through the nose or mouth and guided directly into the trachea; a component of the tube can be inflated to fully seal the trachea. This prevents contamination from bodily fluids such as blood or gastric reflux, which are common obstacles in respiratory emergencies. When used with a demand valve, normal flow rates should be lowered if the need for CPR arises.

Transport
These are automatic ventilators that vary between high and low pressure. They provide consistent air flow at timed, constant pressures. These are useful in situations where the patient requires more care than just airway management and ventilation. If the patient is spontaneously breathing, automatic ventilators are able to adjust to accommodate and assist the patient.

Pediatric Patients
In pediatric patients, the same ventilation techniques can be utilized but certain aspects of delivery will differ. These differences include:

Mouth-to-Mouth and Cardiopulmonary Resuscitation (CPR)
In pediatric patients, especially in those under one year of age, a mouth-to-nose seal should be formed, due to the small size and obligate nasal breathing preference demonstrated by infants. Chest compressions can often hinder progress. If they are absolutely necessary, they should be performed at a rate of 15 compressions per two breaths. Compressions are delivered below the sternum using the index and middle fingers.

17

Bag valve mask (BVM)

Airway adjuncts will likely need to be used with pediatric patients to maintain a patent airway, due to the size of the tongue and throat. Different masks are available for use with children and infants; they are more circular in nature. Bags are also smaller to reduce the risk of hyperventilation. Children should be ventilated at a rate of 16 to 20 breaths per minute. Infants should be ventilated at a rate of 20 to 30 breaths per minute.

Laryngeal Mask Airway (LMA)

As with BVMs, smaller mask sizes exist for pediatric patients, including neonates weighing at least two pounds.

Tracheal Tube

Pediatric patients rarely require the use of an inflated cuff to seal the trachea, as their tracheas are narrow enough to be sealed with a non-cuffed tube. Cuffed tubing may be beneficial if the patient is over eight years old. With all tubing, stabilizing the patients is important. With pediatric patients, however, it is especially vital, as small movements in tube placement can result in a host of undesired effects. Small tubal movements generally do not have the same far-reaching effects in adult patients. Pediatric patient tube size can quickly be estimated using the patient's smallest finger as a parallel. A more precise method to selecting tubing size is to add 16 to the child's age and divide that sum by 4.

Normal vs. Abnormal Breathing

Respiration processes and rate gradually change over the course of the lifespan. They also change in acute situations, such as with illness or trauma. Respiration rate is a common biomarker used to identify pathologies such as general pulmonary dysfunction (such as an obstruction, asthma, infection, or lung fluid), as well as more specific conditions like cancer, cardiovascular disease, cystic fibrosis, and even acute anxiety. Some instances of abnormal breathing are easily visible, such as a patient who is gasping or has discolored, bluish skin. Other instances may be less visible, but can easily be heard by placing a stethoscope over the patient's bare chest, back, and the space between the second and sixth intercostal muscles. A stethoscope can amplify sounds that indicate wheezing, a narrowing of the bronchial tubes, or stridor—a narrowing of the trachea. It can also be used to detect low- and high-pitched sounds in the lungs. A pulmonary function test measures the pace of inhalations and exhalations, as well as the volume of air intake and expulsion in a single breath.

Adult Patients

Normal resting respiration in healthy adults ranges from 12 to 16 breaths per minute. Elderly adults may breathe anywhere from 10 to 30 times per minute. Respiration rates outside of 12 to 25 breaths per minute for adults under 65-years-old is considered abnormal. Common abnormal respiratory conditions that may lead to an emergency situation include:

Apnea

This refers to temporary pauses in breath in which the lung volume stagnates. The musculature involved in respiration temporarily ceases function. Apnea can be caused by distress, laughing, trauma, or neurological disease. It is also a common sleep condition, in which a patient can stop breathing up to 30 times per hour. Without detection or treatment, sleep apnea can greatly tax the cardiovascular system and lead to cardiac events, due to the long periods of time without oxygen circulation. Sleep apnea is often an undetected condition.

Dyspnea

This refers to shortness of breath that may feel like tightness in the chest or impending suffocation. In emergency contexts, it can occur suddenly in patients facing cardiac events, trauma, hernias, asthma, pulmonary embolisms, pneumonia, extreme temperatures or altitudes, or from vigorous activity, especially if the patient is ill-prepared. Obese patients may feel **dyspnea** from mild or moderate activity, which does not necessarily lead to an emergency context. Patients with chronic respiratory, heart, or lung conditions—such as asthma, cardiomyopathy, or chronic obstructive pulmonary disease (COPD)—may also regularly experience bouts of dyspnea.

Hyperventilation

This refers to any context where there is more oxygen entering the blood than there is carbon dioxide being released. It is characterized by deep, often rapid, breathing lasting approximately half an hour. As a result, the patient might experience a pounding heartbeat, vertigo, numbness in the extremities, and chest tightness. Acute **hyperventilation** is often caused by anxiety, panic, or stress; it can often be managed by practicing slower breathing techniques (which may require coaching from someone other than the patient). Hyperventilation can also be caused by serious issues such as high blood glucose levels or aspirin overdoses. More serious acute cases may result in loss of consciousness, but this is relatively rare. Chronic hyperventilation is often associated with lung diseases such as emphysema or cancer. Supplemental oxygen may be needed. If a patient is hyperventilating they need to be seen by a physician and thus require transport to a medical facility.

Hypoxia

This refers to any instance where the body's tissues are receiving insufficient quantities of oxygen, due to dysfunction in any part of the process of transporting air from the nasal and oral orifices to the lungs to the tissues. Generalized **hypoxia** affects the body holistically; it is often seen in high altitude settings or in underwater resurfacing situations where the patient's body fails to adjust to the differences in air pressure. Generalized hypoxia is characterized by lightheadedness, nausea, heart palpitations, and fatigue. In severe cases, these symptoms precede more serious symptoms such as hallucinating, cyanosis, low blood pressure, and potentially, complete cardiac failure. There are both early and late signs of hypoxia. Early signs include anxiety, tachycardia, and restlessness. Late signs include cyanosis; weak, thready pulse; and changes in mental status. Localized hypoxia occurs when only certain tissues stop receiving adequate oxygen. This is characterized by cold, pale, and sometimes hard tissue. In severe cases, necrosis, especially gangrene, may present. Hypoxic patients should be provided with high-flow oxygen using a nonrebreathing mask. The same treatment can be administered to prevent hypoxemia.

Hypoxemia

This specifically refers to hypoxic situations where blood oxygen content is insufficient. Any cardiovascular dysfunction or obstructions will cause some level of **hypoxemia**; these contexts can be triggered by neurological issues, such as strokes that affect the control centers in the brain that manage the frequency and depth at which the body respires. Hypoxemia is characterized by dyspnea, chest pain, abdominal pain and contractions, cyanosis, and chronic coughing.

Anoxemia

This refers to cases of extreme hypoxemia.

Hypercapnia/Hypercarbia

This refers to high levels of carbon dioxide in the blood, which results from poor carbon dioxide expulsion or low oxygen inhalation. When this occurs, the brain normally commands pulmonary

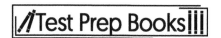

responses leading to hyperventilation. If this doesn't occur, hypercapnia can be deadly. This condition is characterized by elevated blood pressure, flushed skin, twitching, excessive muscle contraction, confusion, lethargy, and headache. Severe cases may lead to convulsions.

Pediatric Patients

Normal resting respiration in healthy children changes as the child ages. Newborns to six-month-old infants will take between 30 to 60 breaths per minute. Six-month-old to 12-month-old infants will take between 24 to 30 breaths per minute. Children between the ages of one year and five years old will take between 20 to 30 breaths per minute. Children between the ages of six and twelve years old will display respiration rates similar to an adult, breathing between 12 and 20 times per minute. In newborns, infants, and toddlers, normal breathing can sound much different than that of an older child or adult. Coughing, choking, and whistling sounds can be normal at this age, but are concerning if they occur for successive and prolonged periods of time, are deep and raspy in nature, sound like a bark, or if the baby looks visibly distressed. Children with diagnosed asthma may know how to manage symptoms with an inhaler. However, if the child has severe wheezing, chest pain, feels flush or faint, cannot clear their throat, cannot stop coughing, or is unable to talk or stand, it is an emergency situation.

Signs of abnormal, and potentially dangerous, respiration problems include:

Hyperventilation

Over 60 breaths per minute is cause for concern. Bouts of rapid breathing, especially in newborns and infants, is common but usually doesn't exceed 40 breaths per minute. This can occur in overheated or stressed babies. Breathing rates greater than 40 breaths per minute may be due to fluid in the lungs or the beginning of pneumonia, which can be fatal at this young age. In older children, hyperventilation that seems to be occurring without the child engaging in physical exertion proportional to such effort is concerning.

Hypoxia

This condition may be seen in premature newborns, and is potentially life-threatening. If a baby is not receiving adequate air intake, he or she may exhibit flared nostrils, a depressed chest, and a bloated belly.

Hypercarbia/Hypercapnia

This condition is believed to be a contributing factor in sudden infant death syndrome (SIDS). Infants may rebreathe carbon dioxide (if they sleep on their stomach or under a blanket, for example) or may not have developed the reflex or neck strength to hyperventilate or turn their head in the context of hypercarbia.

Physical Changes

Bluish, pale, and cold skin and lips are a sign of an emergency. Any instance where a pediatric patient's chest and abdomen are not level with one another (one is depressed while the other is distended, similar to the angle of a seesaw) is also a sign of an emergency.

Respiratory Distress

Respiratory distress refers to any difficulty in breathing, even when adequate respiratory rates and tidal volume are present. This difficulty can be due to physiological or psychological reasons. Delivering

oxygen in this situation prevents instances of respiratory distress from progressing further, often by relieving the burden of compensatory breathing by the patient.

Adult Patients

In all respiratory emergencies, the order of assessment for adult patients is as follows:

- Initial Assessment: Begins when the patient is in view. The rescuer should survey the environment for safety.

- Airway, Breathing, and Circulation (ABC) Assessment: The rescuer should determine if the patient seems to have adequate circulation (i.e., not experiencing a cardiac event), an open airway, and is breathing. If the patient is able to talk, the EMT should ask the patient if he or she feels hot, feverish, or clammy. Loss of consciousness, inability to breathe, and bluish skin require immediate attention to prevent a cardiac event.

- Assess Work of Breathing (WOB): The rescuer should notice the effort required for the patient to breathe. The inability to speak, lie flat, or maintain consciousness requires immediate attention. In emergency settings, EMTs should take special care with auscultation and assessing the details of distress. For example, a patient may have labored breathing, but noticing whether the patient is struggling to inhale or to exhale can guide the EMT to deliver the best intervention.

Other signs of respiratory distress in adults include:

- Bluish skin, lips, or nails
- Chest pain and tightness, often marked by the patient grabbing at their chest
- Elevated blood pressure
- Feelings of panic or anxiety
- Gasping, wheezing, and ragged sounding breaths
- Hyperventilation
- Rapid breathing
- Visibly labored breathing

Acute Respiratory Distress Syndrome (ARDS) refers to any condition where an injury of the lung prevents it from effectively functioning. Its onset is rapid, sometimes developing with hours. If untreated, it will quickly lead to lung failure. A wide array of causes can trigger ARDS. These include direct lung trauma such as the inhalation of poisonous or noxious vapors, drowning, pneumonia, aspiration, or infection within the lung. These causes can also include indirect lung trauma such as heart failure, blunt force on the head, chest, or stomach, surgeries near the lungs (such as heart bypass surgeries), drug overdose, and sepsis.

It is important to note that these situations may not always lead to ARDS. ARDS is characterized by hyperventilation, a feeling of suffocation, and low blood oxygen levels. The condition is diagnosed through arterial blood gas tests, chest x-rays, or CT scans. It is treated by mechanical ventilation until the lungs heal, and usually requires that the patient receive tubal feeding and hydration until healing is complete. ARDS is a severe condition that often does not result in a complete recovery, with most patients experiencing some level of lung damage. Recovery is an ongoing process that usually takes months or years. Over 40% of ARDS patients succumb to the condition.

Pediatric Patients
In all respiratory emergencies, the order of assessment for pediatric patients is as follows:

Initial Assessment
Begins when the pediatric patient is in view. The rescuer must survey the environment for safety.

Pediatric Assessment Triangle (PAT)
This is a brief assessment lasting under sixty seconds, where the practitioner establishes a relationship (if possible) with the patient and notices any outward physical symptoms without ever touching the patient. The mnemonic TICLS covers the aspects that the practitioner should notice when conducting a PAT: Tone, Interactiveness, Consolability, Look/Gaze, Speech/Cry. Next, the EMT should notice the pediatric patient's breathing and whether it is labored or if any abnormal sounds are present, such as wheezing or gasping. Last, the rescuer should observe the pediatric patient's skin for pallor or mottling. Bluish- or grayish-tinged skin is a late stage of hypoxia in pediatric patients. The PAT is often the first reliable indicator of whether the pediatric patient's airway is open and patent.

Airway, Breathing, Circulation, Disability, Exposure (ABCDE) Assessment
This is a hands-on assessment performed sequentially as listed. First, the airway should be inspected and assessed to see whether it needs to be opened. Then, breathing is assessed. The EMT should count the respiratory rate for 30 seconds and listen to the lungs. Note that an elevated respiratory rate may be due to anxiety and panic that the child feels from the situation. A respiratory rate between 20 and 60 breaths is acceptable. Next, circulation is addressed by noting pulse rate, skin temperature, and blood pressure. Then, the rescuer should note whether any disabilities are present and determine the child's level of consciousness. This can be assessed using the AVPU scale, a descending scale that stands for Alert, responsive to Verbal stimuli, responsive to Painful stimuli, and Unresponsive. The assessment ends by assessing the child's body. This may require exposing the torso, arms, and legs; these should be assessed one part at a time and ideally with the assistance of a trusted caregiver, for the child's warmth and comfort.

Other signs of respiratory distress in pediatric patients include:

- A sunken chest
- Accelerated heart rate
- Cold, clammy, bluish or grayish tinted skin, lips, or nails
- Fatigue
- Flared nostrils
- Loud wheezing
- Rapid breathing
- Stridor
- Poor alertness and inability to focus

Additionally, pediatric patients in respiratory distress tend to lean the torso forward, often propping themselves up with their hands in front of them, to provide extra space for diaphragmatic movement. This is referred to as the tripod position. Consequently, pediatric patients assuming this posture should not be laid down in a prone or supine position. Patients might assume the sniffing position instead, with the head forward and chin and nose up as if sniffing the air.

Infant Respiratory Distress Syndrome (IRDS) is similar to ARDS in that it refers to a rapid onset of deteriorating respiratory function, but the condition relates to pediatric patients under the age of one. It usually occurs in premature newborns due to the lack of fully formed respiratory structures, which prevent complete inhalation and exhalation from occurring. IRDS is the leading cause of death in the first month of life. It is also treated by mechanical ventilation, and sometimes with the administration of glucocorticoids to speed up the infant's lung development. Without effective treatment, IRDS can lead to a collapsed lung, hemorrhage, sepsis, blindness, kidney failure, mental retardation, and/or cerebral palsy.

Respiratory Failure

Respiratory failure refers to any instance where one's respiratory system is unable to provide enough oxygen and remove enough carbon dioxide for the body's cells and tissues to perform life-sustaining metabolic processes. When a patient is in respiratory distress and is unable to compensate for the distress (either on their own or with emergency assistance), it usually leads to respiratory failure. The slowly decreasing levels of oxygen in the blood create a positive feedback loop that eventually diminishes the brain's ability to continue mechanisms—such as rapid breathing—that try to compensate for the lower oxygen levels.

Respiratory failure patients will either be in a state of hypoxemia (type I) or a state of hypercapnia (type II). Type I respiratory failure is more common. These failures are often caused by COPD, pneumonia, asthmatic attacks, pulmonary edemas or embolisms, ARDS, or pulmonary arterial hypertension. Type II respiratory failures are usually caused by COPD, asthmatic attacks, drug overdose, muscular disorders, head injuries, tetanus, or poliomyelitis. Respiratory failure can result from an acute condition (such as choking on a piece of food) or a chronic disease (such as a lung disorder). Acute respiratory failure comes on suddenly and is usually due to an obstruction or the presence of fluid in the alveoli. These types of respiratory failures are the most likely to lead to emergencies; without quick treatment, they can result in death. Chronic respiratory failure is usually the result of a permanently debilitating lung disease, such as emphysema. While this is a serious condition that usually requires continuous oxygen supplementation and lifestyle changes, it is relatively predictable and therefore less likely to suddenly escalate to a life-or-death situation.

Adult Patients
Signs of respiratory failure in adults are similar to those of respiratory distress and include:

- Anxiety
- Confusion
- Loss of consciousness
- Dyspnea
- Sleepiness
- Sweating

Adults with arterial blood oxygen tension lower than 60 mmHg are considered to be in a state of type I respiratory failure. Adults with arterial carbon dioxide tension higher than 50 mmHg are considered to be in a state of type II respiratory failure.

Pediatric Patients

Pediatric patients experiencing respiratory failure show signs similar to those of respiratory distress. These patients are inherently at a higher risk of respiratory distress progressing to respiratory failure. Premature infants, younger infants and toddlers, immunocompromised pediatric patients, and those with anatomic or physiological deficiencies are especially vulnerable. Pediatric patients with a history of chronic disease, especially congenital conditions, are also at an increased risk of respiratory failure. Pediatric patients experiencing respiratory failure will likely require extra airway support, such as through a nasopharyngeal or oropharyngeal airway, and intubation to maintain a patent airway.

After three weeks of age, infant arterial blood oxygen and carbon dioxide tension level requirements are approximately the same as an adult's.

Upper Airway Respiratory Emergencies

Upper airway respiratory emergencies refer to conditions affecting the nose, the nasal sinuses, and the pharynx. It is unlikely that the EMT will need to diagnose the exact condition causing the emergency, and many upper airway respiratory emergencies present in the same manner and require similar interventions.

The most common adult and pediatric upper airway respiratory emergencies are detailed below.

Adult

COPD

This is an umbrella condition that can refer to the presence of chronic bronchitis, emphysema, and/or other pulmonary diseases that all contribute to the progressive deterioration of the lungs' ability to breathe. It is most common in long-term smokers, but can also be caused by prolonged toxic inhalation (e.g., coal miners or factory workers that are frequently exposed to foreign elements in the air).

COPD is characterized by decreased elasticity of the airways and alveoli, deterioration of the walls of the alveoli, inflammation of the airways, and/or overproduction of mucus in the airways. It presents as productive, wet coughing, wheezing, chest tightness, and dyspnea. COPD patients may also have the appearance of a large, barrel chest due to the presence of trapped air in the lungs. COPD's onset is slow, so often the symptoms are initially attributed to something else, such as obesity or heart disease.

Mild and moderate COPD may be managed with anticholinergic bronchodilators (which decrease lung tissue inflammation and mucus production) and lifestyle changes, whereas severe COPD will require ongoing oxygen therapy (usually through a nasal cannula or mask) or a lung transplant. EMTs may be able to help administer prescription bronchodilators as part of the primary intervention process if working with such a patient. Supplemental oxygen should be delivered, but intubation and high flow techniques should be avoided, as they may further inflame the airway. Respiratory emergencies in patients with COPD may result from sudden lung failure, improper disease management, or complications from a common respiratory infection.

Chronic Bronchitis

Bronchitis, an inflammation of the bronchial membranes that can cause narrowing of the bronchioles, is considered chronic when a cough related to the condition (which may originally be diagnosed as an acute case) presents for at least three months within a two-year period. It may also be characterized by sputum. Swollen bronchioles or sputum independently can create an airway obstruction, but the presence of both together increases the risk of a respiratory emergency. In chronic bronchitis cases, the

cells of the upper airway are more likely to become inflamed in response to common allergens or foreign bodies.

Emphysema
This condition is characterized by the breaking down of the alveolar walls. Once these structures degrade, the excess burden placed on the bronchioles causes them to collapse and obstruct the airway. This condition is irreversible.

Epiglottitis
This refers to inflammation of the **epiglottis** and the base of the tongue, which can cause swelling so severe that the airway can become blocked. This condition may start out as a simple respiratory infection or sore throat. Patients often drool excessively as the case becomes more severe. When it leads to epiglottitis that results in a respiratory emergency, primary emergency care should be simply to provide oxygen. In these cases, oxygen should be administered utilizing slower flow techniques, such as with slow bag valve mask ventilation. High flow techniques and manual examinations can further irritate the tongue and epiglottis, and lead to more swelling.

Foreign Body Airway Obstruction (FBAO)
Often characterized by choking, FBAO refers to any blockage in the airway caused by the presence of an unrecognized or unwanted entity. It often occurs when eating too quickly. Elderly patients with neurological disorders or dental problems are vulnerable to this issue. FBAO cases are often not complex situations, but can progress to critical conditions such as loss of consciousness and cardiac arrest within minutes. Mild cases may resolve themselves by involuntary coughing by the patient, but emergency services are often called when the case progresses past that point.

EMTs may attempt to ventilate using a BVM, but if ventilation interventions fail, back blows and abdominal thrusts should be delivered. Five back blows should be administered by hinging the patient's torso forward at the waist, supporting the patient's chest with one hand, and using the heel of the other hand to strike between the shoulder blades. These should be followed by five abdominal thrusts, where the hand on the patient's chest should be brought over the patient's navel. This hand should be made into a fist while the rescuer's opposite hand pushes the fist into the patient's abdominal wall, then upward. The back blows and abdominal thrusts should be stopped immediately if the foreign object becomes dislodged. If ventilation, back blows, and abdominal thrusts fail to improve the patient's condition, or if the patient becomes unconscious, a straight or curved blade laryngoscope can show whether the obstruction still exists in the airway. Forceps can be used to remove the obstruction if it is visible.

Pediatrics
Croup
Croup is a symptom of a pediatric respiratory infection. It is characterized by inflammation and swelling of the entire upper airway, including the larynx, trachea, and bronchioles. It is distinguished by a "barking" cough, due to the swollen larynx; this changes the vibration of the cough's sound as it passes. Most cases of croup are not serious, but if swelling is severe, it can result in an airway obstruction. In emergency cases, croup will need to be treated with humidified oxygen, possibly through intubation.

Bacterial Tracheitis
This refers to an infection of the trachea, which can result in excessive swelling, leading to airway obstruction, low blood pressure and cardiac arrest, sepsis, or pneumonia. It is extremely rare in adults.

25

When it occurs, it tends to do so after a viral respiratory infection. In severe cases, intubation may be required.

FBAO

FBAO cases are most common in children under five years of age, as this demographic often puts items directly into their mouth or fails to chew foods completely. Some foods, such as hot dogs, popcorn, and nuts, can be hazardous to children in this age group as they can easily become lodged in the child's narrow airway. However, even well-supervised children can unintentionally swallow small items such as toy pieces, coins, beads, or hazardous foods. These cases should be oxygenated up to 100 percent. If ventilation does not help the patient, children under 12 months old should be given five back blows followed by five chest thrusts using the index and middle fingers. Children over 12 months should be given abdominal thrusts. Sweeping of the airway should only be conducted with a straight blade laryngoscope and forceps, removing the object with the forceps if it is visible. Otherwise, the foreign object could be lodged further.

Respiratory Arrest

Respiratory arrest refers to the complete cessation of breathing while the heart muscle is still able to function. However, a period of prolonged respiratory arrest will likely lead to a cardiac event. Respiratory arrest is characterized by imminent or presenting loss of consciousness.

Adult Patients

In adults, respiratory arrest is often caused by airway obstruction, neurological events (such as a stroke), drug abuse that inhibits nervous system functioning (such as opioid abuse, alcohol abuse, or sedative abuse), or weakness of the musculature involved in respiration (such as in cystic fibrosis patients). When respiratory arrest lasts longer than five minutes, irreversible brain damage and/or cardiac damage is likely.

Respiratory arrest is usually obvious as the patient has stopped visibly breathing and may be unconscious, but other symptoms include muscular retraction, cyanosis, choking (and potentially pointing toward the neck), and abnormal end-tidal volumes. Treatment includes clearing the airway and re-establishing breath through assisted ventilation. If cardiac treatment is also needed, chest compressions or defibrillation may also be utilized.

Pediatric Patients

In pediatric patients, respiratory arrest is most commonly caused by airway obstruction, especially in infants who are susceptible to nasal blockages. Infants are vulnerable to respiratory arrest without warning. This is attributed to the small size of the nostrils, the fact that infants are obligate nasal breathers for at least six months, and the cone shape of the trachea through pre-adolescence. Symptoms of respiratory arrest in the pediatric patient may include limp muscles, brachycardia, lack of chest and rib movement, and cyanosis. Treatment includes clearing the airway and re-establishing breath, usually through intubated ventilation. Cardiac arrest is highly correlated with respiratory arrest in pediatric patients. If cardiac treatment is needed, chest compressions should be administered immediately.

Lower Airway Respiratory Emergencies

The vocal cords are normally considered to be the physical marker distinguishing between the upper and lower airways. The conditions listed below are common emergency situations affecting the lower

airway. As with upper airway respiratory emergencies, it is unlikely that an EMT will have to specifically diagnose these conditions; emergency treatments in these situations are similar, with oxygen administration serving as the primary course of medical care.

Adult
Asthma
Asthma is normally a chronic respiratory condition, and patients typically are aware of the diagnosis and the means to manage it (such as an inhaler). Occasionally, severe bouts of asthma do not respond to the patient's medication, which can lead to a respiratory emergency. These instances are normally acute and unpredictable, resulting from an external allergen. Adults may also experience emotional asthma, triggered by mental, emotional, or physical stress (such as job problems, a romantic breakup, or overexertion). Wheezing is normally present immediately in patients experiencing an asthma attack, as exhalation becomes a taxing process that can quickly lead to respiratory arrest. Wheezing, followed by an abrupt cessation of wheezing, is an extremely critical development, as this indicates that airflow into the bronchioles has ceased altogether. Even with oxygen supplementation, critically ill asthma patients may not reach adequate blood oxygen levels. Alert and engaged patients should receive CPAP ventilation; unconscious patients should receive slowly-administered BVM ventilation in order to prevent lung injury caused by excess air placement. Oxygen should be humidified.

Acute Pulmonary Edema
Most commonly seen in patients with congestive heart failure, **acute pulmonary edema** is caused by excessive fluid levels in the lungs that block oxygen and carbon dioxide exchange between the alveoli and the capillaries. Non-cardiac instances of acute pulmonary edema usually result from ARDS. CPAP ventilation provides a high enough flow pressure to force gas exchange, but should only be utilized if the patient is conscious, can follow commands, and is still breathing autonomously. Otherwise, a BVM should be used. Patients should be kept upright until hospitalized.

Cystic Fibrosis
This is a genetic disorder that affects multiple organs, but pulmonary failure is the most common emergency situation that tends to result from **cystic fibrosis**. This disease is characterized by excess mucus production. Patients often face repeated lung dysfunction, ranging from excess fluid in the lungs to tissue scarring. Consequently, emergencies can range from pulmonary obstruction cases to complete respiratory failure as the lungs gradually weaken over time.

Toxic Inhalation
This is a broad term that refers to any instance of chemical, gaseous, or other noxious substance inhalation that hinders the lungs' ability to adequately respire and ventilate, or that structurally damages any physical component of the pulmonary system. The inhalation of toxins such as carbon monoxide, cyanide, and natural and/or industrial gases commonly results in the need for emergency services. Visibly hazardous events such as a home fire or chemical explosion can also result in the inhalation of noxious substances. However, even engaging in normally safe activities, such as painting or performing home repairs that require commonly used solvents or glues, can result in emergencies if they're performed in enclosed, small spaces without adequate ventilation.

The resulting consequences from toxic inhalation can vary. Carbon monoxide inhalation, for example, can quickly result in death since it is difficult to detect and also affects hemoglobin's ability to transport oxygen. Milder concentrations of inhaled toxins may result in less severe symptoms such as lightheadedness or nausea, which can alert an individual that a more serious condition is imminent.

27

When providing care to patients affected by toxic inhalation, it is extremely crucial to assess the environment and ensure that EMTs are not exposed to harmful toxins, or that they have the proper safety equipment to deal with such an environment. Treatment for **toxic inhalation** normally involves delivering pure oxygen using a non-rebreather mask.

Pulmonary Embolism

This refers to the occurrence of a blockage in the pulmonary arteries. Although it is usually caused by a clot, it can also result from fat, fluid, or foreign objects in the artery. This blockage prevents adequate blood flow into the lungs. Severity of a **pulmonary embolism** depends on the size of the blockage; larger blockages will lead to highly visible signs of respiratory distress, such as sudden chest pain and dyspnea.

Pediatrics

Asthma

Pediatric patients differ from adults in asthmatic events in that their emergencies are almost always triggered by an external allergen or irritant. It is rare that a non-allergenic event (such as stress) causes an emergency asthmatic event in a pediatric patient. Most emergency cases occur in patients over two years old and will respond to epinephrine treatment.

Respiratory Syncytial Virus (RSV)

Pediatric patients are more vulnerable to viral infections leading to respiratory emergencies. **RSV** is a common, highly transmissible virus that causes inflammation of the lower airways and lungs. While many children experience only symptoms similar to the common cold, RSV in infants can progress to pneumonia. One common sign of RSV in infants is dehydration. The EMT can monitor the airway and breathing, provide supplemental humidified oxygen if needed, and transport the child to the hospital. ALS backup may be needed to provide IV fluids.

Bronchopulmonary Dysplasia

Bronchopulmonary dysplasia refers to a neonatal chronic lung disease, to which premature newborns are most susceptible because their bronchioles are not fully developed. As the newborn's lungs are not developed to fully handle this stress, the patient may experience lifelong respiratory problems, weakness, and infections.

Cystic Fibrosis

See "Cystic Fibrosis" under the Adults section above for a description of the disease. Note that the lifespan for those with this disease tends to be in the 30s, though often younger, so pediatric **cystic fibrosis** patients are common. Children with cystic fibrosis often have symptoms such as wheezing, sinus congestion, a chronic cough with thick mucus, and dyspnea. The EMT can provide suction and oxygen for a patient with cystic fibrosis.

When to Oxygenate and Ventilate

Knowing the appropriate time to deliver supplemental oxygen and assisted ventilation is a fundamental skill for EMTs. Delivering these practices too late can result in poor health outcomes for the patient, but delivering them too early, when they may not be necessary, can also cause patient discomfort and extreme complications. For example, a patient that is suffering from shortness of breath may not be experiencing a respiratory emergency at all, since shortness of breath can result from a number of physiological conditions. Delivering oxygen at a high flow rate during a serious cardiac event such as a myocardial infarction may actually injure the heart muscle. Over-oxygenating can also cause

28

complications in obese patients. Monitoring oxygen saturation throughout the intervention and noticing the movement of the patient's chest and accessory muscles are ways to determine whether oxygen therapy and ventilation are appropriate for the situation. Oxygen therapy devices are attached to oxygen cylinders upon which flow rates and concentration levels can be adjusted by the EMT.

Adult Patients

The average healthy adult has a blood oxygen saturation level between 96% and 98%. In emergency situations, oxygen saturation levels below 94% should be noted, monitored, and may require oxygen therapy. Older adults often have blood oxygen saturation levels below 94%, as this tends to diminish slightly with age. If a patient's blood oxygen saturation level rapidly falls (normally marked by at least a 3% decrease over a 30- to 60-minute period), it likely indicates the need for oxygen therapy. Additionally, if the patient suddenly develops dyspnea that is visibly worsening, especially if they have a history of diabetes or kidney disease, oxygen therapy should be delivered.

The following devices are commonly used in emergency settings:

- **Nasal cannulas**: These deliver oxygen through tubal prongs placed directly into the nostrils at a flow rate ranging from 1 liter to 6 liters of oxygen per minute. This is a lower level oxygen concentration delivery system, delivering oxygen concentrations between 24% and 44%. They can be used in patients that are experiencing mild respiratory distress but are otherwise alert.

- **Non-rebreather masks**: This mask is placed over the patient's mouth and nose and delivers oxygen while transporting the patient's respired breath out of the device, so that it cannot be re-consumed. It is a higher flow and oxygen concentration device, delivering at a flow rate of 10 to 15 liters per minute and at a concentration of up to 90%. This is a good option for patients who are in critical, hypoxic conditions (blood oxygen levels of 90% or lower) but have the physical ability to breathe autonomously.

- **BVM**: This mask is similar to a non-rebreather mask—it is a one-way air flow mask placed over the mouth and nose, but oxygen delivery is controlled by a provider who squeezes an attached bag to release oxygen to the patient. It provides the highest oxygen flow rate, at 15 or more liters per minute, and also delivers oxygen at a concentration of 90% or more. This option is best for unconscious, non-breathing, and critically-hypoxic patients.

Pediatric Patients

The average healthy full-term newborn, infant, or child has a blood oxygen saturation level similar to an adult. It may be anywhere from 95% to 100%. Premature babies normally have blood oxygen saturation levels between 84% and 90%, which is considered moderately hypoxic and requires oxygen supplementation. However, providing oxygen therapy to a newborn should always be delivered at a lower flow and concentration rate. Over-oxygenating at this age can lead to blindness.

Older, conscious pediatric patients may be frightened by oxygen therapy devices or by having these devices near their faces. It is important to keep the pediatric patient calm to prevent the detrimental effects of anxiety from further exacerbating the respiratory emergency. If it seems unlikely that the pediatric patient will accept or maintain the placement of a nasal cannula or mask, a BVM can be gently waved over the patient's face, above the nose and mouth, so that the oxygen supply is available for the patient to inhale. This is called the **blow-by technique**.

Indications and Contraindications of Interventions

There are instances where the interventions that have been discussed in this section should and should not be used.

Manual Airway Management

- *Use of a nasal cannula:* This intervention is indicated in cases where blood oxygen saturation levels are low and when the patient is in a mild state of hypoxia. This intervention is contraindicated if the patient has nasal congestion or obstruction, has facial or nasal injuries, or is unwilling to wear or maintain the cannula.

- *Use of a non-rebreather mask*: This intervention is indicated in cases of moderate to severe hypoxia or respiratory distress. This intervention is contraindicated in patients vulnerable to hypercapnia, who have facial injuries, or who are unwilling or unable to wear and maintain the mask.

- *BVM ventilation*: This intervention is indicated in cases of respiratory failure, when intubation does not work or will not stay, and in cases where both high oxygen flow rate and high levels of oxygen concentration are needed. This intervention is contraindicated if the upper airway is blocked, if the EMT is inexperienced, if there is risk of aspiration or other fluid in the patient's mouth or airway, or if the patient is over 57 years of age, has a beard, is missing teeth, or has maxillofacial deformities.

- *Use of a rebreather masks*: This intervention is indicated in cases of mild hypoxia or respiratory distress where the patient is able to maintain their own breathing. This intervention is contraindicated in cases where the patient is vulnerable to hypercapnia, has fading or loss of consciousness, or is unwilling to wear or maintain the mask.

- *Use of tracheal tubing*: This intervention is indicated if the patient is experiencing a cardiac event, is unable to breathe autonomously, is unconscious, or is in a severely critical, traumatic condition. This intervention is contraindicated in cases where there is maxillofacial trauma, tracheal or pharyngeal blockages, or if there is a possibility that the patient has an injury to the cervical spine. Tracheal tubing may be necessary when spinal injury is present, in which case, the patient's head and neck should be completely stabilized and secured before placing the tube.

Suctioning

- **Endotracheal suctioning**: This type of suctioning is indicated when an artificial airway is in place and if fluid or other secretions are obstructing the tracheal pathway. This type of suctioning is contraindicated if it will aggravate the patient's condition; however, in a true emergency where endotracheal tubing is necessary, there will rarely be an actual contraindication due to the benefit of the endotracheal tubing procedure over the risk.

- **Nasotracheal and nasopharyngeal suctioning**: These types of suctioning are indicated when fluids or other obstructions (such as mucus, blood, food, etc.) are in the nasal-tracheal path or lower airway and cannot be otherwise removed. This type of suctioning is contraindicated if the patient has epiglottitis, croup, head or neck injury, is experiencing a cardiac event, or has trauma to the nasal area (including a bleeding nose).

- **Oropharyngeal suctioning**: This type of suctioning is indicated when fluid obstructs the oral cavity or the upper airway. This type of suctioning is contraindicated in the presence of maxillofacial trauma, if the patient is conscious and gagging, if the patient is able to cough, or if the patient has a foreign body obstruction.

Humidifiers

Humidifiers are used to moisten oxygen used in medical emergencies. They work by delivering sterile mist into the oxygen supply. Humidifiers are always used if oxygen therapy is delivered to the lower airway and/or is delivered through intubation. Humidifiers are often used when supplemental oxygen or oxygen therapy is delivered in arid climates, when the patient requires prolonged supplementation (usually meaning beyond a 24-hour period), or if the patient requests one. High flow oxygen supplementation can feel physically drying and uncomfortable, so EMTs may choose to humidify the oxygen in these instances if the patient is not able to request it.

Some types of respiratory emergencies, such as asthma, indicate oxygen humidification. For example, asthma emergencies should deliver humidified oxygen, as mucus plugs that are present may dry up during oxygen therapy, which can cause additional complications. Some studies have indicated that humidifiers do not increase patient comfort or airway moisture, and that alternative methods may work better for such purposes. These methods include using nasal cannulas with wider tubing (which decreases the pace of the air flow) and ensuring that the patient is sufficiently hydrated.

Humidifiers must be sterilized and dried after every use, as bacteria can easily grow in their warm, damp environments and infect patients.

Partial Rebreathers and Non-Rebreathers

A partial rebreather mask is a unique type of ventilation mask. Rather than allowing the patient's exhalations to completely pass out of the constructs of the mask, a partial rebreather mask stores a portion of the patient's exhalation in an attached bag. The patient "rebreathes" this air, and the flow of carbon dioxide serves to naturally stimulate the lungs. These may be used in less severe respiratory cases, and only when the patient is not at risk of hypercapnia.

Comparatively, a non-rebreather mask is only composed of a one-way flow path. It also consists of an attached bag that collects the contents of the patient's exhalation, but the bag is secured and carbon dioxide does not travel back to the patient. Emergency situations typically warrant the use of a non-

rebreather mask, as these are used to deliver high concentrations of oxygen in critical conditions such as bleeding and cardiac events, respiratory distress and arrest, shock, and trauma. Patients should be able to physically breathe on their own, but require a higher concentration of oxygen than what is naturally available to them.

Venturi Masks

The venturi mask is a high-flow oxygen delivery system that delivers calibrated levels of oxygen. This system mixes air present in the room with a concentration of pure oxygen; this concentration can be precisely calibrated. A venturi mask has holes on either side into which color-coded nozzles can be secured. Each nozzle will deliver a different concentration of oxygen. These can range between 24 and 60 percent, flowing at a rate ranging between four to 15 liters per minute. Venturi masks are typically used in patients with severe lung diseases, and are most commonly seen utilized in COPD patients. COPD patients will require an oxygen concentration delivery between 28 and 40 percent. Additionally, EMTs may choose to use venturi masks when the patient's respiratory ability cannot be gauged, as venturi masks will work exclusive of the patient's respiratory rates and tidal volumes, or when it appears the patient may be experiencing hypercapnia. Oxygen does not need to be humidified when it is delivered through a venturi mask.

Venturi Mask Specifications

Venturi valve colour	Inspired oxygen concentration (%)	Oxygen flow (l/min)	Total gas flow (l/min)
Blue	24	2 - 4	51 - 102
White	28	4 - 6	44 - 67
Yellow	35	8 - 10	45 - 65
Red	40	10 - 12	41 - 50
Green	60	12 - 15	24 - 30

Manually Triggered Ventilator (MTV) and Automatic Transport Ventilators (ATV)

MTVs are also referred to as flow-restricted, oxygen-powered ventilation devices. An MTV delivers oxygen, but has the ability to restrict flow speed. It must be attached to a pressurized oxygen source in order to work. It is important to maintain cricoid pressure when using an MTV due to the relatively high flow rate, which can cause abdominal distention and lung tissue damage if improperly monitored. MTVs

deliver oxygen concentrations up to 100% at a rate of up to 40 liters per minute. These devices are contraindicated in patients that have chronic lung disease, chest injuries, or spine injuries.

ATVs are also powered by pressurized oxygen. They are quite similar to MTVs in function; the main difference is that ATVs are computerized. Ventilation rates can be pre-set and the EMT is able to perform other necessary tasks while monitoring the ATV. ATVs will adjust to the patient's respiratory rate and tidal volume. They are contraindicated in pediatric patients under age five, in situations where the patient experienced lung pressure issues (such as in scuba divers who ascend too quickly), and in patients with a pneumothorax.

Oral and Nasal Airways

Oral and nasal airways are external devices that assist with maintaining an open and patent patient airway. They are flexible and tube-shaped devices that come in a number of sizes in order to accommodate a range of patients.

Oral airways are sized based on the diagonal length of the patient's cheek, measuring from earlobe to mouth. After selecting an oral airway that is closest to this size, the provider will then open the patient's mouth, and slide the curved portion of the airway against the top palate. Once the airway makes contact with the throat, it must be rotated 180 degrees before sliding it into the throat. In a pediatric patient, the oral airway is rotated 90 degrees before sliding it into the throat. The EMT should ensure that the tongue is not blocking the path. In unconscious patients, an oral airway can be instrumental in keeping the tongue down, rather than blocking the upper airway.

Note that oral airways are contraindicated in conscious patients, as they require the patient to have no gag reflex, which is normally only achieved when the patient is unconscious. These devices are also contraindicated in patients with oral or maxillofacial trauma, or if the patient has a foreign body obstruction. If the patient does vomit, the airway will need to be removed, the patient's oral cavity and upper airway will need to be swept and suctioned, and a new, unused oral airway will need to be inserted as long as the victim has not regained consciousness.

Nasal airways are sized by measuring across the cheek the distance from the earlobe to the correlating nostril. They should be lubricated before use, then inserted against the bottom wall of the nostril. Nasal airways should slide in easily. If not, the other nostril should be used. Nasal airways should never be forced into place. These airways are contraindicated only in the event of skull, nasal, or facial trauma.

Note that these types of airways usually are associated with the need to suction, so once the airways are in place, EMTs should monitor patients for secretion build-up or other obstructions.

Pulse Oximetry

Pulse oximetry is a quick, easy, and cost-effective method of measuring and monitoring a patient's oxygen saturation levels. A pulse oximeter is comprised of a sensor that is attached to a small screen that displays its readings. The sensor detects oxygen saturated hemoglobin molecules using photo detection and delivers the reading as a percentage.

The sensor is normally placed on the patient's earlobe, fingertip, or other area where skin is relatively thin. Readings may be affected by bright lights in the area, poor perfusion, a hyperactive/flailing victim, nail polish, swelling of the sensor site, hypothermia, or if the patient is a smoker, has sickle cell disease, anemia, or carbon monoxide poisoning (due to these conditions' affect on hemoglobin). Pulse oximetry

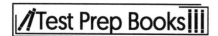
is not 100% accurate when compared to more invasive blood gas measurement techniques, but this tool is still extremely reliable when used to determine if a patient needs oxygen therapy. It is important to note that this method only deals with oxygenation and provides no indicators of ventilation.

Pulse oximetry is based off the oxygen-hemoglobin dissociation curve, which graphs the percentage of oxygen saturation against the arterial pressure of oxygen. As pressure rises, so do oxygen saturation levels. When oxygen saturation levels are low, as indicated by pulse oximetry readings, arterial pressure will also drop, indicating that hypoxic conditions can occur. The lowest functional limit of arterial pressure before respiratory problems occur is 60 mmHg, associated with 90% oxygen saturation levels.

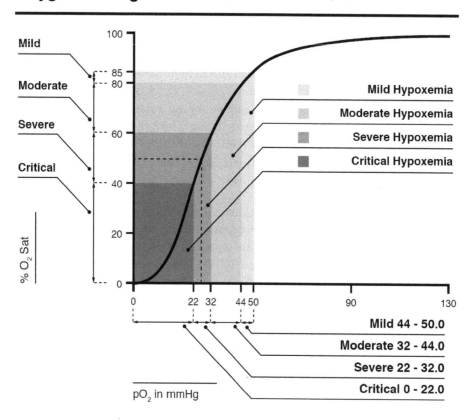

Blood Pressure

Blood pressure can be measured manually or automatically. Automatic readers are most commonly used. Blood pressure is affected by caffeine, stress, smoking, exercise performed just before measuring, temperature, a full bladder, and certain medications. Normal blood pressure is a systolic reading between 90 and 120, and a diastolic number between 60 and 80. The systolic pressure indicates how forcefully blood is traveling against arterial walls when the heart contracts, and the diastolic pressure indicates arterial blood force between heart beats (when the heart is at rest).

Manual

A manual blood pressure monitor utilizes a stethoscope, an arm cuff, and a manually-operated pressure gauge called a sphygmomanometer. With the stethoscope earpieces in, the EMT should find the brachial pulse (toward the inside of the elbow) using their index and middle fingers or the stethoscope. The head of the stethoscope should be placed over the pulse point, and the arm cuff should slide over the stethoscope head, just above the inside of the elbow. The cuff should be tightened to a snug fit. The pressure gauge is attached to a bulb with an airflow valve with a cap. The practitioner should tighten the cap completely before beginning the reading.

When ready, the practitioner should squeeze the bulb. With each squeeze, the cuff will tighten. The provider should keep squeezing the bulb until the gauge reads approximately 150 mmHg and the pulse is no longer audible. Pressure is then released by slowly opening the airway valve on the bulb. This will deflate the cuff and relieve pressure on the patient's arm. When the practitioner begins to hear the pulse again, the pressure reading should be noted as the systolic pressure (top number). As the cuff is further released, the sound of the patient's pulse will eventually no longer be audible. At this point, the pressure reading should again be noted and the value serves the diastolic pressure (bottom number).

Automatic

An automatic blood pressure monitor has a cuff that should be placed above the patient's elbow, then tightened to a snug fit. After powering on the device, the provider should wait until the screen reads "0". Then, the provider should press start, which will automatically inflate the cuff. The device should make an audible sound to indicate that the reading is complete or that there has been an error. It will show the reading or an error symbol on the monitor, then begin to deflate so that the practitioner can remove the cuff or redo the reading.

Practice Questions

1. In the event of an untreated respiratory emergency, how quickly can the emergency result in brain damage or turn fatal?
    a. Within twelve minutes
    b. Within fifteen minutes
    c. Within ten minutes
    d. Immediately

2. The "ABCs" of first-responder treatment are an abbreviation referring to which order of operations?
    a. Airway management, Breathing, Circulation
    b. Access, Breathe, Continue
    c. Administer, Bypass, Call
    d. Airway management, Bypass, Cooperate

3. What is the primary benefit of placing an adult patient in the sniffing position?
    a. It inherently supports the ability for the patient to autonomously take in deep breaths through the nostrils.
    b. It aligns the oral, pharyngeal, and laryngeal axes, decreasing resistance in the airway and allowing for ease of intubation.
    c. It ensures that a cardiac event does not occur.
    d. It stabilizes the cervical spine to protect against injury.

4. What is the name for the sac-shaped structures in which carbon dioxide and oxygen exchange take place?
    a. Kidneys
    b. Medulla oblongata
    c. Alveoli
    d. Bronchioles

5. Which is the most common ventilation technique used in emergency management?
    a. Bag valve mask
    b. CPAP
    c. Negative pressure
    d. Mouth-to-mouth

6. Janet, an EMT, is called to the home of an elderly woman who seems to live alone. Her neighbor stopped by and noticed the woman seemed to be in distress. The woman is conscious, but is having great difficulty speaking. She tries to speak, but gasps and begins violently coughing. Her cough sounds wet. She frantically points to a stack of paper on her counter. Janet rifles through the papers and discovers the woman, named Susie, is 76 years old and was diagnosed with grade 2 COPD the previous week. There are also some over-the-counter cold and flu medications with the paperwork. Janet quickly measures Susie's oxygen saturation with her pulse oximeter, and it reads 87%. What should Janet's next steps be?
   a. Place Susie in the sniffing position and suction out whatever is causing the wet cough.
   b. Call her supervisor.
   c. Immediately defibrillate Susie to prevent the occurrence of a cardiac event, then ventilate using a BVM.
   d. Keep Susie upright, and prepare to administer concentrated oxygen using a venturi mask.

7. Collin is an EMT who is part of a team that is transporting a car accident victim to the hospital. The patient received a severe blow to the head and is not alert. Collin is monitoring the patient's arterial gas tension. The patient's arterial oxygen tension is staying constant at 70 mmHg, and the patient's carbon dioxide tension is staying constant at 60 mmHg. Why should Collin be concerned?
   a. The patient is experiencing Type I respiratory failure.
   b. The patient is experiencing Type II respiratory failure.
   c. The patient is experiencing cardiac arrest.
   d. The patient is a pediatric patient, and susceptible to certain problems in transportation.

8. Chronic obstructive pulmonary disease refers to a collection of lung diseases including which of the following?
   a. RSV and pneumonia
   b. Chronic bronchitis and emphysema
   c. Acute bronchitis and chronic bronchitis
   d. RSV, acute bronchitis, and emphysema

9. Cardiac arrest almost always correlates with respiratory arrests in which type of patients?
   a. Male
   b. Pediatric
   c. Elderly
   d. Obese

10. Tim and Tom are two EMTs treating a patient, Joe, who is in respiratory distress. Joe is conscious and can gesture to respond, but he is having trouble speaking and keeps rubbing the outside of his throat. Tim and Tom open Joe's mouth and notice his tongue and epiglottis are red, inflamed, and very swollen. The opening of Joe's airway is still open, but barely so. What course of action is contraindicated in this case?
   a. Keeping the patient calm
   b. Monitoring Joe's physical appearance
   c. Monitoring Joe's pulse oximetry
   d. Manually sweeping the oral cavity before placing a tracheal tube

11. Which assessment is usually the first reliable indicator of whether a pediatric patient's airway is open and patent?
    a. PAT
    b. AVPU
    c. CAB
    d. WOB

12. Maya, an EMT, is at a scene where an eight-year-old pediatric patient is in respiratory distress. The patient needs to be intubated. What size endotracheal tube should Maya select?
    a. 8 ETT
    b. 1 ETT
    c. The smallest one available
    d. 6 ETT

13. Pediatric patients that are intubated with an endotracheal tube can benefit from a cuffed tube if they are what age?
    a. Over eight years old
    b. Between three years and seven years old
    c. Under ten years old
    d. Newborn patients only

14. EMT Nick is working with a visibly inebriated patient that is drifting in and out of consciousness. The patient is sitting upright, but will slump over for periods of 10 to 12 seconds before returning to consciousness. The patient's oxygen saturation level just fell from 94% to 90%, and Nick is preparing to deliver supplemental oxygen. Nick notices the patient's tongue is causing an obstruction, especially when the patient drifts off. Which of the following actions is contraindicated in this situation?
    a. Placing a nasal cannula into the patient's nostrils
    b. Keeping the patient upright in a tripod stance
    c. Placing an oral airway into the patient's mouth to keep the tongue down
    d. Talking to the patient in a calm, comforting voice

15. Which of the following respiratory conditions may be a leading contributor of sudden infant death syndrome (SIDS)?
    a. Emphysema
    b. Hypercapnia
    c. SARS
    d. Asthma

16. Which of the following contexts can cause a low pulse oximetry reading?
    a. Carbon monoxide exposure
    b. Sickle cell disease
    c. A long-term smoking habit
    d. All of the above

17. What is considered normal resting respiration rate in healthy adults?
    a. 12 to 16 breaths per minute
    b. 30 to 35 breaths per minute
    c. 40 to 45 breaths per minute
    d. 5 to 9 breaths per minute

18. Andy, who lives in Phoenix, Arizona, has been diagnosed with asthma. Which of the following would be a useful therapy technique for him?
    a. Exercising only at nighttime, when it is less hot outside
    b. Moistening supplementary oxygen with a bubble humidifier
    c. Monitoring his heart daily with a home blood pressure machine
    d. Gatorade

19. EMT Donnie arrives at the scene of a respiratory emergency. He notices that the environment is safe and attends to a patient who is lying on the floor. The patient looks to be middle-aged, and his face looks anxious and drawn. Donnie asks if the patient can say his name. The patient tries, but no sound comes out. He opens and closes his mouth a few times, and begins gasping. Donnie has quickly assessed what about the patient?
    a. The patient's WOB
    b. The patient's PAT
    c. The patient's heart status
    d. The patient's kidney status

20. A patient's blood oxygen saturation level correlates closely with what other factor?
    a. Whether or not the patient is following a vegetarian diet
    b. The patient's blood glucose and triglyceride levels
    c. The patient's arterial oxygen pressure
    d. The patient's family history of diabetes

Answer Explanations

1. C: Although it may take longer, lack of oxygenated blood to the heart or to the brain can become fatal as soon as ten minutes from the start of the respiratory emergency. It is almost never immediate, though.

2. A: The rescuer should follow these steps when attending a respiratory emergency. They should make sure that the airway is open and patent, that the patient is breathing, and that adequate circulation is occurring. If not, those are the problems that need to be addressed immediately. The other options listed do not apply or make sense.

3. B: The sniffing position aligns these three axes in a way that best opens the airway. The sniffing position does not relate to the patient's ability to breathe through the nose, nor does it prevent an impending cardiac event from occurring. The sniffing position is often contraindicated in instances where the cervical spine is injured, as it actually destabilizes this area.

4. C: The alveoli are small sac-shaped structures at the end of the bronchioles where gas exchange takes place. The bronchioles are tubes through which air travels. The kidneys and medulla oblongata do not directly affect oxygen and carbon dioxide exchange.

5. A: The bag valve mask technique is the most common method of ventilation due to its ease of use and its ability to deliver high flow rates and high concentrations of oxygen. CPAP is often used in more complex cases. Mouth-to-mouth is typically used when equipment is not available, such as when a nonmedical bystander who has limited first aid experience is the first responder. Negative pressure ventilation is virtually obsolete at this time.

6. D: Venturi masks are often the best course of action when treating COPD patients, and since Susie is able to sit upright, this will assist in keeping her airway open. If Susie is alert while upright, there is no need to place her in the sniffing position in this case. There is not a vital need for Janet to call her supervisor, and defibrillation, which jump-starts a heart in cardiac arrest, is an unnecessary course of action at this stage.

7. B: The patient's carbon dioxide tension is above 50 mmHg, which indicates hypercapnia, or Type II respiratory failure. The patient's arterial oxygen tension is above 60 mmHg, indicating that hypoxia is not yet a concern. There is no indicator that the patient is experiencing cardiac arrest or is a pediatric patient.

8. B: These diseases are referred to as chronic obstructive pulmonary diseases due to their long-term burden on the pulmonary system. RSV is an acute infection that normally resolves itself, and pneumonia may be acute as well. Acute bronchitis does not apply for the same reason, as it normally resolves itself.

9. B: Pediatric patients that experience cardiac arrest almost always do so as a result of first experiencing respiratory arrest, due to the lack of compensatory mechanisms in the pediatric body when they are unable to breathe. Male, elderly, and obese patients may experience cardiac arrest from respiratory arrest, but it is not a highly correlated cause.

10. D: Joe is showing symptoms of epiglottitis, such as his inflamed epiglottis and tongue. Touching these areas or inserting a tube is likely to irritate the area further, and may cause it to swell shut, leading to a complete obstruction. Tim and Tom should keep Joe calm and monitor his appearance and stats as they attend to and transport him.

11. A: The Pediatric Assessment Triangle (PAT) consists of the initial judgment that a provider makes upon seeing and hearing the pediatric patient. It can usually be conducted in under a minute, and establishes a relationship with the patient and takes note of any obvious physical, outward symptoms. The AVPU (alert, verbal, pain, unresponsive) is a scale that measures the child's level of consciousness. CAB (chest compressions, airway, breathing) is not an airway assessment, but an order of actions for resuscitation. WOB (work of breathing) refers to an assessment used for adult patients.

12. D: Sizing a pediatric patient's endotracheal tube is most accurately done by adding 16 to the patient's age and dividing by 4. Since the patient is eight years old, $8 + 16 = 24$ and $24 \div 4 = 6$.

13. A: Patients under eight years of age have tracheal pathways so narrow that an un-cuffed tube will still likely create a barrier seal, which is the benefit of the cuff.

14. C: The patient is conscious, so placing an oral airway is contraindicated as the patient's gag reflex is likely to prevent any benefit of the airway and may even cause the patient to vomit. In this case, since the patient is somewhat conscious with only mild hypoxia, a nasal cannula may work best, and keeping the patient upright and soothed/cooperative may be useful to providing care as well.

15. B: Infants that roll onto their stomachs or accidentally cover their noses are susceptible to rebreathing their exhalations and becoming victims to hypercapnia, since they are usually too weak to roll over or clear obstructions from their nasal paths. Emphysema is an irreversible lung disease correlated with smoking, and is normally seen in older adults. SARS and asthma are respiratory conditions, but they are not related to SIDS.

16. D: Carbon monoxide, sickle cell, and smoking (which also introduces some carbon monoxide into the body) affect hemoglobin, which is what a pulse oximeter examines. The actual content of blood oxygen saturation as measured in a more invasive blood gas test may read differently in these cases.

17. A: 30 to 45 breaths per minute would be considered mild to moderate hyperventilation in an adult of any age, and under ten breaths per minute would be considered mild to moderate hypoventilation in an adult of any age.

18. B: Due to the arid climate and the asthma diagnosis, moistening Andy's oxygen would likely be more comfortable for him physically and prevent mucus clots (common in asthmatic patients) from drying up, which can cause complications. Exercising at nighttime may feel better physically, but won't have much of an effect on Andy's asthma. Monitoring his heart rate and consuming sugar and electrolytes will also not have a direct effect on Andy's asthma.

19. A: WOB stands for work of breath, which refers to how hard the patient is laboring to breathe. In this case, Donnie is able to assess that the patient is laboring to breathe. PAT is a pediatric assessment. From this initial visual encounter, Donnie isn't able to gather accurate information about the patient's heart or kidneys.

20. C: A person's oxygen saturation level is closely correlated with their arterial oxygen pressure, as illustrated by the oxygen-hemoglobin dissociation curve. As one increases, so does the other. Blood oxygen saturation level is not directly correlated with any of the other listed options.

Cardiology and Resuscitation

Adult and Pediatric Cardiology and Resuscitation

Cardiology is a component of healthcare focused on the heart, including vascular systems associated with the heart (such as cardiac arteries and veins). **Cardiac arrest** refers to cessation of heart contraction due to a failure of the heart's internal electrical system. Healthcare providers who specialize in cardiology focus on preventive cardiovascular treatments, as well as managing and treating conditions such as cardiovascular disease, cardiac arrests, congenital cardiac and cardiovascular disorders, and cardiac traumas.

Adult and pediatric cardiology are two highly distinct fields, and providers are rarely interchangeable. This is due to the fact that the anatomy and physiology of adult and pediatric cardiovascular systems are different and require different interventions, even when experiencing the same condition (such as cardiac arrest). Most conditions and pathologies in adults differ significantly from the issues that present in pediatric patients.

Pediatric patients are more likely to present congenital heart conditions or respiratory issues that lead to a cardiac event. While adult resuscitative practices in emergency situations usually focus on immediately "jump starting" the heart through chest compressions or defibrillation, pediatric resuscitative practices often center first on correcting respiratory conditions to prevent or diminish the severity of cardiac events.

Cardiac System

The cardiac system's main component is the **heart**, a hollow muscle located in the middle of the chest with four chambers separated by thick walls. The thickest of these walls, the **septum**, runs vertically down the heart and separates it into left and right halves. In a healthy individual, blood cannot flow between these halves. This is important because the septum separates oxygenated from deoxygenated blood. Each half of the heart consists of a top chamber, called an **atrium**, and a bottom chamber, called a **ventricle**. The ventricles are responsible for pumping blood out of the heart. They receive blood from the two atria; in healthy individuals, blood only flows through one-way valves from the atria to the ventricles and cannot flow backward.

The heart works in tandem with the circulatory system; collectively, they are referred to as the **cardiovascular system**. The heart's primary purpose is to act as a pump for blood, moving it through a vast network of blood vessels. Two primary loops, originating from the heart, are responsible for the main circulation of blood through the body. The **pulmonary loop** pumps deoxygenated blood from the heart to the lungs and oxygenated blood from the lungs to the heart. The **systemic loop** takes oxygenated blood from the heart to various tissues throughout the rest of the body. The primary vessels that circulate blood are **veins** (which carry deoxygenated blood), **arteries** (which carry oxygenated blood), and **capillaries** (thin vessels that assist in carrying both types of blood to their final destination and are involved in gas and nutrient exchange at the tissue level).

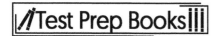

When oxygenated blood enters the heart from the lungs, it first enters the left atrium and flows into the left ventricle through the **mitral valve**. The left ventricle pumps oxygen-rich blood through the **aortic valve** into the primary and largest artery, called the *aorta*. The aorta distributes blood to smaller connecting arteries, which transport the blood further away from the heart to capillaries that are able to deliver oxygenated blood directly to tissues that need it. As tissues use the oxygenated blood, deoxygenated blood is removed by capillaries that transport it to veins.

The two largest veins in the circulatory system are the **inferior vena cava**, which is the final collection point for deoxygenated blood from the lower extremities of the body, and the **superior vena cava**, which is the final collection point for deoxygenated blood from the upper extremities of the body. Both veins end in the right atrium, and the blood flows into the right ventricle through the **one-way tricuspid valve**. The right ventricle pumps deoxygenated blood back toward the lungs to become oxygenated. The blood then returns to the left atrium to begin the loop again. Both the left and right halves of the heart work simultaneously, so that oxygenated blood is distributed from the left ventricle to the rest of the body while deoxygenated blood is distributed from the right ventricle to the lungs with just a single cardiac contraction.

Pulmonary and Systemic Circulation

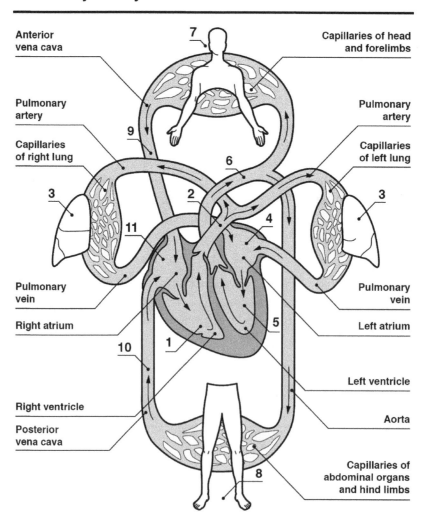

Blood Pressure

As mentioned, **blood pressure** refers to the force of blood exerted on the primary cardiovascular arteries as it is pumped through them. It is considered to be a vital sign; abnormally high or low blood pressure is often indicative of pathology. Blood pressure readings consist of two numbers: the systolic blood pressure written over the diastolic blood pressure. **Systolic blood pressure** refers to the pressure exerted on blood vessel walls when the heart contracts. **Diastolic blood pressure** refers to the pressure exerted on blood vessel walls when the heart relaxes between beats. Blood pressure is easily affected by sudden movement, caffeine or alcohol intake, stress, nervousness, smoking history, overall daily activity levels, and age. Sudden, unanticipated spikes or drops in blood pressure are usually indicative of a critical health status that should immediately be examined and treated. In emergency situations, blood pressure should be continuously monitored for this reason.

Assessing Normal versus Abnormal Cardiovascular Findings in a Patient

When called to the scene of an emergency, an initial cardiovascular assessment may be made by involving the patient or a relative. If possible, the patient's medical history should be obtained. Pediatric patients may have congenital heart defects. These most commonly include improper separation of the chambers (such as atrial septal or ventricular septal defects), improper arterial growth, or issues with the valves in the chambers. In adult patients, EMTs should look for cardiovascular risk factors such as previous heart attacks, strokes, hypertension, high cholesterol, smoker status, obesity, and current medications.

The patient may report abnormal chest sensations, such as pain, tightness, shortness of breath, a sensation of pressure over the rib cage, tingling or numbness in the jaw and back, or heaviness in the chest. Patients who are experiencing abnormal cardiovascular functioning, such as cardiac arrest, may also report digestive problems, hiccups, or stomach pain, as these areas are innervated by the same region responsible for the heart. They may also be able to provide a timeline of when symptoms began. Symptoms that should always be considered indicative of a critical cardiovascular event, even in the absence of chest pain, are nausea, vomiting, dizziness, and loss of motor control and strength. This is especially true in patients with a history of cardiovascular risk factors.

If the patient is unable to communicate appropriately with the **Emergency Medical Technician (EMT)** team, the EMT may need to rely solely on their own findings. The EMT should determine vital signs, including respiratory rate, temperature, heart rate, blood pressure, and appearance of skin. **Tachypnea**, an increased respiratory rate, and cold, greyish skin are both indicative of tissues not receiving enough oxygen, and may be present in patients suffering from stroke or embolisms. Flushed skin may be indicative of an irregular heart rate. Both abnormally high (**tachycardia**) and abnormally low (**bradycardia**) heart rates are indicative of abnormal cardiovascular functioning and often lead to cardiac arrest. Blood pressure often provides the most comprehensive indicator of the patient's overall health status. A high systolic blood pressure reading indicates that the left ventricle specifically is overcompensating, while a high diastolic blood pressure reading shows the blood vessel's elasticity and blockage. Abnormal blood pressure is linked to myocardial infarctions.

It is important to note the patient's overall health and the holistic context of the emergency when assessing vital signs. Endurance athletes, for example, naturally have lower heart rates, as do elderly patients. These do not necessarily mean these patients are suffering from bradycardia.

Chest Pain

Chest pain is a frightening experience, and therefore a common cause for summoning emergency care. However, the presence of chest pain can be attributed to several reasons, ranging from the quickly resolvable to the potentially fatal. For example, the pectoral muscles can be injured or strained during strenuous exercise or improper load bearing, and this can present as chest pain. This is a less urgent cause for concern than many other cases of chest pain and can usually be remedied with simple treatments like icing the affected area and administering over-the-counter pain relief medication.

Chest pain can also result from mental conditions such as high stress, anxiety, and panic attacks. In these instances, the patient may also report feeling unable to breathe properly and the sensation of a rapid heart rate. Patients typically make a full recovery in these cases once the stressor or panic trigger passes, and EMTs can assist in calming and soothing the patient, especially if the patient has a history of any such mental conditions. Because these symptoms are similar to that of serious cardiac events, it is important to rule out critical diagnoses such as cardiac arrest.

Cardiac ischemia is the result of no blood or oxygen reaching the heart, and can (but not always) result in chest pain referred to as **angina pectoris**. This is a temporary but painful experience, involving pressure across the chest, torso, arm, and/or back. It usually occurs acutely—triggered by exercise, excitement, or any other activity that causes an increase in heart rate. It may feel like the symptoms associated with a heart attack; the primary difference is that the symptoms do typically diminish without leading to any **tissue infarction** (an irreversible death of the tissues).

Cardiac ischemia is caused by blockages in the blood vessels (**atherosclerosis**) or hardened arteries (**arteriosclerosis**). Both conditions are the result of poor lifestyle behaviors, such as diets high in processed food, sedentary activity levels, and smoking. However, arteriosclerosis is also a natural byproduct of aging. Both conditions lead to a narrowing of the pathway through which blood can flow; when oxygenated blood is unable to reach the heart in time, cardiac ischemia may occur. Any instance of angina is indicative of cardiovascular disease or deterioration. It increases the risk for a more serious cardiac event. Therefore, if a patient appears to be in cardiac distress and has a history of angina or other cardiovascular events, it is an indicator that a critical intervention will be likely. Prolonged ischemia will likely result in cardiac arrest.

Silent cardiac ischemia, which doesn't present physical symptoms like angina, is common in women and diabetic patients. Over time, this weakens the heart and can lead to heart failure. Often, these patients do not realize they have any risk factors for heart failure and the cardiac event can come as an unfortunate surprise.

Cardiac Rhythm Disturbances

Cardiac rhythm is governed by cardiac muscle itself, which uses electrical conductivity to manage heart rate and chamber pressure. This electrical system is found in the right atrium and called the **sinoatrial node,** which signals to both atria to contract. The impulse then stimulates fibers in the ventricles to contract.

The Heart's Electrical Pathway

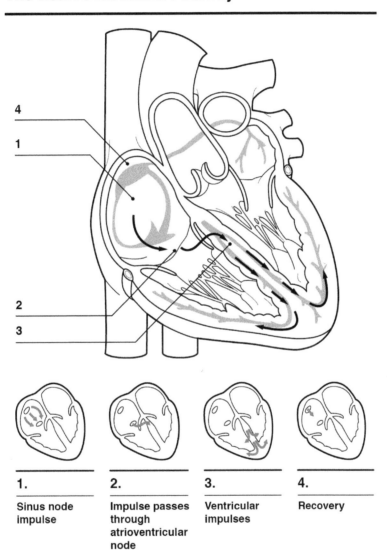

1.
Sinus node impulse

2.
Impulse passes through atrioventricular node

3.
Ventricular impulses

4.
Recovery

Disturbances to a healthy, normal cardiac rhythm are referred to as **arrhythmias.** These can be influenced by both congenital and lifestyle factors. Arrhythmias are characterized by fatigue, chest pain, inability to sweat, hot flashes, and dizziness. The most common congenital arrhythmia is **Wolff-Parkinson-White Syndrome**, a group of physical cardiac defects that lead to a disruption of how the heart's electrical signals function, consequently resulting in a dysfunctional heart rate and chamber pressure.

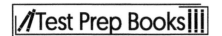

Several external and lifestyle factors can lead to arrhythmias. Some arrhythmias are temporary and not dangerous; for example, some people experience a brief increase in heart rate after drinking caffeinated beverages. Prolonged temporary arrhythmias, such as increased heart rate due to drug abuse, smoking, or constant exposure to high levels of cortisol can be extremely damaging to the heart muscle and its vascular network over time. These arrhythmias can slowly cause weakening of the heart and its vascular network. Heart attacks can also lead to permanent damage of the heart muscle; inactive or scarred areas of the heart disrupt electrical transmission as well.

Arrhythmias physiologically occur in a few different ways. Some affect the functioning of the atrial chambers. These are called **atrial fibrillation**, which is a dysfunction in certain muscle fibers in the atria that causes erratic atrial blood flow. Because the atria are mainly storage chambers for blood, this disruption can cause blood to flow to the ventricles in a disorderly manner. The result can be blood clots, because the blood does not move out of the chamber quickly enough. **Supraventricular tachycardia** refers to increased heart rate in the atrial chambers only, causing a differentiation between the pumping rates of the atria and the ventricles.

Ventricular fibrillation and **ventricular tachycardia** are similar dysfunctions to atrial fibrillation and supraventricular tachycardia, except they occur in the ventricles. They also lead to erratic blood flow and a disorganized, erratic, and fast-paced heart rate. These dysfunctions are most commonly treated with medication. If that does not work, the patient will usually receive an implanted pacemaker device. If surgery is necessary, the patient receives the Maze Procedure, which attempts to disrupt and reset the electrical pathways of the heart. Without proper management, arrhythmias often lead to cardiac arrest.

Cardiac Arrest

Cardiac arrest refers to cessation of heart contraction due to a failure of the heart's internal electrical system. In adults, cardiac arrest may come on without warning. In symptomatic patients, cardiac arrest is marked by chest pain, nausea, vomiting, tingling in the arm and back, and weakness. Patients quickly lose consciousness. For EMTs, a lack of a carotid pulse is the most obvious sign that a patient is in cardiac arrest. Without treatment, cardiac arrest usually becomes fatal in eight minutes or less.

In adult cases, cardiac arrest is most likely caused by **coronary artery disease**. Over time, coronary artery disease causes weakening of the left ventricle to the point where it can no longer pump. It can also block adequate amounts of blood flow to the heart, which disrupts the electrical signaling that allows the heart to pump in an orderly manner. Cardiac arrest can also result from inherited diseases that affect the heart's electrical system.

In pediatric patients, cardiac arrests are most likely due to respiratory complications. Pediatric patients are highly vulnerable to the effects from choking, drowning, neglect, and other respiratory complications, due to the smaller, less developed structure of their respiratory systems. Lack of oxygen quickly leads to cardiac arrest in this population. Additionally, congenital heart issues, traumas (such as infection at birth), and undetected disorders can lead to pediatric cardiac arrests.

For patients who are at especially high risk for cardiac arrest, or those patients who experience cardiac arrest and survive, almost all are treated with medication and some form of surgery. Some patients may receive an implantable cardioverter-defibrillator in their chest. This medical device monitors the heart and will internally defibrillate the heart if an arrhythmia is detected. Others who have high levels of

arterial blockage may undergo coronary angioplasty—a procedure that uses an inflated balloon to open blocked arteries, or a coronary bypass surgery, which reroutes blood flow away from blocked passages.

Stroke-Like Symptoms

A **stroke** results when a blood vessel in the brain becomes blocked or damaged, preventing oxygenated blood from reaching the brain. The risk factors for stroke include taking birth control pills, high cholesterol levels, diabetes, smoking, family history, sitting for long periods of time, and age. A stroke can result in damaged brain cells, leading to long-term loss of motor functions, thought processes, or speech. The specific effects of a stroke will depend on the location within the brain in which it occurred and the degree to which the brain tissue was damaged. It is important to ask patients or relatives how long their symptoms have lasted; treating strokes within three hours may provide the ability to reverse any damage and prevent long-term disability.

Strokes are characterized by an acute headache, numbness in the extremities, vision issues, slurring of speech, and muscle weakness, especially in the face and arms. Several conditions can mimic the symptoms of a stroke, and these conditions are especially common in the elderly. This can lead some patients to downplay the symptoms of an impending stroke, or even cause them to fail to realize that they have had a minor stroke. **Transient ischemic attacks** occur when a blood clot reduces blood flow (and thus oxygen supply) to the brain for a short period of time but then resolves. However, the symptoms can mimic that of a major stroke, although they do not last as long. These events increase the risk of suffering a major stroke. Some patients may "blank" for a few moments when having a minor stroke, and attribute it to forgetfulness or aging. More serious conditions that may cause stroke-like symptoms include migraines and seizures (which can both cause vision loss, speech problems, and muscle weakness), brain tumors, and **Bell's palsy**—a nerve condition that causes sudden, but temporary, paralysis.

Post-Resuscitation Care

Because patients who experience a cardiovascular event are often resuscitated before being admitted to the hospital, and because these patients are at increased risk of another event, post-resuscitation care is a crucial component of preventative care, increasing the patient's life expectancy, and eliminating or limiting cardiovascular and neurological damage. Post-resuscitation care encompasses aspects of monitoring and managing the patient's vitals, blood lipid and glucose panels, oxygenation and ventilation, and rehabilitation after discharge (to also include education for family and caregivers).

Patients who suffer cardiac arrest can benefit greatly from carefully administered therapeutic hypothermia, a practice which intends to reduce the patient's internal body temperature to between 89.6 degrees and 93.2 degrees Fahrenheit. This can be accomplished with ice packs, ice baths, or administering cold fluid through an infusion; the lowered body temperature may need to be maintained for up to 24 hours, depending on the patient and the context of the case. Because cardiac arrest prevents oxygenated blood from reaching the brain, the brain compensates by attempting to perform anaerobic metabolism. However, this causes cellular waste that leads to further oxygen depletion, which can make impending tissue damage worse.

Even if cardiac function is reestablished by the EMT team, any presence of necrotized (dead) brain or heart tissue will result in a flood of immune system activity, which may cause inflammation that the organ cannot handle. As the body's temperature is lowered, brain activity slows considerably. This effectively decreases metabolism, since it requires less oxygen, so it prevents the loop described from

occurring, while still keeping the patient alive. This is a newer practice, and specific procedures are governed by the administrating hospital. Some organizations have not yet adopted this practice. Avoiding hyperthermia is of utmost importance when caring for a patient who has experienced a cardiovascular event.

Once the situation is stable, patients are rewarmed slowly and monitored for fluid loss, electrolyte imbalance, and vasodilation. At this point, it is likely that the patient will be suffering from electrolyte imbalance and abnormal glucose levels, both of which are deterrents to optimal recovery. Both should be consistently monitored through blood testing, because unconscious patients inherently mimic signs of poor electrolyte balance and hypoglycemia. Insulin and electrolyte fluid solutions will likely need to be administered.

Finally, patients may need consistent mechanical ventilation support. Rescuers will need to consistently monitor respiratory indicators such as respiratory rate and the extent to which the patient's breathing is labored. While patients who experience cardiac events are often unable to circulate oxygenated blood throughout their bodies, hyperventilating the patient can cause more harm than benefit. Arterial blood oxygen saturation is easily affected by changes in pressure, and hyperventilation can lead to vasoconstriction in the vessels serving the heart and the brain; counterintuitively, hyperventilation may actually lead to further oxygen depletion of these organs.

Assuming successful transport to a clinical setting and patient recovery, post-resuscitation best practices also focus on treatment of patients for the duration of their stay in the clinical setting. It further involves educating patients about the causes of their condition and how to prevent reoccurrences, and counseling patients' household members, caregivers, and friends in nurturing supportive lifestyle behaviors for the patient.

Hypotension/Hypertension from Cardiovascular Causes

A patient's blood pressure can provide a wealth of insight to the patient's overall health status. Normal blood pressure is a systolic reading of less than 120 mmHg and a diastolic reading of less than 80 mmHg (written as 120/80). A systolic reading of 140 mmHg or higher, or a diastolic reading of 90 or higher, is considered **hypertensive** (high blood pressure). Hypertension is considered the most dangerous risk factor for cardiovascular deaths, and can be a direct cause of heart failure, heart disease, and an enlarged heart. It is also the primary cause of at least 50 percent of stroke incidences.

Prolonged hypertension gradually damages blood vessels in two ways. First, the high force exerted on blood vessel walls damages their smooth inner lining and weakens the cellular structure. Second, the vessels dilate as the body compensates for the extra pressure and tries to lower it, but this dilation causes the vessels to lose their elasticity over time. As a result, they become hardened. Additionally, high blood pressure can be damaging to the cardiac muscle itself. When the vessels are unable to efficiently transport blood, the heart has to pump harder. This can cause a thickening of the left ventricle, which causes it to pump more inefficiently; or, the heart simply wears out to the point of failure. When the actual heart muscle is weakened or damaged, the patient may experience cardiac arrest or heart failure (due to the inability of the muscle to effectively contract), while damaged blood vessels can lead to a heart attack or stroke (due to the inability of oxygenated blood to reach these areas).

A number of factors can cause high blood pressure. Smoking, obesity, a sedentary lifestyle, a diet high in processed foods and trans fats, alcohol abuse, age, kidney disease, sleep apnea, genetics, and

unmanaged stress are the most common causes for prolonged or chronic hypertension. Acute periods of hypertension may be caused by less harmful contexts such as temporary stress and vigorous exercise. However, hypertensive crises are situations when blood pressure suddenly spikes and does not return to an acceptable level. Patients who monitor their blood pressure at home are instructed to call emergency services if they receive a reading of 180/110. This often precedes a stroke or a cardiac event. It can result from ongoing cardiovascular degeneration or from a temporary event, such as overdosing on a stimulant drug. High blood pressure in pregnancy (**preeclampsia**) is usually an emergency that may require immediate bed rest or induction of labor.

Hypotension (low blood pressure) refers to a systolic reading under 90 mmHg and a diastolic reading under 60 mmHg. **Orthostatic hypotension** is a common, harmless drop in blood pressure that takes place when people quickly stand up. It is characterized by a few seconds of lightheadedness. Unless the patient feels prolonged symptoms such as lightheadedness, dizziness, nausea, or fainting, chronic hypotension is not necessarily as worrisome as chronic hypertension. Most hypotension readings are temporary, and can be due to something as simple as dehydration. Many endurance athletes have consistently lower blood pressures, and some medications, alcohol, sedative drugs, and diabetic complications (such as permanent nerve damage) can also cause hypotension. However, some acute instances of low blood pressure are an emergency. Severe blood pressure drops are also seen in instances of hemorrhage and shock. Decreases of blood pressure by more than 10 points is a red flag. In these situations, the patient is at risk of heart failure or cardiac arrest.

Shock

Shock refers to any context where the body is unable to circulate an adequate amount of blood to carry out essential physiological functions. It commonly occurs in emergencies of the cardiovascular system. **Cardiogenic shock** occurs as a result of direct cardiac muscle damage. It often presents due to heart attack or heart failure. **Hypovolemic shock** occurs as a result of heavy bleeding and overall low blood volume, which prevents adequate circulation from occurring. Shock patients will always exhibit low blood pressure. They may also present with cold, clammy, bluish skin; dehydration; shallow breathing; chest pain; and abnormal pulses. Patients in a state of severe shock may be unconscious. Shock patients will likely need to be treated with chest compressions if they aren't breathing and don't have a pulse, suctioning and mechanical ventilation, and/or defibrillation before or during transport. Pediatric patients under three months of age and all immunocompromised patients who appear to be in shock should be treated as septic.

Resuscitation

Cardiopulmonary resuscitation (CPR) addresses cardiac functioning, respiratory assistance, and circulatory issues. It is used in emergency situations where the patient is unresponsive and lacks a pulse or is experiencing agonal breathing. Though CPR employs chest compressions, it will not restart a heart in arrest or reset any presenting arrhythmias, but it may be able to affect electrical impulses in the heart in a way that will respond positively to external defibrillation. The goal of the procedure is to provide enough oxygen to the heart and the brain to prevent long-term damage, until the patient is able to receive more comprehensive treatment.

To administer CPR to adults, rescuers should make sure the environment is safe. Then, if possible, the patient should be laid in the supine position. Chest compressions—conducted by placing the hands on top of one another, interlacing the fingers together, positioning the heel of the bottom palm over the sternum, and pressing forcefully down about five centimeters in depth—should be conducted at a rate

51

of one compression per half second. Airway management and appropriate assisted ventilation should also be employed, but proper chest compressions should take precedence if both cannot be conducted simultaneously.

In pediatric patients, however, airway management and ventilation are often more crucial than chest compressions. Because most pediatric cardiac events occur as a result of a respiratory issue, the respiratory issue should be addressed. Chest compressions can often cause more harm than good, especially if any objects are lodged in the airway. For children experiencing a cardiac event, an **automated external defibrillator (AED)** (rather than chest compressions) should be utilized as soon as possible. If an AED is not available, the heel of one hand should be used to deliver chest compressions at a rate of just under two per second. In pediatric patients under one year of age, just two fingers should be used to deliver chest compressions.

CPR Hand Positioning for Compressions, Infants and Adults

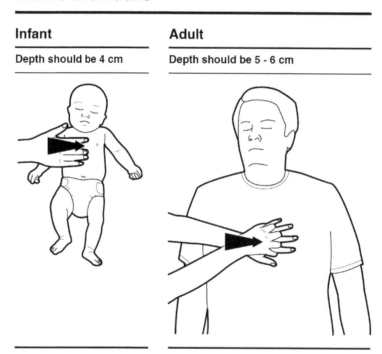

Infant	Adult
Depth should be 4 cm	Depth should be 5 - 6 cm

Automated External Defibrillators (AEDs)

An automated external defibrillator can play a crucial role in preventing cardiac arrest. Found as part of most first responder kits in places where large groups gather (such as community centers, restaurants, hotels, sports venues, entertainment venues, et cetera), AEDs are small, portable, and come with instructions that can be utilized effectively even by bystanders. The primary purpose of an AED is to detect ventricular cardiac arrhythmias and deliver electrical stimulation that resets a healthy cardiac rhythm. It will only work effectively on patients experiencing ventricular fibrillation or ventricular tachycardia. AEDs can be used on pulseless patients; however, they cannot provide any beneficial function to patients whose hearts are already in arrest and are not producing any electrical activity.

Because AED treatment is limited to reestablishing ventricular cardiac rhythms only, cardiopulmonary resuscitation (CPR) may be required beforehand.

In addition to written instructions, AED devices provide audio instruction when powered on. The instructions will inform the user to expose the patient's chest (scissors are included in the kit, in case clothing needs to be cut), remove all metal objects (such as jewelry and undergarments with metal components), and shave visible hair (razors are included in the kit in case for this purpose). Sticky electrode pads, which come in adult and pediatric sizes, are adhered to the patient's chest, and the AED will detect if the patient can receive a shock. If so, the machine will instruct users to stand back, and it delivers shocks through the pads. Most models will administer additional shocks if needed or instruct the user to perform CPR (if shocks will not be of benefit). AEDs will also store data that can be provided to the hospital upon arrival.

AED devices should be regularly checked for proper functioning, battery strength, and expiration of parts.

Acting on Potential Cardiovascular Issues

There are a number of cardiovascular issues that can result in emergencies, and the first line of defense for each of them varies. Knowing distinct symptoms of cardiovascular emergencies can help responders quickly deliver the most effective intervention. Heart attacks are characterized by chest pain, pain in the shoulder, back, and neck, shortness of breath, and collapse. However, some patients (for example, many women) do not show any symptoms and simply collapse. If a heart attack is suspected, adult aspirin may be given. The patient should be placed in a comfortable position and may then require oxygenation, ventilation, and defibrillation. The rescuer should also prepare to provide chest compressions if the AED cannot detect an appropriate rhythm.

Arrhythmias may be the result of a congenital disease or an impending cardiac event due to coronary artery disease or drug abuse. Irregular heart rhythms may be characterized by flushed skin, anxiety, nausea, and vomiting. An abrupt change in blood pressure is also likely. If possible, it is important to first get the patient's medical history (such as if they have any diagnosed arrhythmias or an implanted pacemaker device) and an account of recent events, including when symptoms began. Oxygenation and ventilation should be provided and an AED should be at hand, as defibrillation may be needed. Again, the rescuer should be prepared to deliver chest compressions if the AED cannot detect an appropriate rhythm.

If the patient is experiencing heart failure, he or she may show low blood pressure and may have fluid in the lungs. Such patients may also experience high blood pressure that is unproductive, and may experience chest pain and shortness of breath. The patient should be placed in a comfortable position. However, if the patient is experiencing excessively high blood pressure, he or she should be placed in a seated position, if possible.

If a patient is in cardiac arrest and not exhibiting a pulse, the EMT should begin CPR and prepare to utilize the AED. Patients that are hemorrhaging or appear to be in some sort of shock should be treated with a focus on maintaining adequate blood oxygen saturation.

Practice Questions

1. What is the primary cause of cardiac emergencies in adult patients?
    a. Congenital issues
    b. Poor lifestyle behaviors
    c. Vegetarian diets
    d. Genetic predisposition

2. What is the primary cause of cardiac emergencies in pediatric patients?
    a. Congenital issues
    b. Poor lifestyle behaviors
    c. Vegetarian diets
    d. Genetic predisposition

3. If a patient appears to be experiencing a cardiac event and fluid can be heard in the lungs, what condition are they likely experiencing?
    a. A heart murmur
    b. A heart attack
    c. Heart failure
    d. A stroke

4. CPR and use of an AED is likely the first course of action that responders should take for which of the following patients?
    a. A young man who experienced chest pain and tingling in the arms before losing consciousness
    b. A middle-aged woman who is grabbing her chest, gasping for air, and has a slight greyish tinge to her skin
    c. A pregnant woman with an abnormally high blood pressure reading
    d. A young child who is gasping for air and has a slight greyish tinge to her skin

5. Silent cardiac ischemia is common in which demographic of patients?
    a. Pediatric patients
    b. Female patients
    c. Male patients
    d. Patients over the age of 65

6. What is the pathway of oxygenated blood from the lungs?
    a. Lungs to the left atrium, through the mitral valve into the left ventricle, pumped into the aorta upon contraction, then dispersed to tissues via a network of arteries and capillaries
    b. Lungs to the right atrium, through the mitral valve into the right ventricle, pumped into the aorta upon contraction, then dispersed to tissues via a network of arteries and veins
    c. Lungs to the left atrium, directly to the right aorta, then dispersed to tissues via a network of arteries and capillaries
    d. Lungs to the left atrium, through the septum valve, stored in the left ventricles, then dispersed to tissues via a network of arteries and capillaries

7. What procedure uses a small inflated balloon to treat arterial blockages?
   a. Coronary bypass surgery
   b. Defibrillation
   c. Coronary angioplasty
   d. Laparoscopy

8. What procedure involves rerouting blood flow away from dysfunctional blood vessels to healthier blood vessels?
   a. Coronary bypass surgery
   b. Coronary angioplasty
   c. Yoga therapy
   d. Splinting

9. Therapeutic hypothermia provides which of the following benefits?
   a. It puts the patient to sleep so that rescuers can perform necessary interventions without obstruction.
   b. It reduces a fever in febrile patients.
   c. It decreases the brain's metabolic activity.
   d. It is a cost-effective intervention.

10. Which of the following are risk factors for cardiovascular events?
    I. History of heart attack
    II. History of stroke
    III. History of smoking
    IV. Obesity
    a. Choices I and II
    b. Choices I, II, and IV
    c. Choices I, II, and III
    d. All of the above

11. Pediatric patients under three months of age and immunocompromised patients who appear to be experiencing shock should also be treated for which of the following conditions?
    a. Hypothermia
    b. Sepsis
    c. Tachycardia
    d. Apnea

12. What blood pressure reading should always be considered an emergency?
    a. 120/80
    b. 140/90
    c. 110/70
    d. 180/110

13. What is the primary function of an AED?
    a. To provide oxygen to the brain during heart failure
    b. To detect ventricular cardiac arrhythmias and deliver electrical stimulation
    c. To detect if a patient is about to have a stroke or heart attack
    d. To provide cardiac support to conscious patients only

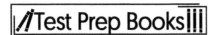

Cardiology and Resuscitation

14. What supporting items are included in an AED kit?
   a. Electrode pads of various sizes, scissors, and razors
   b. Electrode pads for adults only, a bag ventilator, and instructions for performing CPR
   c. Bandages, antiseptic creams, and aspirin
   d. A blood pressure monitor, aspirin, and instructions for performing CPR

15. A sudden drop in blood pressure could indicate that a patient may be about to experience which of the following?
   a. Shock
   b. Hemorrhage
   c. Cardiac failure
   d. All of the above

16. Jason is a 58-year-old male who has a history of cardiovascular disease, hypertension, and periods of high unmanaged stress in his life. After a particularly difficult day, he receives a phone call about a large outstanding bill of which he was not aware. He is about to end the call when he drops his phone and his arm goes limp at his side. Jason's wife hears the crash and comes into the room. She calls his name, but he does not appear to hear her and gazes blankly into the distance. His mouth is slightly agape. Suddenly, he seems to "snap back." He turns to look at his wife and is momentarily confused, but then seems to regain himself and verbally tells her he is okay. What condition is Jason exhibiting symptoms of?
   a. A major heart attack
   b. A transient ischemic attack
   c. Shock
   d. Heart failure

17. Jenny, an EMT, needs to deliver chest compressions to a 10-month-old infant. What is the appropriate hand placement to deliver compressions to this patient?
   a. Heel of one palm over the infant's sternum
   b. Hands stacked, fingers interlaced, with the heel of the bottom hand over the infant's sternum
   c. Two fingers over the infant's sternum
   d. None of the above because a 10-month-old infant should not receive chest compressions

18. What is the primary cause of at least half of all stroke incidences?
   a. Hypertension
   b. Congenital conditions
   c. Smoking
   d. Age

19. Maria is discharged from the hospital after receiving care for a major heart attack. When she returns home, her two adult children arrive to help with physical household tasks that Maria cannot do until she fully recovers. Her husband goes to the grocery store and pharmacy, and he returns with foods to prepare heart-healthy meals that Maria's hospital nutritionist recommended, as well as the heart medications that her physician prescribed. Maria's family is helping with what aspect of her treatment?
   a. Positive psychology
   b. Post-resuscitation care
   c. Federally mandated caregiver requirements
   d. Physical therapy

56

20. Which of the following is a condition that refers to hypertension in pregnancy that may require immediate bed rest or induced labor?
    a. Gestational diabetes
    b. Second trimester hypertension
    c. Preeclampsia
    d. Gestational tachycardia

21. Which structure serves as the electrical stimulator of the cardiac muscle?
    a. The sinoatrial node
    b. The left ventricle
    c. The aorta
    d. The tricuspid valve

22. Which condition involves a hardening of the arterial walls?
    a. Stents
    b. Atherosclerosis
    c. Arteriosclerosis
    d. Plaque bypass

Answer Explanations

1. B: Most cardiac emergencies in adult patients result from poor lifestyle behaviors such as diets high in processed foods and trans fats, smoking, high stress, sedentary behaviors, and obesity. Congenital issues are more likely to cause cardiac emergencies in pediatric patients, especially newborns and infants. Genetic predisposition may cause some cardiac problems, but it is not the cause of most emergencies. Vegetarian diets are not positively correlated with cardiac emergencies.

2. A: Congenital issues are more likely to cause cardiac emergencies in pediatric patients, especially newborns and infants. Most cardiac emergencies in adult patients result from poor lifestyle behaviors. Genetic disposition may cause some cardiac problems, but they are not the cause of most emergencies. Vegetarian diets are not positively correlated with cardiac emergencies.

3. C: Fluid in the lungs, especially when heard in conjunction with low blood pressure, is primarily associated with heart failure. This occurs when the heart is unable to effectively pump blood out of the heart, so blood pools into the lungs. This situation does not occur with the other outcomes listed.

4. A: The young male is exhibiting symptoms of cardiac arrest. CPR and use of an AED is the first course of action for someone who is unresponsive and may be in cardiac arrest. The pregnant woman may require bed rest or induction of labor. The middle-aged woman and the young girl should not have CPR performed, or an AED used, while they are still conscious.

5. B: Female patients are most likely to experience silent cardiac ischemia— a cardiac event that exhibits no distinctive symptoms. Female patients, along with diabetic patients, are less likely to show the telltale signs of a cardiac event, such as chest pain or shortness of breath. They often may just feel tired or collapse.

6. A: This path correctly describes where blood flows after leaving the lungs in order to reach the tissues of the body. The other paths listed are incorrect, out of order, and list fictitious structures.

7. C: This procedure inflates a small balloon inside the blocked artery to break down the blockages and widen the pathway through which blood can flow. A coronary bypass surgery reroutes blood from unhealthy vessels to healthier ones. Defibrillation tries to reset the electrical rhythm of the heart. Laparoscopy refers to surgical procedures that take place in the torso.

8. A: This procedure reroutes blood from unhealthy vessels to healthier ones. Coronary angioplasty inflates a small balloon inside the blocked artery to break down the blockages and widen the pathway through which blood can flow. Yoga therapy and splinting are not able to perform the process that is described.

9. C: Therapeutic hypothermia decreases the body's internal temperature enough to decrease the brain's metabolic activity, so the body requires less glucose. This limits overall cellular waste and prevents tissue damage in the case of a cardiac emergency. The other options listed are not relevant benefits of the practice.

10. D: All of the provided choices increase a patient's chance of experiencing a cardiovascular emergency.

11. B: These patient demographics indicate an increased chance of experiencing sepsis when the patient goes into shock. The patient should be treated for sepsis immediately, in addition to receiving treatment for shock. The other conditions do not apply.

12. D: Patients who monitor their blood pressure at home are recommended to immediately call emergency services if they receive a reading of 180/110. Readings of 120/80 and 110/70 are considered normal blood pressure readings; 140/90 is considered high blood pressure, but not a hypertensive emergency.

13. B: An AED can detect these types of arrhythmia and correct them. It cannot perform oxygenation or detect when a patient is about to have a stroke. It also can be used on conscious or unconscious patients.

14. A: AED kits include electrode pads to use on both adult and pediatric patients, scissors in case patient clothing needs to be cut to place the pads, and razors in case the patient requires shaving for the pads to be placed. AED kits do not include any of the other items listed.

15. D: A drop of more than 10 points in blood pressure reading indicates that any of these conditions are occurring or may be imminent.

16. B: Jason has many of the risk factors for a cardiovascular event to occur. In this context, he shows many stroke-like symptoms similar to those that take place during a transient ischemic attack (small stroke-like episodes from which people appear to fully recover). He would not have shown a recovery had he experienced any of the other situations listed.

17. C: Infants only require light pressure during chest compressions, which they are able to receive. Both full-hand options would provide too much pressure and could be dangerous for the infant.

18. A: Hypertension is the primary cause of at least 50 percent of strokes. Smoking and age do also contribute to stroke risk, but are not as directly correlated or significant as hypertension.

19. B: Discharge care, as well as family education and support, are crucial components of post-resuscitation care and ensuring that the patient prevents any repeat events. In this case, Maria's family is supporting her by helping her in the home and with her lifestyle to prevent future cardiac events and strain.

20. C: Preeclampsia is a severe condition that requires immediate attention. Gestational diabetes is diagnosed in the second trimester and can be managed with lifestyle modifications. Second trimester hypertension and gestational tachycardia are not real conditions.

21. A: This node is the primary stimulator of electrical activity in the heart. The other structures listed play a role in blood flow, but do not deal with electrical stimulation.

22. C: This condition refers to arterial walls losing their elasticity due to age or lack of care (such as from long-term smoking). Stents are medical devices that can be implanted in the body. Atherosclerosis refers to blocked arteries. Plaque bypass is not a real condition.

Trauma

Adult and Pediatric Trauma

Trauma refers to the occurrence of any event where a transfer of energy causes a negative, intolerable effect on an individual's tissues, bones, or organs. Adult and pediatric trauma emergencies are categorized on a scale that ranges from Level 1 to Level 3. This distinction corresponds with the type of trauma center to which the patient should be transported. Along the continuum, Level 1 trauma centers have the ability to provide a wide range of high quality care at any time of the day, while Level 3 trauma centers may have fewer resources. Level 3 cases are typically ones where trauma was experienced, but the scope of the patient's case falls outside of the more severe requirements established for Level 1 and 2 parameters. Depending on the case, Level 3 admittances may later be transferred to a facility of another level. Treatment centers are often designated as serving adult or pediatric patients, although some centers do serve both populations. This distinction is important, as adult and pediatric interventions vary widely, and care providers are rarely interchangeable.

Multisystem Trauma

Trauma patients are characterized by physiological criteria including low systolic blood pressure, low respiratory rate, and a **Glasgow Coma Scale** (a neurological scoring test that determines a patient's level of consciousness) assessment of under 14. Anatomic indications may include amputation; two or more visible fractures; paralysis; any injury to the head, neck, torso, or pelvis; or a depressed chest (often indicative of broken ribs). **Multisystem trauma** refers to any instance where the patient has injuries affecting multiple systems of the body. It is considered one of the leading causes of death, and the number one cause of death in pediatric patients. Most traumatic incidents involve body or organ penetration (such as a bullet wound), toxic inhalation, poisoning, drowning, suffocating, explosions, or crushing from a heavy object. All of these situations can easily affect multiple systems in the body. Head traumas, spinal cord injuries, and aortic injuries are the primary causes of patient fatalities when multisystem trauma is present.

When EMT rescuers arrive at a scene involving a patient who likely suffered multisystem trauma (for example, in major vehicle accidents, which are the most common sites of multisystem trauma cases), their primary goal is to prevent further injury or decline of the live patient. While EMTs will follow usual protocols of addressing any immediate concerns (such as managing the patient's airway, ventilation, and oxygenation; managing symptoms of shock or hemorrhage; and stabilizing any skeletal injuries), it is vital that there is thorough and accurate communication with the receiving hospital in order to prepare the attending medical team. The ability of the EMT team to adequately stabilize the patient and communicate comprehensively with the receiving hospital is positively correlated with how well the patient recovers once in the hospital.

It is also important that the EMT team is aware of problems that can arise from certain traumatic injuries and prepares for the appropriate response. For example, a patient who experiences trauma near the heart is at an increased risk of also experiencing a cardiac event, so the EMT team should be prepared to manage that event. A patient who has lost a limb may be stabilized temporarily, but the potential volume of blood loss could cause symptoms of shock or heart failure. It is important that the EMT team is able to anticipate these changes and can quickly address various emergency situations, as

trauma cases can be unpredictable and volatile in terms of the chain of reactions that can occur within the patient.

Pediatric patients make up the majority of multisystem trauma cases. Almost any time a pediatric patient experiences a head injury, another system is likely to be affected, due to pediatric patients' skull anatomy and brain physiology. Behaviorally, pediatric patients of all ages are more likely than adults to make riskier decisions that increase their chances of experiencing trauma. Pediatric cases can be divided into three classes, where Class 1 multisystem traumas are the most critical and Class 3 multisystem traumas indicate that the patient was able to be stabilized by EMT services before being admitted to the receiving hospital; Class 2 multisystem traumas fall in the middle.

Relating the Mechanism of Injury to Injury Patterns

Different types of trauma correlate with different visible signs and physiological symptoms. Blunt force trauma and penetration traumas most commonly occur as a result of falls, crashes, or violence. The travelling speed before impact of the object that causes the trauma, the mass of the object that caused the trauma, and the distance at which the object that caused the trauma or the patient travelled (for example, in a fall or if being thrown in a collision), the location of the trauma, and any protective factors (such as the presence of an airbag) are all aspects that influence how severe the injury will be.

For example, if a patient wearing a seatbelt is travelling at a low speed in an average mid-sized sedan with functioning airbags runs off the road and hits a small tree, any trauma is likely to be much less severe than a motorcyclist who is not wearing a helmet, traveling at 80 miles per hour, and collides with an oncoming car going approximately the same speed. A patient who is forcefully hit in the head by an assailant is likely to experience more trauma to that area than a patient who slips and bumps their head against drywall.

In response to direct blunt force or penetration, most solid anatomical structures (such as bone) will shatter or crack. Other structures that are filled with air or fluid (such as the lungs, stomach, or blood vessels) will most likely burst or tear.

Vehicular accidents are one of the most common cases for which EMT services will be required. In these cases, knowing the specific way the crash occurred can provide EMTs with clues as to how injury patterns will present. Frontal impacts, where the patient's vehicle is hit head-on, most commonly result in injuries primarily on the upper half of the body (specifically, rib fractures, heart injuries, or aortic injuries) or primarily on the lower half of the body (specifically, pelvic fractures, or knee or hip dislocations). Lateral impacts, where the patient's vehicle is struck on the side, are likely to cause ruptures of organs in the torso area.

These impacts can also cause head, neck, and spinal injuries. Rear impacts, where the patient's vehicle is struck from behind, commonly result in spinal injuries that can range from minor to severe. Rolled vehicles can affect the occupants in unpredictable ways. Motorcycle accidents, however, involve different patterns. If a motorcycle is involved in a frontal accident, the patient is likely to have been ejected from the motorcycle. Depending on where the patient landed, or if he or she was hit by any other objects, the patient can be expected to have cervical spinal injuries, injuries to the organs in the torso, and broken bones. If the motorcycle is hit laterally, patients are likely to experience effects of crush-type injuries—where the area in question becomes compressed. Crush injuries can vary widely in severity, with symptoms ranging from mild bruising that can heal without medical intervention to tissue ischemia so severe that it necessitates amputation of the area.

Environmental Emergencies

Environmental emergencies refer to situations that occur as a result of what is occurring around the patient. Common instances of environmental emergencies include patients suffering from natural disasters, overheating or hypothermia, drowning and diving accidents, or animal or insect bites. In these instances, diligently surveying the scene upon arrival is crucial, as environmental emergencies can affect multiple people, including EMT personnel.

Natural disasters include somewhat unpredictable events like earthquakes, flooding, hurricanes, tsunamis, tornadoes, blizzards, and landslides. Hazards that result from natural disasters include things like noxious fumes, downed—yet live—electrical wires, fires, weakened residential and commercial structures, excessively hot or cold temperatures, and higher than normal instances of motor accidents.

EMT personnel may experience increased exposure to patients' bodily fluids (especially in instances where many injuries occurred simultaneously), and debris management to which they may not be accustomed. As always, EMT personnel should ensure that the scene and conditions are safe before they begin to treat patients. In natural disaster contexts, many large teams of EMTs can be expected to work with other rescue agencies (such as fire and police departments) to effectively help communities. Patient injuries and the necessary interventions can vary widely at the scene. For example, a community that has been hit by a tornado may have patients who need treatment for anything from superficial lacerations, to being struck by lightning, to serious crush injuries. Rescuers should anticipate this level of unpredictability.

When responding to a patient who is suffering from excess heat in some way—elevated body temperature not due to an internal fever, heat rash, heat exhaustion, etc.—such patients will likely need to be immediately cooled. This can be achieved by removing clothing, misting cool water on the patient, fanning the patient, placing cool rags on the patient's body, or administering cool fluids if the patient is able to take them. In severe cases, a water and electrolyte mix may be administered intravenously. Many overheated patients will need pressurized oxygen.

Patients suffering from excess cold should be removed from the source of cold. The patient should be undressed only if their clothing is wet. It is important to note whether the patient is experiencing a localized cold issue or general hypothermia. The area affected should be actively rewarmed only if there is a superficial injury and there is no chance that the area could be affected by the cold again. Otherwise, the area should simply be kept clean and sterile until the patient is admitted. Patients suffering from general hypothermia may need pressurized oxygen as well. The body temperature for mild hypothermia is 90 to 95 degrees Fahrenheit, 86 to 92 degrees for moderate hypothermia, and less than 86 degrees for severe hypothermia. When treating a patient with hypothermia, the intent is to keep the patient from losing any more heat. Warm, humidified oxygen can be delivered to help maintain internal temperature. After removing any wet clothing, blankets should be used to cover the patient, and then they should be transported to the hospital. Hypothermic patients should be handled lightly, since ventricular fibrillation could occur if they are handled too roughly.

Patients suffering from drowning or diving accidents will need a patent airway immediately, followed by cardiopulmonary resuscitation. Conscious patients should receive assisted ventilation.

Patients who have been attacked by an animal or insect should be kept calm. Ice and an antiseptic can be applied to the bite, and the area should be kept stationary. If possible, the animal or insect that caused the attack should be brought to the emergency department as well.

Secondary Assessment Related to Trauma Patients

The primary assessment of a trauma patient follows what is known as the **ABCDE approach**, which stands for Airway, Breathing, Circulation, Disability, Exposure. The goal of this approach is to notice and provide intervention for all conditions that could be considered life-threatening in a short-term period. The ABCDE approach is a systematic process that should be implemented upon contact with the patient (unless the patient appears to be in cardiac arrest), and thereafter at any periods of sudden deterioration (such as a spontaneous blood pressure drop or spike over 10 points).

The **secondary assessment** of a trauma patient takes place after the critical issues discovered from the primary assessments have been addressed and the patient has been relatively stabilized. Depending on the severity of the case, EMT personnel may not always reach the point of conducting a secondary assessment. It may take place later in the hospital by the patient's long-term medical team. These assessments, however, provide a great deal of information about the patient. Most deaths from trauma occur within three time frames: within minutes, within the hour (known as the **Golden Hour**, a period during which effective medical intervention is most likely to reduce or eliminate the possibility of a fatal outcome), or within days or weeks from the event.

If a patient has not succumbed to a traumatic event immediately, most responders will be intervening during the Golden Hour and all information that can be obtained about the patient will only serve to positively influence the patient's outcome. A secondary assessment may include gathering data about the patient's medical history; this information can come from the patient, bystanders, family or friends, or an electronic medical record. It should include items like potential allergies, previous or current medical conditions, and previous or current medications. Additionally, this inquiry can provide information about what led to the traumatic incident.

Next, the secondary assessment focuses on physical aspects of the patient. It includes taking and monitoring vital signs and examining the patient from head to toe. The head should be examined for bleeding from any orifices and any tenderness. The patient's pupils and general alertness of the eyes can provide insight to neurological issues. The neck should be examined for tenderness, but should otherwise be kept stable until admitted to the hospital, due to the inability to see the cervical spine without an x-ray.

The chest should be examined for any depressions or physical unevenness, and a stethoscope should be used to listen to the lungs and heart to note any arrhythmias or fluid buildup. Both the abdomen and the area running the length of the spinal column should be examined for distention, protrusions, and tenderness. Extremities should be examined for broken bones and ischemic tissues. Private areas should not be examined before hospital admittance unless there is visible bleeding or some other reason that warrants pre-hospital examination. It may be possible to conduct some functional exams at this time, including testing the patient's sensory awareness. All findings should be documented and reported to the admitting hospital.

Bleeding

A person **bleeds**, or **hemorrhages**, when an artery or a vein is either punctured or damaged. Bleeding must be controlled until the patient arrives at an emergency care facility. Patients who lose too much blood are at risk of death. Both adult and pediatric patients are treated for bleeding in the same manner. In cases of severe bleeding, vital signs should be assessed every five minutes and high-flow

oxygen is usually indicated. It is important to document the approximate amount of blood loss and indicate the amount of time it took to lose that volume of blood.

In normal circumstances, a clot will form to close the area and bleeding will cease; however, there are times that the bleeding is so profuse that it must be addressed in the field. Bleeding can be either external or internal, and a patient may be bleeding externally and internally at the same time. The patient may be bleeding externally, through a break in the skin or through a body orifice, or may be bleeding internally, into an organ, a cavity, or in between tissues. An injury usually causes hemorrhage, but it may also occur as the result of an illness. **Hemophilia** and **von Willebrand's disease** can both cause the patient to suffer from bleeds. Severe bleeding can lead to hypovolemic shock, a condition that can be life-threatening.

Hypovolemic shock is a state of physical collapse and prostration caused by excessive blood loss, circulatory dysfunction, and inadequate tissue perfusion. If a patient loses approximately one-fifth of their total blood volume, then he or she may go into hypovolemic shock. Various conditions may cause hypovolemic shock, such as severe diarrhea, excessive perspiration, intestinal obstruction, acute pancreatitis, peritonitis, as well as severe burns, all of which can deplete body fluids. Symptoms of shock include rapid pulse; irritability; cool, clammy skin; lethargy; restlessness; and a pale appearance of the skin, or pallor.

When treating a patient who is in hypovolemic shock, the volume of blood and fluid must quickly be replaced. EMTs must determine where the bleeding originated and then control its flow. If the patient does not have a head injury, shock can be treated by raising the patient's legs 8-10 inches above the head so that the flow of blood is concentrated in the torso and toward the head. The heart, brain, and lungs are most affected by shock, and irreparable damage can occur to the patient in as little as 4-6 minutes. Excessive bleeding can be quite traumatic to the patient, so one of the goals for EMTs is to keep the patient calm so that the bleeding can be addressed quickly and efficiently. A non-rebreathing mask can be used to deliver high-flow oxygen, and suction should be performed as needed.

External Bleeding

External bleeding is bleeding that can be seen coming from an open wound on the skin or may come from an orifice, such as the ears, nose, mouth, or anus. Excessive external bleeding may present with symptoms such as cold and clammy skin, rapid and thready pulse, restlessness, thirst, drop in blood pressure, and a decrease of the level of consciousness. **Capillary bleeding** is the most common type of external bleeding. Scratches, minor cuts, and scrapes can cause capillary bleeding. **Venous bleeding** occurs when a vein is punctured or otherwise damaged and is characterized by slow leakage of dark red blood. **Arterial bleeding** is the most serious type of bleeding and this occurs when an artery is punctured or otherwise damaged. Spurts of bright red blood characterize arterial bleeding; the spurting is a result of the heart pumping blood through the arteries.

The primary way to stop external bleeding is to apply firm, steady pressure to the site from which it is occurring; this pressure can stop or slow the flow of blood. A pressure bandage is made from sterile or clean material, such as gauze. Once the pressure bandage is applied, it should not be removed, even to place additional bandaging to the wound. Instead, the new bandage should be placed over the one that is already in place. The bandages should be removed only upon arrival at the emergency care facility by the physician who is caring for the patient. If the pressure bandage is removed, bleeding may reoccur and make the situation worse.

If the pressure bandage is not working, pressure can be applied to various parts of the body to slow the flow of blood. These places are called **pressure points** and are sites on the body where an artery is close to the skin. Once compressed, the blood flow is slowed to the area and is more easily controlled. Pressure points include the **temporal artery** in the middle of the scalp, the **brachial artery** in the inner side of the upper arm, the **radial artery** near the wrist, and the **femoral artery** in the leg. The bleeding may also be slowed by elevating the extremity above the heart. In correct order, bleeding should be addressed with direct pressure, then digital pressure, then the extremity should be elevated, and finally, a tourniquet can be used to control heavy, life-threatening bleeding.

A **tourniquet** is defined as a device used to stop the flow of blood through a vein or an artery, typically by compressing a limb with a cord or a tight bandage. A tourniquet is easily made by using a triangular bandage, rolling it longways into a 1-2-inch band that encircles the limb, and then tying it into a knot. Tourniquets should be applied 2-3 inches closer to the torso from the bleeding area. Tourniquets are effective in saving the patient's life if direct pressure and/or elevation does not control bleeding, especially if the patient is in a remote area and cannot get to an emergency care facility quickly. Tourniquets are wrapped tightly around the extremity and often knotted so that blood flow is controlled and lessened. If necessary, a second tourniquet can be applied closer to the torso than the first tourniquet. The time of application should be noted and the bleeding should be reassessed periodically.

Once the bleeding has slowed, direct pressure may be used to further control blood flow. The tourniquet should not be removed until the patient arrives at the emergency care facility and is under a physician's care. Tourniquets can cause permanent tissue damage, so they must not be used unless the patient is in danger of bleeding to death. Although using a tourniquet does not ensure that the limb will not be lost, it should be considered a last resort in the field.

Internal Bleeding

Internal bleeding is usually a medical emergency requiring rapid transport to the emergency care facility. A bruise is a contusion and indicates that bleeding has occurred between the layers of the skin. Internal bleeding may be caused by **blunt trauma**, which occurs when a patient collides with something at a high speed, or by **penetrating trauma**, which occurs when a foreign object penetrates the skin, such as gunshot wounds or stabbing injuries. If internal bleeding occurs in the brain, the patient may demonstrate symptoms of stroke, may enter a coma, and may die. Bruises on the neck, groin, or trunk may be symptomatic of severe internal bleeding, which may flow into the peritoneum or into the internal organs of the body, such as the liver, spleen, intestines, or kidneys.

Patients who have an internal bleed may exhibit symptoms such as nausea and vomiting; excessive thirst; cold, clammy skin; drop in blood pressure; and/or decreased consciousness. Additionally, they may experience bright red blood in the mouth, rectum, or other orifice. A coffee-ground appearance of vomitus and/or black, tarry stools called **melena** may appear. The patient may also experience dizziness or fainting (**syncope**) while sitting or standing or may experience orthostatic hypotension, which, as mentioned, is an abnormal decrease in blood pressure when a patient stands up. Patients must be monitored using the ABC's of assessment until they are transported to the emergency care facility.

General Assessment

Once the EMT arrives at the scene, an assessment must be performed so that each injury can be sufficiently addressed. First, the EMT must assess whether the patient and EMT can be safe in the area where the patient was found. Then, the ABCDE mnemonic is used to assess the condition of the patient.

The patient is assessed as follows:

- A – Airway
- B – Breathing
- C – Circulation
- D – Disability
- E – Exposure

When assessing the airway, the EMT should look for the rise and fall of the chest. If the chest does not rise and fall consistent with a good **airway** and normal breathing, then the EMT must check for breath sounds by **auscultation**, which can indicate that the patient is **breathing**. It is possible that some type of obstruction is preventing normal breathing in the patient. When assessing **circulation**, the radial and/or femoral pulse should be detected. Skin color is also important when assessing circulation; for example, a patient whose skin feels cool and/or clammy may be going into shock. **Disability** includes assessment of the pupils, their size, and their reactivity. The EMT should then disrobe the patient to look for injuries. During this **exposure** portion of the assessment, the EMT should search for bleeding or other wounds.

The ABCDE assessment is the first assessment performed upon the patient. Once the initial ABCDE assessment is completed, the EMT should conduct the secondary assessment, beginning with the head, and working downward toward the feet. When performing a secondary assessment of young children, the EMT should proceed from toe to head; older children are assessed in the same way that adults are, from head to toe.

Chest Trauma

According to the Centers for Disease Control and Prevention, trauma is the leading cause of death for individuals between the ages of 1-44. **Chest trauma** can result from an accident, or may be the result of a puncture wound. **Blunt trauma** is a serious injury that is caused by a blunt object or a collision with a blunt surface. Because the chest cavity houses several vital organs, such as the heart and lungs, injury to this area can be life-threatening. Patients may suffer chest trauma because of broken bones, such as fractures of the ribs or the sternum. The clavicle is the most common broken bone seen in pediatric and adult patients.

The seven upper ribs are called **true ribs**, while the lower five ribs are called **false ribs**, because they do not connect to the sternum. A **flail chest** exists when the patient has three or more fractured ribs in two or more places; the mortality rate for a patient with a flail chest is high because injuries may exist that are not readily seen. The **sternum**, or breast bone, is often broken when patients have open heart surgery. The sternum consists of three bones, including the manubrium, the body of the sternum, and the xiphoid process.

Chest trauma presents as a variety of different conditions. For instance, **atelectasis**, or the collapse of lung tissue, can occur because of **crepitus**, which is the grating of bone upon bone. Respiratory or diaphragmatic splinting are causes of complications from broken ribs.

Several types of chest sounds can be heard upon auscultation, including stridor, wheezing, crackles, and rhonchi. **Stridor** is usually heard upon inspiration but may occur during exhaling, and is characterized by a high-pitched breath sound, often because of an obstruction in the airway. Stridor can be heard without a stethoscope. **Wheezing** can be mild, moderate, or severe, and is a whistling sound most often heard during exhalation; this breath sound is commonly present in patients with asthma. **Crackles** are

66

defined as short rattling or crackling sounds that may be indicative of emphysema. **Rhonchi** are low-pitched sounds heard in conditions such as pneumonia, when there are thick secretions that hinder normal breathing.

Several other conditions can interfere with the normal operation of the heart and/or lungs. **Pericardial tamponade** occurs when tears in the chambers of the heart begin to leak and the blood fills the thoracic cavity, causing the patient to die from bleeding. **Beck's triad** consists of three symptoms that indicate pericardial tamponade, including muffled heart sounds, hypotension, and elevated central venous pressure. This elevated pressure distinguishes pericardial tamponade from hemorrhagic shock. Other symptoms of pericardial tamponade include respiratory distress and tachycardia. The patient may experience pulsus paradoxus, in which the systolic blood pressure is less than 10-15 mmHg during inspiration. Pericardial tamponade is always a medical emergency. If the bleeding is not quickly stopped, the patient is likely to die.

Myocardial contusions and myocardial ruptures are additional injuries to the chest area. A **myocardial contusion** is a bruise to the muscle of the heart that often happens during a car accident. A **myocardial rupture** is usually fatal; it occurs when there is enough force to lacerate or tear the wall of the atria or ventricles. An **aortic rupture** is a condition in which the aorta tears or is ripped open. Like the myocardial rupture, aortic rupture is often fatal because the aorta is the largest artery in the body. Because so much blood is lost from wound, the patient will rarely recover.

A **pneumothorax** is defined as the presence of air or gas in the cavity between the lungs and the chest wall. This condition can cause a lung to collapse, and can be either open or closed. An **open pneumothorax** can be the result of a ruptured emphysematous vesicle on the surface of a lung, an open chest wound that allows air inside, or a severe case of coughing; some happen without any apparent reason. An open pneumothorax often produces a sucking or gurgling sound. A **closed pneumothorax** indicates that air is present in the pleural space. This type of injury may be caused by broken ribs or may occur without broken bones.

A **tension pneumothorax** occurs when air that has entered the thoracic cavity cannot get out. This condition can cause death quickly if it is not recognized soon enough to treat. The EMT can provide high-flow oxygen to avoid hypoxia. Added air will put pressure on the chest so this must be done cautiously. If possible, the EMT should make an early call ALS to perform chest decompression. Otherwise, the patient should be transported immediately to the hospital. A **hemothorax** is an accumulation of blood in the pleural space, while a **hemopneumothorax** is a combination of air and blood in the pleural space. Half of the patients who develop a hemothorax die within one hour of the injury.

Lung tissue in pediatric patients is fragile, and they have a smaller residual lung capacity. Because of this, **hypoxia**, which is a deficiency in the amount of oxygen at the tissue level, can develop quickly in the pediatric patient. The EMT should be prepared for respiratory failure if any of the following symptoms occur:

- Increased respiratory rate with signs of distress;
- Inadequate respiratory rate, especially with depressed mental status; and/or
- Cyanosis even while on oxygen.

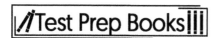

Abdominal/Genitourinary Trauma

The abdominal cavity houses several vital organs, such as the liver, spleen, stomach, diaphragm, intestines, pancreas, kidneys, and appendix. Trauma to any of these organs can lead to death. Additionally, injury to one or more of these organs may not be recognized during the ABCDE assessment. Abdominal organs may be injured by compression or by shearing forces; **shearing forces** are unaligned forces pushing one part of the body in one direction and another part of the body in the opposite direction. Injuries to solid organs, such as the liver or spleen, can result in quick blood loss and the patient can bleed to death. Injuries to hollow organs, such as the stomach, intestines, or kidneys, may go unnoticed for a time and may produce infection, abscess, or sepsis.

Because the liver is a large organ and takes up a large amount of space in the abdomen, trauma to this area can pierce the liver and this can result in the patient's death. The **liver** filters blood from the digestive system and metabolizes drugs in the body. The **spleen** stores and filters blood, and helps to guard the body against infection. In children, as in adults, the liver and spleen are larger organs, but the child's liver and spleen are injured more often than those of the adult patient. The **retroperitoneal space** houses the **kidneys**, which function as filters that remove waste from the bloodstream. Patients who have a kidney or bladder infection may feel pain in the right and/or left hypochondriac regions of the body. The **bladder** and **urethra** are pelvic organs that can be damaged in car accidents, but may also be injured during a fall. A rupture of the bladder is more likely when the bladder is full at the time of the injury.

Signs and symptoms of abdominal trauma include pain and swelling in the abdominal area, back pain, chest pain, and painful urination. The patient may also experience signs of shock, or may exhibit signs of seatbelt restraint, such as bruising. When arriving on scene, the EMT should make note of any disarray in the vehicle or any obvious trauma at the scene. The patient may show signs of **peritonitis**, an inflammation of the peritoneum, which can be painful. **Grey Turner's sign**, which is characterized by bruising of the skin of the flanks or loin in acute hemorrhagic pancreatitis, is a strong sign of abdominal trauma. **Cullen's sign**, which is indicated by irregular hemorrhagic spots on the skin around the umbilicus, is also a sign of abdominal trauma.

Evisceration is defined as the extrusion of the viscera outside of the body, which can happen during an accident, injury, or after surgery. The viscera are the soft internal organs of the body, such as the intestines. If an evisceration happens prior to transporting a patient to a hospital, the wound should be covered with a sterile gauze that it slightly moist. As in other bleeding injuries, the gauze should not be removed once soaked through; instead, the EMT should add additional sterile gauze on top of the first application and continue to apply pressure to slow or stop the bleeding.

Orthopedic Trauma

The human body contains 206 bones, and is made of other types of tissue, including nerves, vessels, ligaments, joints, muscles, and tendons. The human body comprises two types of skeletons—the axial skeleton and the appendicular skeleton. The **axial skeleton** includes the skull, hyoid bone, thoracic cage, and vertebral column. The **appendicular skeleton** is made up of the upper and lower extremities and the girdles, which attach the extremities to the rest of the body. The skeleton and muscles work together to move the body and maintain an upright posture. Several types of muscle are found throughout the body, including cardiac, smooth, and skeletal. Skeletal muscle is the most common type of muscle found in the body.

Fractures are breaks in the continuity of a bone or cartilage and can be open or closed, as well as complete or incomplete. An **open fracture** exists when a protruding bone or other object causes a soft tissue injury. **Closed fractures** are breaks that have not penetrated the skin. A **greenstick fracture** is one that is broken on one side of the bone and intact on the other side. A **transverse fracture** occurs at right angles to the long axis of the bone. A fracture is said to be **comminuted** when it is splintered into pieces, while a **spiral fracture** is twisted, affecting the length of the bone as opposed to the width. **Oblique fractures** are neither parallel nor at a right angle to a specific or implied line. At the ends of the long bones sit the **epiphyseal plates**; fractures involving the epiphyseal plates are common childhood breaks. As children get older, hormones thicken the cartilage in long bones and they become harder and less susceptible to breaks.

Bones that are broken are often secured by a splint until the patient is under the care of a physician at a hospital or trauma center. **Splints** are used to immobilize an injury and can also decrease pain, bleeding, and contamination at the site of the injury. Soft or formable splints can be made into a variety of shapes to secure the injured body part. Rigid splints cannot be changed; for example, a board or plastic splint is not easily manipulated and can usually be classified as a rigid splint. **Traction splints** are designed to stabilize fractures in the middle of the femur. The traction splint is a temporary fix that will stabilize the fracture and will help to align the break until the patient arrives at an emergency care center and is under the care of a physician.

Most of the support of the chest wall in children comes from muscles, and because of this, infants and children have higher oxygen consumption rates and tire more quickly than older children and adults. The chest wall also offers less protection than in older children and adults. The EMT must pay close attention to the possibility of traumatic injury, and should provide full immobilization of the injury, especially when the patient is a young child. Additionally, when performing a secondary assessment on children, the assessment should proceed from head to toe in older children and from toe to head in younger children.

Sprains involve a twist of a ligament that causes pain and swelling, but not dislocation. Sprains are diagnosed by severity, beginning with a first-degree sprain, which results in minimal swelling; second- and third-degree sprains are progressively more serious. The ligaments in third-degree sprains are completely torn. A **strain** is the resulting injury that affects a muscle or tendon after overexertion or overextension. Because bones are softer in pediatric patients, possible sprains and strains should be treated as if they were actual fractures.

Shoulder injuries often happen in older adults, especially geriatric patients, whose bones are more brittle. Some injuries, such as **rotator cuff tendon injuries**, can be acute or chronic, and often happen because of a fall onto an outstretched arm. Although this is a common reflex, it is not wise to stretch the arm outward to lessen the effects of a fall, and this can make the injury worse.

Elbow and forearm injuries are common among children and athletes, and both injuries can be managed by using a splint and elevating and applying ice over the injured area for twenty minutes on, and then twenty minutes off.

Hand and finger injuries may be the result of sports, exercise, work-related injuries, and/or violence; these areas of the body should also be splinted, iced, and elevated, whenever possible. Injuries are usually more severe in the lower extremities because there is often a greater force used in the creation of the injury. These injuries are often accompanied by significant blood loss and are more difficult to manage because they can inhibit walking or moving about.

Joints can be dislocated; dislocations happen to the shoulders, elbows, hips, knees, fingers, and ankles, most often. Hip injuries are common among geriatric patients, and many die within one year of suffering the injury, often due to pneumonia, thromboembolism, and/or infection.

Patients with **musculoskeletal injuries** can be placed into one of four following classes:

- Life- or limb-threatening injuries or conditions, including life- or limb-threatening musculoskeletal trauma

- Other life- or limb-threatening vascular injuries and only simple musculoskeletal trauma

- No other life- or limb-threatening injuries but with life- or limb-threatening musculoskeletal trauma

- Isolated injuries that are neither life- nor limb-threatening

Patients who have **femoral injuries** are in danger of losing so much blood that even lightning-fast efforts cannot fix. Fractures in the femoral area can cause the broken bones to rub together, and contractions in the leg increase the patient's pain level. Swelling in the area is probable, so the leg needs to be immobilized and the patient should be watched for signs of shock. If dictated by local protocols, a **pneumatic antishock garment (PASG)** should be used to immobilize the injury. It should be noted that a femoral injury in children younger than four years old is often an indicator of child abuse, and should be reported to the appropriate authorities.

Knee, patellar, tibial, and fibular injuries should be immobilized with a rigid or formable splint, iced, and elevated, if possible. Finger and toe (**phalangeal**) injuries can be aided by "buddy splinting," which is done by taping the injured finger or toe to an adjacent one. These injuries should also be iced and elevated.

Fractures heal in several stages, depending upon the size and the severity of the injury. First, a hematoma forms at the site of the fracture, and then scar tissue forms. A **hematoma** is a collection of extravasated blood that has escaped from the vessel into the tissue and then is trapped in the tissues of the skin or in an organ, resulting from trauma or incomplete hemostasis after surgery. **Osteoblasts**, or immature bone cells and cartilage cells, form on the fracture site. Last, immature bone cells grow and mature. Most small fractures heal in a matter of weeks, while larger fractures, especially those in the legs, can take months to heal. Even small fractures in the hands may cause pain for years after the site has healed.

Soft Tissue Trauma

Soft tissue trauma (or **surface trauma**) may be obvious to the eye or may exist underneath the skin, sometimes without any bruising or contusions that would alert an EMT to the injury. A **contusion**, or bruise, does not disrupt the continuity of the skin; instead, the patient or EMT may notice bruising or other discoloration, swelling, and pain. The largest organ in the body is the **skin**—a layered covering that consists of the **outer epidermis, inner dermis**, and a deep layer of fibrous tissue called the **hypodermis**, which exists beneath the dermis. The skin includes openings of sweat and sebaceous glands and serves as the body's primary defensive structure. The epidermis is made up of thin epithelial tissue and has five layers. These layers include the outermost stratum corneum, the stratum lucidum, the stratum granulosum, the stratum spinosum, and the innermost layer—the stratum basale. The outermost layer comprises many layers of dead skin cells, which contain keratin. **Keratin** is a sulfur-containing fibrous

protein that forms the chemical basis of epidermal tissues, such as hair and nails. **Melanin** is the pigment in the skin that gives it color.

The **dermis** is the vascular, thick layer of skin that lies beneath the epidermis and contains elastic fibers, lymph vessels, blood vessels, connective tissue, as well as motor and sensory nerve endings. The dermis also contains an extracellular matrix composed of proteoglycans and glycoproteins along with collagen and elastin fibers. **Collagen** is a protein and is the major component of connective tissue that gives the skin strength and flexibility. Skin helps to protect the body from bacterial infections and to maintain fluid balance. The blood vessels in the dermis help to regulate body temperature, while its nerve tissue promotes responses to stimuli such as heat, cold, pain, and touch. The dermis also helps to cushion the body from stressors and strains. The hypodermis lies beneath the dermis and serves several functions; for instance, it provides further cushioning and insulation for the body. It also supports and protects organs and other structures underneath.

When an injury happens to the body, bleeding may occur; **hemostasis** is the stoppage of blood flow or the stoppage of bleeding, often by use of a hemostatic agent or drug. Four separate functions occur during hemostasis. First, during **vasoconstriction**, vasomotor action narrows blood vessels' lumens, which slows the flow of blood. Platelets then form at the site of the injury; **platelets** are minute, colorless, anucleate biconcave disks of cytoplasm that are released from bone, then adhere to other platelets and damaged epithelium. The platelets are then called **thrombocytes**. The third process is that of **coagulation**, which is the change from blood in liquid form to a thickened solid. This is commonly known as **blood clotting**. Finally, the platelets stick to the injured vessels, and collagen and other secretions create a seal over the injured vessels called a **platelet plug**. Coagulation is a quick process. When a blood vessel is damaged, prothrombin activator works to change prothrombin to **thrombin**, which is an enzyme that forms fibrin threads, and those threads form the clot.

The Inflammation Process
Soft tissue or surface trauma can interfere with the normal physiological functions of the body by way of inflammatory and/or vascular responses, which are an important part of the body's ability to heal. An **inflammatory response** is a tissue reaction to injury or an antigen that may include pain, swelling, itching, redness, heat, and/or loss of function. The response may involve dilation of blood vessels and leakage of fluid, which causes swelling, and the release of plasma proteases and vasoactive amines, such as histamine. **Histamine** is a chemical that may promote a vascular response. A **vascular response** usually happens after cellular injury and there is a dilation of the surrounding arterioles, venules, and capillaries. **Hyperemia**, which is an engorgement of blood in an organ or in surrounding areas, is the increase in pressure and capillary permeability that causes fluid to leak from the vessels into the interstitial space. Thus, the fluid produced by this leakage is called **interstitial fluid** and it often creates redness and swelling, and the skin may feel warm to the touch.

The inflammation process is a local response to cellular injury that is marked by capillary dilatation, leukocytic infiltration, redness, heat, pain swelling, and often loss of function. The body attempts to remain in a state of **homeostasis**, which means that it tries to maintain a relatively constant condition in the internal environment while continuously interacting with, and adjusting to, changes originating within or outside of the body system. Although it may be logical to think when applying this theory that the goal of the body is to stay the same, the reality is that the body is not in a static or fixed state; it is a state of continuous motion, adaptation, and/or change in response to the stimuli in the environment. **Equilibrium** is a state of chemical balance in the body, reached when the tissues contain the proper proportions of various salts and water.

71

During this process, **leukocytes**, which are white blood cells, rush to the infected or inflamed area of the body to fight off infection. The metabolic processes of tissues during healing, as well as the movement of lymphocytes, macrophages, and granulocytes, cause the skin to take on a red appearance and feel warm to the touch.

The Wound Healing Process and Scar Formation

A **wound** is defined as any physical injury involving a break in the skin, usually caused by an act or accident (rather than by a disease), such as a chest wound, gunshot wound, or puncture wound. At the point of healing, **scar tissue**, which is also known as **cicatrix**, forms as an avascular, pale, contracted tissue, and feels firm. The area around the scar is notably red and soft. Not all wounds heal at the same rate, and some are impeded by the patient's medical condition, drug use, and various other anatomical factors.

However, some wounds heal within a few days and do not leave any sort of scar. As mentioned, various medical conditions and diseases can affect the timing of healing, such as advanced age, diabetes, malnutrition, liver failure, severe alcoholism, cardiovascular disease, and peripheral vascular disease. While the EMT is in the field with the patient, a wound history should be made and kept within the patient's medical record. The EMT should record the approximate time of the injury, where it occurred, the mechanism of the injury and likelihood of any associated injuries, approximate blood loss, and level of pain felt by the patient, as well as information about the patient's most recent tetanus immunization.

Some people develop keloids or hypertrophic scarring, both of which are abnormal scar formations. **Keloids** (sometimes spelled **cheloids**) occur when there is an excessive growth of collagenous scar tissue that extends beyond the borders of the original wounds. **Hypertrophic scars** are formed from an excessive formation of new tissue in the healing of a wound.

Several types of wounds need closure, including wounds over joints or other tension areas, gaping wounds, and skin tears. A soft tissue wound can be considered open or closed. **Open wounds** include bites, abrasions, lacerations, punctures, and avulsions. Crush injuries, contusions, hematomas, and amputations are all types of **closed wounds**.

Open Wounds

Patients may receive bites from humans, animals, or insects, and various diseases can be spread through a bite wound. Bites are usually superficial, but they can involve structures deep within the body, including muscles and bones. The patient may experience complications from bite wounds such as abscesses, cellulitis, hepatitis B, and tetanus. All bites should be evaluated and treated by a physician.

An **abrasion** is defined as the scraping or rubbing away of the surface of the skin by friction. Abrasions may be the result of trauma or of some type of treatment, such as debridement following a burn. Abrasions should be kept clean and dry to help prevent infection.

Lacerations are wounds produced by tearing body tissue and often result in a great deal of bleeding. They can occur at the surface of the skin, but can also happen within the body when an organ is compressed or moved out of place by an external or internal force, such as a blow that does not break the skin. Surgery is usually necessary to repair an injury severe enough to wound internal organs.

Puncture wounds are usually made by sharp, pointed objects. Such wounds can be quite deep and can interrupt the normal continuity and function of involved organs. The patient may arrive at the emergency care center with the object that caused the wound still lodged in place; the attending

physician should determine the best way to remove the object and repair the wound. Items that cause puncture wounds should never be removed in the field by the EMT. Patients are usually given antibiotics after the injury is repaired to help avoid subsequent infection. If infection remains after treatment, it is possible that there is a retained foreign object in the patient's body.

An **avulsion** is defined as the forcible tearing away of a body part by trauma. This type of injury often happens when the patient is working with industrial equipment. Avulsed fingers, toes, limbs, or other separated tissues should be saved and taken to the emergency department or trauma center with the patient. If possible, the body part should be placed in a plastic bag with ice so that it can remain as clean and preserved as possible. A **degloving injury** is a type of avulsion that happens when soft tissues down to the bone—including the neurovascular bundles and sometimes tendons—are peeled off of the body part. Degloving injuries happen most often to appendages but can also happen when the hair is caught or entangled in machinery, which causes a scalp avulsion.

Closed Wounds

A **crush injury** is defined as a break in the external surface of the body due to a severe force applied against the tissues. Crushing injuries can be severe and life-threatening, and may present with symptoms such as the destruction of both muscle and bone tissue, hemorrhage, and fluid loss, which can lead to hypovolemic shock, hematuria, renal failure, and/or coma. The patient with a crush injury may have ruptured an organ, suffered a major fracture, and might experience hemorrhagic shock, even if the skin over the injury remains intact. A patient can die quite quickly if the crush injury is serious enough. Crush injuries are often seen in car accidents, industrial accidents, and in injuries that happen during war.

Crush syndrome, although rare, is a life-threatening, severe condition caused by extensive crushing trauma. It is characterized by destruction of muscle and bone tissue, hemorrhage, and fluid loss, resulting in hypovolemic shock, hematuria, renal failure, and coma. The patient experiencing crush syndrome needs intensive care with close monitoring of all vital functions, as well as administration of fluids, electrolytes, antibiotics, analgesia, and oxygen.

Although the patient with a crush injury may appear to be stable for a while, complications will occur once the patient is removed from the trapping environment that caused the injury. First, blood rich in oxygen returns to the body part that has been crushed. This is called **reperfusion**, defined as the restoration of blood flow to an area that was temporarily ischemic. This process can lead to shock, because it reduces the circulation of blood throughout the body. Second, the oxygen-rich blood moves back through the body and waste products and toxic substances are circulated throughout the body systems, which causes **metabolic acidosis**; this is a condition in which excess acid is added to the body fluids or bicarbonate is lost from them.

This process results in:

- **Hyperkalemia**: a greater than normal amount of potassium in the blood;
- **Hypocalcemia**: a deficiency of calcium in the blood serum;
- **Hyperphosphatemia**: a low phosphorus level in the blood; and/or
- **Hyperuricemia**: abnormally elevated levels of uric acid in the blood.

The third complication that can occur when a patient has a crushing injury is the release of myoglobin from damaged muscle cells in the injury area, which is filtered through the kidneys. This process can cause acute renal failure.

Compartment syndrome is a surgical emergency and can be a complication of a crush injury; symptoms may begin within a few hours of the injury or may appear up to forty-eight hours afterward. The most common causes of compartment syndrome, in addition to crushing injury, include tibial fractures, forearm fractures, hemorrhage, constrictive casts, prolonged limb compression, and burns. This condition results from elevated pressures within a confined muscle compartment, most commonly in the leg and forearm.

The Five P's of compartment syndrome include pain, paresthesia, pallor, paralysis, and pulselessness; however, the patient may not have all five of these symptoms, yet he or she can still have compartment syndrome. The patient will likely complain of severe pain and may also experience nerve dysfunction. The compartment is often firm, swollen, and tender when palpitated. Normal compartment pressure is less than 10 mmHg. The **delta pressure**, which is the diastolic blood pressure minus the tissue pressure, is the best predictor of irreversible muscle damage. Compartment syndrome is diagnosed when the delta pressure is ≤ 30 mmHg. The patient will likely undergo a surgical fasciotomy to correct this condition; until surgery, the affected limb should be placed at the level of the heart, supplemental oxygen should be administered, and constrictive casts or dressings should be removed.

Contusions are defined as injuries to tissues with skin discoloration without the breakage of skin; contusions are often called bruises. In these injuries, blood from broken vessels leaks into the surrounding tissues. The patient usually experiences swelling, pain, tenderness, and discoloration. These symptoms may be reduced by applying ice immediately after the injury.

As mentioned, a **hematoma** is a collection of extravasated blood trapped in the tissues of the skin or an organ resulting from trauma. At first, there is bleeding into the space containing the hematoma, but if space is limited, the pressure of the blood flow slows and eventually stops. The hematoma can often be felt and may be quite painful. If necessary, hematomas can be drained once the patient reaches the emergency care center, but precautions must be taken for infection.

An **amputation** happens when a patient experiences complete or partial loss of a limb. This may happen during an accident or may be medically necessary due to the progression of a disease in a limb. Bleeding must be controlled after an amputation because it can be extensive, and vital signs must be monitored continuously. The wound should be bandaged with additional dressings placed on top of previous bandages once they are soaked. A tourniquet may be used to help the bleeding to slow or stop.

Head, Neck, Face, and Spinal Trauma

Head

Head injuries to the scalp, skull, and/or brain can be dangerous and can cause mental impairment and permanent disability. Head injuries may be caused by vehicle accidents, participation in sports, home accidents, industrial accidents, intentional violent acts, and falls. When an object hits or penetrates the head, the patient is said to have a **direct injury**. When acceleration and/or deceleration forces result in the movement of the brain within the skull, the patient is said to have an **indirect injury**. Head injuries can also be open, such as bleeding wounds, or closed, with no visible signs of injury present. The EMT should follow criteria for spinal immobilization. All patients with head trauma should be quickly assessed and the EMT may assume that the patient has a spinal injury until examination and diagnostic procedures at the emergency care center have ruled out such injury.

Patients may have soft tissue injuries, concussions, skull fractures, and traumatic brain injury, as well as other types of head trauma, all of which must be carefully monitored by the EMT until the patient is

placed under the care of an attending physician. Head injuries are usually traumatic to the patient because the brain is such a vital organ; it is possible that some injuries to the brain may not be properly diagnosed for months or years because the symptoms can be quite subtle in nature. The EMT should be reassuring to the patient and keep them as calm as possible.

The internal and external carotid arteries and their branches provide the blood supply to the face; because of this vascularity, head injuries may bleed profusely, adding to the patient's anxiety. It is important that a clear airway is maintained in the event of a head injury, which may mean that suction should be used to ensure that the patient can breathe. Obstructions—such as broken teeth, dentures, and foreign objects—must be carefully removed so that the airway remains clear.

There are many signs and symptoms of head injury, including:

- Inability to wake the patient
- Short-term memory loss
- Loss of consciousness
- Dizziness
- Confusion
- Very high blood pressure
- Persistent headache
- Dilation of pupils
- Slurred speech
- Loss of coordination
- Convulsions
- Seizures
- Agitation or restlessness
- Inability to concentrate
- Ringing in the ears

Not all head injuries result in symptoms, and closed head injuries can be much more serious than those that are open. The EMT must determine and document the mechanism of injury as well as the events that led up to the injury, in addition to all symptoms. Patients with a head injury may vomit, and if this happens, the airway must be cleared immediately. The EMT must continually assess the patient for the need for spinal immobilization, and monitor the patient's vital signs and level of responsiveness every fifteen minutes when the patient is stable, and every five minutes if unstable.

Concussions

A **concussion** is defined as a head injury that results from violent jarring or shaking; it alters the way that the brain functions, although its effects may be temporary. Concussions are classified in three different grades, each with specific symptoms. **Grade 1 concussions** result in no loss of consciousness, temporary confusion, and the symptoms clear within fifteen minutes of the injury. **Grade 2 concussions** also result in no loss of consciousness and temporary confusion is present, but the symptoms last longer than fifteen minutes. **Grade 3 concussions** result in loss of consciousness for any length of time. Permanent brain injury may occur in the patient with a grade 2 or grade 3 concussion. Concussions are a type of **diffuse injury**, and are the most common types of brain injury; these are injuries in which the **neural processes (axons)** prevent the nerves from communicating with each other. Situations in which the patient gets worse after a concussion are cause to further evaluate the patient for more serious head injuries, such as those caused by contusion or hemorrhage.

Two types of amnesia may accompany concussions. Retrograde amnesia is a loss of memory of events or information that happened before the injury. Anterograde amnesia is a loss of ability to create new memories after the injury.

There are many signs and symptoms of concussion, including:

- Combativeness
- Temporary visual problems
- Issues with equilibrium
- Changes in vital signs
- Coordination problems
- Dizziness
- Fatigue
- Slurred speech
- Nausea and/or vomiting
- Headache
- Ringing in the ears
- Delayed response to questions

It may be difficult to diagnose concussions in infant or toddler patients because they are unable to communicate their symptoms. In addition to the symptoms experienced by adults with concussions, infants and toddlers may cry excessively, and seem dazed, irritable, or listless. Anyone who suffers a head injury should see a physician.

Moderate and Severe Diffuse Axonal Injuries
A patient with a **moderate diffuse axonal injury** will initially be unconscious and will experience confusion and amnesia of the injury event. Patients may also have difficulty concentrating, and be anxious and/or moody. They should be reassessed frequently for levels of consciousness. **Severe diffuse axonal injury** is the most severe form of brain injury, involving severe mechanical shearing of many axons in both cerebral hemispheres extending to the brain stem.

Skull Fractures
Several types of skull fractures are possible with a head injury, including those that are linear, depressed, basilar, and open vault. The EMT must continually consider the possibility of spinal injury while assessing the patient, so care must be taken when moving the patient during examination and treatment in the field. Several complications may occur with skull fractures, such as infection, cranial nerve injury, and underlying brain injuries.

Linear fractures are defined as those that resemble a line and do not displace the bone tissue. About 80 percent of skull fractures are linear. Most linear fractures do not involve a laceration, but infection is possible if a laceration is present. **Depressed fractures** are those in which fragments of bone are depressed below the normal surface of the skull.

Basilar fractures occur when the mandible condyles perforate the base of the skull; more commonly, this occurs when a linear fracture extends into the floor of the anterior and middle fossae. If a patient is bleeding from the ears or nose, gauze can be used for a halo test. If a lighter colored halo of fluid appears around the blood on the gauze, cerebrospinal fluid is present, which indicates that there is a skull fracture.

Several symptoms of basilar fractures exist, including:

- **Battle's sign**, which is ecchymosis over the mastoid process resulting from a temporal bone fracture

- **Ecchymosis** of one or both orbits, commonly called raccoon's eyes, resulting from fracture of the base of the sphenoid sinus

- **Cerebrospinal fluid leakage**, which can cause meningitis

- **Hemotympanum**, which is blood behind the tympanic membrane caused by fractures of the temporal bone

Battle's sign and raccoon's eyes are rarely seen in the emergency care center unless the bruising comes from an earlier injury. **Open vault fractures** are often the result of a small object striking the head at a high speed and are common with scalp lacerations.

Traumatic Brain Injuries

A **traumatic brain injury (TBI)** occurs when sudden trauma damages the brain. There are two categories of TBI: primary brain injuries and secondary brain injuries. Direct trauma to the brain causes a **primary brain injury**, while intracellular and extracellular derangements cause a **secondary brain injury**. Derangements, such as hypoxia and hypercapnia, are defined as an organ or part not functioning properly due to dislodged or injured parts. The severity of injury can be measured using the Glasgow Coma Scale (GCS) and is classified as mild, moderate, or severe; it can be further classified focal or diffuse. Contact usually causes **focal injuries**, such as skull fractures and brain hemorrhage, and such issues are often detectable to the naked eye. **Diffuse injuries** are those that are usually caused by acceleration/deceleration forces, but can also be from meningitis and hypoxia. They involve larger or more widespread brain regions, often with microscopic levels of damage, making them often more difficult to detect or define. Falls are the leading cause of traumatic brain injuries in both adults and children. Vehicle accidents and sports injuries are also common causes of traumatic brain injury.

The EMT should watch for signs and symptoms of a traumatic brain injury, and determine the mechanism and time of injury. The EMT should note any periods of unconsciousness that the patient experiences and how long they last, mental status, seizure activity, verbalization problems, and the patient's ability to move the extremities. The EMT should remember that patients may be confused and may not remember the events leading up to and during the injury. Information may need to be collected from family and/or friends who are present to determine the patient's medical history, drugs that the patient takes on a regular or an as-needed basis, and drugs and/or alcohol that the patient may have taken leading up to the injury.

Traumatic brain injury may occur in infants, whose responsiveness may be reduced. The infant may experience asymmetry in the pupils and/or face, as well as abnormalities in the motor function of the extremities.

Other signs and symptoms of traumatic brain injury in infants include:

- Lethargy
- Vomiting
- Seizures
- Bradycardia
- Decreased sucking reflex
- Apnea

Older children who experience traumatic brain injury may experience:

- Nausea
- Vomiting
- Headache
- Visual changes
- Hypertension
- Motor weakness
- Bradycardia
- Respiratory distress

An **Acquired brain injury (ABI)** occurs at the cellular level and is most often associated with pressure on the brain. It can be the result of a growth or tumor, or the result of neurological illness, such as a stroke. Like traumatic brain injuries, acquired brain injuries disrupt the brain's normal functioning. An ABI happens after birth and is not related to a congenital or a degenerative disease.

Focal Injuries

Focal injuries are defined as specific, grossly observable brain lesions. These injuries can result from contusions, edema, ischemia, and hemorrhage. Focal injuries occur in one region of the brain.

When the brain is bruised, producing a structural change in brain tissue, the patient usually has a **cerebral contusion**, which can result in more serious deficits and abnormalities than concussions. Local damage that occurs at the site of impact is called **coup**, and an injury that occurs at a site opposite the side of impact is called **contrecoup**. The patient may lose consciousness if the brain stem is contused. Patients who are comatose after such injury may experience prolonged comatose states. Usually, cerebral contusions heal on their own, although the length of time to heal may vary and the level of improvement may differ from patient to patient. Most patients who die from head injuries are shown to have cerebral contusions during the autopsy.

Cerebral edema is the swelling of brain tissue and can lead to increases in **intracranial pressure (ICP)**. ICP can prevent blood from flowing into the brain, depriving it of the oxygen it needs to function. Swelling is a serious matter because the excess fluid has nowhere to go in the limited spaces inside the brain. This condition may be treated with medications, removal of small amounts of fluid from the brain, and/or surgery.

Ischemia is defined as an inadequate blood supply to an organ or a part of the body and can be chronic or acute. When the brain is not getting enough oxygen, the resulting condition is called **brain hypoxia**. While this is always a serious condition, depending upon the length of time that the patient has been without oxygen, it may be treated by just placing the patient on oxygen therapy. Ischemia can be caused

78

by choking, drowning, cardiac arrest, carbon monoxide poisoning, and stroke, among other conditions. The brain can survive for approximately six minutes after the heart stops beating.

Brain hemorrhage, also called **intracranial** or **intracerebral hemorrhage**, is bleeding in or around the brain. There are several causes of brain hemorrhage. Hypertension is the most common cause of this condition; therefore, it is important that hypertensive patients take their blood pressure medication exactly as prescribed. Over time, the walls of vessels can weaken, which can lead to rupture and bleeding. **Aneurysms**, which are defined as sacs or weak spots in the walls of arteries, veins, or the heart, may also cause brain hemorrhage. **Arteriovenous malformation (AVM)**, which is a tangle of abnormal blood vessels connecting arteries and veins, may cause bleeding in the brain, although it is a rare disorder and is usually congenital. Smoking and drug abuse, especially that of cocaine, can also lead to bleeding in the brain. The symptoms of brain hemorrhage depend upon what part of the brain is involved; they may come on abruptly and worsen quickly or may progress slowly over hours or days. Types of brain hemorrhages are usually classified based upon their location; these types include cerebral, epidural, subdural, and subarachnoid hematomas.

Cerebral hematoma, most commonly found in the frontal or temporal lobes of the brain, can be caused by deceleration, increased intracranial pressure, and/or skull fractures. Symptoms can include headache; weakness, tingling, or paralysis on one side of the body; balance and/or coordination problems; lethargy; and confusion. Cerebral hematoma symptoms can appear suddenly and the patient can deteriorate quickly.

An **epidural hematoma** takes place between the cranium and the dura mater, and although it is a serious condition, injury to the brain may not be severe. Patients who experience an epidural hematoma often have a temporary loss of consciousness followed by a lucid period. While half of the patients with this type of hematoma do not recover consciousness, the other half do recover and their neurological status returns to normal; however, recovery will differ from patient to patient.

Patients who are at risk for a **subdural hematoma** include those who have clotting deficiencies, hemophiliacs, and older adults. This hematoma is usually associated with the veins that bridge the subdural space, and it normally occurs between the dura mater and the surface of the brain in the subdural space. The lapse of time between injury and onset of symptoms determines the classification of subdural hematomas. An acute subdural hematoma is one in which the symptoms appear within twenty-four hours. A subacute subdural hematoma is symptomatic between two and ten days, and one that is symptomatic after two weeks is considered chronic.

A **subarachnoid hematoma** refers to bleeding into the cerebrospinal fluid. The most common symptom of a subarachnoid hematoma is a sudden, severe headache that begins in one area and then spreads, becoming dull and throbbing. Causes include trauma, rupture of an aneurysm, or arteriovenous abnormality. The patient may have a brief period of unconsciousness, and severe subarachnoid hematoma may result in continued unconsciousness, coma, and death. Permanent brain damage is common with this type of hematoma.

Neck
The **neck** is the main structure of support of the skull; injuries to this area of the body may involve soft tissue, bone structures, or both. Three zones separate the sections of the neck and are divided horizontally in the human body. Several structures, such as the trachea, esophagus, jugular vein, and carotid artery, are found in more than one zone. Zone I includes the base of the neck, from the sternal notch to the top of the clavicles or the cricoid cartilage. The highest rate of mortality is seen in Zone I,

because of the major thoracic and vascular structures that are located there, such as the jugular vein, esophagus, trachea, and cervical spine. Zone II extends from the clavicles or the cricoid cartilage to the angle of the mandible; this section of the neck contains many of the same structures as Zone I, such as the carotid artery, jugular vein, esophagus, trachea, and cervical spine. Zone III is the section of the neck above the angle of the mandible, and contains the carotid artery, salivary glands, and pharynx.

The neck and its structures may be injured from:

- Violence
- Sports
- Horseback riding accidents
- Diving or other water-related activities
- Stabbings
- Hangings
- Strangulation
- Industrial accidents
- Vehicle accidents
- Blows to the neck

The EMT should remember that injuries to the neck area may result in restriction of the patient's airway, so continual assessment of neck injuries is indicated. The most commonly injured parts of the neck are blood vessels; if they are severed and bleeding is not controlled, the patient may die from excessive blood loss, which is called **exsanguination**. Intubation can help stabilize damaged areas of the neck, provide ventilatory support, and protect the airway. However, airway procedures that involve entry through the neck should be avoided; in most cases, a bag-mask device will provide adequate ventilation for the patient. The EMT should assume that a cervical spine injury is present when the patient has a neck injury.

Face

Facial injuries may be to the soft tissues or may be a result of fractures. Vascularity in the face can cause injuries to look quite serious. Life-threatening injuries in this area are possible, although rare. The facial bones can remain intact under tremendous stress; however, facial fractures may allow absorption of the force from blunt trauma.

Symptoms of facial fractures include:

- Crepitus
- Ecchymosis
- Pain or numbness
- Swelling
- Asymmetry of cheek bone or nasal septum
- Limited movement of the eyes or jaw
- Dental malocclusion

Nasal fractures are the most common facial fractures, followed by mandible fractures.

Le Fort fractures were first described in 1901 as three different patterns that occur in midface fractures. **Le Fort I fractures**, which are horizontal, are found in the region from the maxilla to the nasal fossa. **Le Fort II fractures** are usually triangular, and involve the nasal bones and medial orbits. **Le Fort III**

fractures are more complex than the other two fracture types, and involve separation of the facial bones from the cranial bones. Symptoms of midfacial fractures include an unstable maxilla, nasal flattening, lengthened appearance of the face, and leakage of cerebrospinal fluid from the nose. Patients with Le Fort fractures are hospitalized because of the risk of serious airway issues and the difficulty of correct placement of nasogastric or nasotracheal tubes.

The cranium and maxilla are both supported by the **zygoma**, more commonly known as the **cheek bone**. This bone also articulates with the frontal and temporal bones, as well as the maxilla. Symptoms of **zygomatic fracture** include a flattened cheek area and numbness of the cheek and nasal area. This type of fracture is often seen in combination with orbital fractures.

Eyes

A fracture of the floor and medial walls of the ocular orbit is called a **blowout fracture**, and is usually caused by a blunt object, such as a fist, ball, or rock. It occurs when an object of greater diameter than the orbital rim strikes the globe of the eye and the soft tissue around it. This places pressure on the orbital floor, and if fracture results, the orbital contents may be pushed into the maxillary sinus. Symptoms of **blowout fractures** include swelling, **double vision (diplopia)**, restricted movement of the eye, impaired extraocular movements, and **epistaxis** (nosebleed). Orbital fractures are commonly associated with other facial injuries.

Numerous parts of the eye can be damaged from trauma, including the conjunctiva, iris, cornea, pupillary sphincter, lens, retina, optic nerve, and other intraocular or intraorbital structures.

Injuries to the eyes should be evaluated by a physician in the emergency department or trauma center. Patients may complain of foreign bodies in the eyes, and when this is suspected, the EMT should inspect the inner surface of the upper and lower eyes. If an object is present, it should be removed, using gentle irrigation with sterile water or normal saline. Other injuries to the eye include vitreous hemorrhage and dislocation of the lens; the EMT should control any bleeding with gentle pressure and protect the eye with a metal shield or cardboard cup.

The patient may have a **corneal abrasion**, which is a scratch to the surface of the cornea of the eye. Symptoms of a corneal abrasion include pain, sensation of a foreign body, light sensitivity, and excessive tearing. Patients with contusion injuries experience pain and light sensitivity, along with traumatic dilation or constriction of the pupil. If blood is present in the aqueous fluid in the anterior chamber of the eye, the patient may be experiencing **traumatic hyphema**. There are numerous causes of hyphema, including blunt trauma, sports injuries, missiles, and projectiles, as well as physical abuse. The EMT should use a double patch on the eye to prevent movement, which can cause further aggravation of the injury.

A normal pupil will constrict when exposed to light and dilate when exposed to darkness. **Mydriasis** is defined as the dilation of the pupil of the eye. Abnormal pupillary responses are common after trauma, and are most often caused by direct trauma to the pupillary sphincter muscle. The pupils in their normal state should be black, round, and of equal size. Pupil abnormalities may be caused by drug use, previous surgical procedures, cataracts, and other causes. Patients with fixed and dilated pupils are usually given a poor prognosis, because the symptom usually indicates damage to the third cranial nerve and/or the upper brain stem or brain stem ischemia. The optic nerve and/or globe may also be damaged if the patient shows abnormal response in pupillary dilation. By instructing the patient to follow an object, such as a finger or pen, the EMT can assess and document abnormalities.

Nose

The nasal bones are fragile and easily broken; nasal fractures are the most commonly broken bones on the face. It takes twice the force to fracture the zygoma compared to the force required to fracture the nose. Many injuries to the nasal area consist of severe swelling and epistaxis, but do not result in broken bones. Physicians sometimes wait several days before treating nasal fractures to allow the body to heal on its own; however, many patients will express concern about deformity and disfigurement where the nose is concerned and they may want to consult with a reconstructive specialist.

For nontrauma patients with nosebleeds, the EMT should have the patient calmly sit down and lean the body and head slightly forward to prevent blood flow into the throat, which can cause nausea and vomiting. A damp washcloth or clean tissue can be used to apply gentle pressure to the nasal area, pinching the soft part of the nose together for at least five minutes. If the bleeding has not stopped at that point, it should be pinched together for another ten minutes. After fifteen to twenty minutes of direct pressure, the nose should stop bleeding, but if the bleeding continues, the patient should be taken to the emergency department or trauma center. If there is heavy bleeding from the nose, this could indicate a cervical spine injury. The patient needs to be kept in the position they are in if the airway can be managed in that position.

Spine

The spinal column is made up of 33 vertebrae which are divided into 5 sections; there are 7 cervical, 12 thoracic, 5 lumbar, 5 sacral, and 4 coccygeal vertebrae. **Cervical vertebrae** are the "joint above" when splinting, and the **sacrum** is the "joint below" in splinting. The **spinal cord** is found inside the **spinal canal** and is encased in the **vertebral foramen** and protected by the **spinal column**. Nerve roots from the **spinal cord** emerge from the spinal canal through the vertebral foramen and then travel throughout the body. **Ascending nerve tracts** carry messages from the body up the spinal cord and to the brain. **Descending nerve tracts** carry impulses from the brain through the spinal cord and down to various parts of the body. There are 31 pairs of spinal nerves that all originate from the spinal cord.

The EMT must determine the **mechanism of injury (MOI)** when evaluating a possible spinal cord injury. A positive classification of injury means that forces or impact during the injury suggest that there is a potential spinal injury. A negative classification of injury means that forces or impact during the injury do not suggest a potential spinal injury. If the EMT is uncertain about the forces or impact, the patient's injury should be classified as uncertain.

Once EMTs arrive at the scene and check for patient safety, they should complete an initial assessment. At this point, the EMT may determine that **spinal immobilization** is necessary. Once spinal immobilization has begun, it must be completed. **Extrication** is the process of removing a person from an entrapment, such as a vehicle, after an accident. Extrication or cervical collar application starts the immobilization process. Manual stabilization does not start the immobilization process. If the EMT decides that spinal immobilization is not indicated, he or she must document the reasons that support this decision; for example, an alert adult patient who has had a vehicle accident, can communicate, and has no complaints of injury, would likely not meet the criteria for spinal immobilization.

Spinal Immobilization Criteria

Spinal injury should be suspected if the blunt mechanism of injury is present and should be treated if one of the following criteria is present:

- Altered mental status for any reason, including alcohol or drug intoxication

- Complaint of neck and/or spine tenderness or pain
- Weakness, tingling, or numbness in the trunk or extremities at any time since the injury
- Deformity of the spine not present prior to the incident
- Distracting injury or circumstances that may lead to an unreliable physical exam or history

If the EMT has any doubt about a patient's injuries, spinal injury should be suspected and immobilization should be initiated. A combination of loading and rotational forces is a common mechanism of injury for spinal injuries. When one or more cervical vertebrae are dislocated and forced into the spinal canal, the result is often a spinal cord injury.

Axial loading is defined as the application of weight or force along the course of the long axis of the body; for example, a diver who hits his head on the bottom surface of a pool can incur a compression fracture or crushed vertebral body without a spinal cord injury. Flexion, hyperextension, and hyperrotation can cause fractures, as well as muscle and ligament injuries. **Lateral bending** occurs when sudden lateral impact moves the torso sideways. This type of injury can occur when a car crashes into the driver's side door or in contact sports. Intentional or unintentional hangings are examples of distraction injuries. Blunt and penetrating trauma and/or electrical injury can also cause spinal cord injuries.

Reassessment of Trauma Patients

Trauma patients should continuously be reassessed using the ABCDE method. Because traumatic injuries are often so severe and need immediate intervention, initial assessments of the patient's condition may change as time progresses. Traumatic injuries can cause a cascade of other effects that only appear over time, and regular assessments assist in catching these changes before they progress. Additionally, continuous assessments can catch conditions that may have previously been missed altogether. Some reports indicate that up to 10 percent of traumatic injuries are not caught by the primary assessment.

In general, EMT personnel can expect to reassess trauma patients anywhere from every five to ten minutes, depending on the severity of the case. In addition to continuing to abide by the ABCDE method, EMT personnel are expected to monitor the patient's vital signs, examine how interventions in place are affecting the patient and adjust accordingly, and note if other conditions are presenting. Conditions that require further examination or immediate intervention include sudden drops or spikes in any of the vital signs (blood pressure, temperature, pulse, and respiration rate), or if any new complaints are verbalized by the patient.

Reassessments can also help EMTs determine the best timing for procedures. Some procedures that are critical to survival may need to be done on site, but any procedure that can be performed during transport to the hospital should not be done on site. Transferring the patient to the appropriate trauma center in a timely fashion is the priority.

Differentiating Blunt from Penetrating MOI

As mentioned, blunt and penetrating traumas can cause similar patterns of injury, but they are different forms of trauma. The main difference is that blunt force traumas make contact with a larger surface area, while penetrating traumas usually have only one single point of initial contact (which can ultimately cause a wider spread of injuries). For example, two patients can experience brain injuries—one who experienced a blow to the skull (blunt force trauma), and one who experienced a gunshot

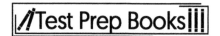

wound to the head (penetrating trauma). Although both affect the same organ, the method of contact is quite different.

Blunt traumas are not only caused by a blow from an object that comes toward the patient. They can also be caused by something dropping or falling on the patient or from a fall itself. Regardless, the impact of a blunt trauma is affected directly by the directional movement of the impact (whether it was head-on, from behind, a lateral hit, or a rotational hit), and the velocity with which the impact took place. Restraining devices can often minimize the effect of blunt traumas, as they greatly reduce the velocity of one of the objects involved (usually of the patient). Many (though not all) blunt traumas are highly visible externally and look aggravated to the naked eye, but there may be hidden injuries.

Penetrating traumas encompass forces that hit the patient in a single point and puncture tissues. In addition to gunshot wounds, other common penetrating traumas include knife stabbings, impacts from particles after an explosion, or impalements from larger objects (including examples where the patient falls onto a sharp object). As with blunt traumas, velocity plays a role in the severity of penetrating traumas. Particles or bullets that hit the body at a faster velocity cause greater localized trauma, while low velocity can cause larger surface area trauma. Additionally, most penetrating traumas cause more internal damage than external damage. A patient may not visibly look as though they are badly injured, but may have an array of deep internal damage (especially to organs or vessels that have been penetrated). These situations can quickly become fatal, especially if the wounds are located between the head and the thighs.

Connecting Obvious and Hidden Injuries

Hidden injuries often occur as a result of obvious injuries, but are not immediately visible or are not visible without the assistance of imaging machinery (such as x-rays, MRIs, or CT scans). Therefore, EMT personnel should never assume that a visible injury is the only condition that will require an intervention. More than likely, there will be additional related injuries that should be anticipated. For example, a pregnant patient may appear to have only experienced mild whiplash from a motor accident, but should always be transported to an emergency department to have the condition of her fetus examined and monitored. A patient with a gunshot wound to the torso may only have an entry wound and not an exit wound, indicating that the bullet is lodged somewhere in their body—potentially in an organ or in a bone, which can cause internal hemorrhage or paralysis as time passes. Facial traumas may correlate with sensory damage. Chest and abdomen traumas often correlate with cardiac or pulmonary events, or sepsis.

Traumatic brain injuries, especially, should be monitored for additional hidden conditions. While a brain injury may be evaluated as stable after intervention and treatment, the effects of brain injury can slowly present and gradually worsen over time. It is common for patients who experience a seemingly mild concussion to succumb to mortality a few hours or days later, even when patients report "feeling fine." Other neurological effects, such as memory loss or personality changes, may be attributed to other causes but are actually the direct result of a prior brain injury. These injuries often cause social and relationship problems when it appears that the patient's personality or intellect has suddenly changed. Unfortunately, many patients who experience head injuries (such as from sports or falls) do not always report it, especially if they don't notice any abnormal symptoms after the incident.

Managing Trauma

Care for a patient who has experienced a traumatic injury goes beyond pre-hospital and in-hospital treatment. It often requires guiding the patient and the patient's support system to understanding the traumatic experience (especially if it was one that was outside of the patient's control); coping with any temporary or permanent physical, emotional, and psychological changes that have resulted from the event; and possibly embarking on a new lifestyle. Many trauma survivors report feeling either unbearable physical or emotional pain or complete apathy; an inability to sleep, eat, or relax; increased anxiety and depression; and common flashbacks of the incident. Trauma survivors may also present changes in hormone and neurotransmitter concentrations and signaling. They are also at risk of exhibiting violence, substance abuse, and other self-destructive behaviors.

Managing these symptoms often requires behavioral-cognitive therapy (not just for the patient, but also for the patient's family and friends) that focuses on comprehending the event that took place, the patient's role in the event, understanding involuntary reactions that arise as a result, and how the patient's support system can best aid in the patient's recovery. These aspects may then be used to teach the patient how to frame the situation, understand their reactions, and implement healthy coping mechanisms that will best serve them in recovery. This type of therapy may be prescribed with other post-trauma care, such as physical rehabilitation. It is important that this educational and healing process begins while the patient is still in medical care, as many people will not voluntarily seek counseling once discharged from the hospital.

Emergency Trauma Care

Spinal Immobilization
Spinal immobilization refers to the practice of stabilizing the cervical, thoracic, and lumbar vertebrae so that the entire column of the spine is unable to move. The procedure is conducted using a stable collar around the cervical vertebrae, and/or a hard board that runs the full length of the patient's spine with the intention of retaining a neutral spinal alignment while in transport. The patient is bound to the board.

Collars that go around the cervical spine are best used on patients that experienced a traumatic, visible head or neck injury, or in patients who experienced an event that places them at a high risk of having trauma to the neck even if no symptoms are immediately showing (such as whiplash in a minor motor accident). Boards that are used in immobilization should not be used as the only method of stabilization in patients at risk of a cervical injury.

Spinal immobilization has a long history in the EMT industry, but recent studies indicate that it may not be an effective practice and that it may cause some degree of harm to most patients, including discomfort, respiratory obstacles, and neurological impingements. As a result, indications for when to use this procedure have shifted significantly. Rather than immobilizing the spine during any trauma case, and assuming the procedure cannot cause additional harm, it is vital for EMTs to make sure this technique is used only when the patient is presenting symptoms or at risk of having experienced a true spinal injury.

Seated Spinal Immobilization
Seated spinal immobilizations take place when a patient is conscious and injuries may be less severe (especially when there are no lower limb injuries), or if a patient must be moved from a seated position

to the emergency vehicle or to a long board. Multiple EMT rescuers will be needed. Whenever possible, the rescuers should communicate their actions to the patient. This can also help the patient autonomously ensure that they do not make large movements with the head, neck, or back. One rescuer should support the patient in maintaining a neutral head and neck alignment to preserve the cervical spine, and another rescuer should place the cervical collar around the patient's neck. A short board—a plastic and rigid piece of support that goes the length of the head and torso—may be placed against the patient's head and back for extra support. X-shaped straps cross the patient's body, and an additional strap goes across the patient's upper chest and collar. There is also a strap that gets secured across the patient's forehead. This strap, along with the collar strap, should be secured last. Straps should be tightened to hold the board securely against the patient.

A **Kendrick extrication device** is also commonly used to employ seated spinal mobilizations *only* in contexts where the patient is not suffering from a life-threatening condition. It combines a flat board, a cervical support mechanism, and supportive head pads into a single device that is shaped like a board, which can easily be slid behind a seated patient. Secured straps cross the patient's body, and the device then wraps around the neck and torso of the patient before being secured. Rods placed within the device maintain the spine's neutral alignment. Again, the head should be secured last.

Long Board
Long boards are used in instances of severe spinal injury. They are usually made out of plastic and are rigid. They are large, but light. Patients can be immobilized onto a long board, usually with the assistance of a cervical collar, side padding to further assist with immobilization, and straps that attach to the board. Additionally, most boards can be used in conjunction with x-ray machines, allowing patients to remain stabilized during testing.

Patients that require long board immobilization should be moved by multiple rescuers onto the board in a logroll fashion, ensuring (before movement) that the patient's head will be completely on the board after placement. Rescuers should work together to ensure all regions of the patient's body (legs, pelvis, torso, neck, and head) move in quick synchronization and without misalignment, twisting, or sagging of any region. This precaution is taken to avoid further injury. Upon placement, small adjustments may be necessary to achieve spinal neutrality on the board. One rescuer should make the adjustments while other rescuers provide support to the patient's body and keep the board secured in place. Then, the patient should be strapped in across the torso, the pelvis (unless there is a pelvic or groin injury), and legs, if needed. During any form of board immobilization, the head should always be secured last.

In recent years, long boards have decreased in usage as the rigidity of the board can cause more harm than good for some patients. Alternatively, vacuum mattresses and extra padding on the long board can help alleviate the discomfort that comes with being immobilized. Many organizations recommend that EMT personnel avoid using a long board when the transport to the admitting hospital is long (over ten minutes), when the patient has gunshot wound related trauma above the waist, or when the patient has physical conditions that would present an obstacle (such as spinal scoliosis, spinal kyphosis or lordosis, late term pregnancy, obesity, etc.).

Extremity Splinting
Extremity splinting refers to a way of immobilizing the patient's limbs (rather than the spinal column). This technique is frequently needed in situations where the patient has a fractured arm or leg. When this is the case, it is quite visible, as limbs will often be at an abnormal angle and the patient will report and display a high degree of pain. The area may also be inflamed, tender, or swollen. In severe cases,

the bone may have ripped through the skin, which may lead to excessive bleeding and shock if not quickly and adequately managed. The most likely scenarios requiring extremity splinting are closed and open fractures, although other, more complicated types of fractures may also be seen.

In cases where extremity splinting is needed, the EMT will likely use one or more rigid boards to stabilize the area. Before administering the splint, the rescuer should try to gather as much information as possible by asking the patient how the area feels, noting color and circulation of the area, if the patient is able to move the area, and if the patient is able to feel any sensation there. Sensory and musculoskeletal cues can indicate whether or not the patient has suffered spinal or nerve injury. The rescuer should try to realign the fracture before splinting, but in severe cases (or in cases where extreme pressure is felt), this may not be possible. Either way, nearby joints should also be splinted to assist with immobilization.

Some splints work in conjunction with a sling for extra support. For example, fractures in the arm are often supported with a sling across the upper body, in which the splinted limb rests during transport.

Traction Splinting

A **traction splint** is most commonly used with large bones where extremity splinting would not provide enough support. Traction splints are used to treat severe, single fractures, most commonly affecting the femur, but can also work with other bones in the hips or legs. Fractured femurs, especially, can cause a host of other issues, including blood loss and involuntary muscle contraction. These muscular contractions can cause the fractured pieces of the bone to move and overlap. A traction splint uses pressure to pull the overlapped pieces away from each other so that the bone can be splinted until treatment is available. If a large bone fracture is suspected, or if the area simply appears abnormal, it should be assumed to be fractured and should be treated with a traction splint.

A traditional traction splint utilizes the pelvis to work effectively. Therefore, broken pelvic bones and other fractures near the affected area are contraindications for using a traction splint. A **Hare traction splint** uses two rods on either side of the fracture, while a **Sager traction splint** uses only one rod against the fracture. One portion of the splint rests against the pelvis on the side of the fracture, and a strap loops around the foot on the side of the fracture. The metal rod supports the site of the fracture, and other straps cross over the leg and rod. The straps are tightened to create pressure that holds the rod in place against the fracture. This general blueprint has advanced considerably since its original inception in the late 1800s. Contemporary versions have both manual and automatic traction capabilities.

Smaller traction splints, called **dynamic traction splints**, work similarly but are intended to treat the small bones of the hand and fingers. These are typically not utilized in emergency situations.

Mechanical Patient Restraint

In some situations, patients will need to be restrained for appropriate care to be delivered. **Mechanical patient restraint** should be a last resort of conduct in emergency cases. Patients who are severely intoxicated or under the influence of substances, are experiencing an episode of psychosis or delusion, exhibiting contagious symptoms that could be life threatening to others, or otherwise threatening harm to themselves or others are examples of cases where mechanical restraint will likely be necessary, especially if verbal negotiation does not work. In situations like these, it becomes more important for the EMT to assess scene safety to ensure the patient is not in possession of, or otherwise able to access, items that could be used to harm rescuers. When working with pediatric patients, the parents or guardians should be the ones to provide restraint whenever possible.

When restraining a patient, it is important for the EMT to use the least amount of physical force necessary and to avoid additional harm or injury to the patient. The patient and their belongings should be treated with respect throughout the entire pre-hospital and transport process. Restraining the patient should not interfere with their ability to accept care. It is also important to note that patients experiencing a seizure should never be restrained, and that pregnant patients should not be restrained in a complete supine or complete prone position.

Additionally, detailed documentation is required any time a patient requires restraint during pre-hospital care. The guidelines for this documentation may vary by organization, but the documentation will typically require detailing what occurred, the nature of the emergency, why the patient needed to be restrained, how the patient was restrained, and any additional injuries that occurred. Laws dictating when patient restraint can be utilized also vary by state, so it is important for the EMT to know the established guidelines of the area where he or she works.

Tourniquets

Tourniquets are used to manage blood flow and circulation in a particular area, using external pressure. Their use is indicated in patients who are hemorrhaging, or at risk of hemorrhaging, due to major artery damage. Applying a tourniquet can save a patient's life or their affected limbs from amputation. Pediatric patients, especially, can benefit from tourniquet administration due to their small size and increased risk of rapidly bleeding out from traumatic injuries. If a medical tourniquet is not available, utilizing the cuff from an available blood pressure monitor is recommended. This should be used as a last resort, however.

Mass manufactured medical tourniquets are easy to use, can be established in under a minute, and can be administered by a single EMT rescuer. Tourniquets are placed close to the location of a wound, without being placed directly over it or near joints. The degree of tightness depends on the location of the wound and the width of the tourniquet. Once placed, the tourniquet should not be moved until the patient reaches the hospital and is in the care of its trauma team. The tourniquet should be monitored to ensure it has not loosened. Generally, tourniquets should not be left on longer than two hours, as irreversible tissue necrosis and nerve damage occurs within six hours.

Although the tourniquet is a life-saving device, the side effects are somewhat severe. The area affected tends to become irritated and deoxygenated, cellular pH levels become imbalanced, the risk of cellular edema increases, and nerve irritation is common. Therefore, removing the tourniquet comes with its own set of intervention protocols. Discharged patients may experience a phenomenon known as post-tourniquet syndrome, which can last anywhere from a few days to six months. This syndrome is characterized by paralysis, tremors, muscle dysfunction, and general weakness in the area where the tourniquet was placed.

MAST/PASG

Military Anti-Shock Trousers (MAST)/Pneumatic Anti-Shock Garments (PASG) are used to treat hemorrhaging patients and patients with pelvis injuries, with the intention of preventing the patient from going into shock or stabilizing the pelvis. Shaped like pants, they fit around the patient's lower half; the device can be wrapped onto the patient, slid onto the patient, or laid flat to where the patient can be placed into it. Sections are inflated to apply pressure to blood vessels (to stop excessive bleeding) or to stabilize broken bones, broken joints, or torn muscles. When used in hemorrhaging victims, the pressure from the device may return enough blood back into circulation to stabilize the patient until he or she is admitted to the hospital. They are best utilized in patients who have severe lower body

bleeding injuries, such as a femoral artery wound. However, recent studies have shown that the amount of blood that recirculates from MAST/PASG application is about one-fourth of what was previously believed.

The use of MAST/PASG devices can present unpleasant side effects. The excess pressure on the torso can negatively affect the patient's breathing, as well as exacerbate injuries to the upper torso, chest, and lung area. While the compression offered by MAST/PASG devices can help reestablish and redirect blood flow in patients that are bleeding out (such as if a limb was severed), it can make internal hemorrhages worse to the point of expediting a fatal outcome. These devices should also not be used on any patients suffering a cardiac arrest or experiencing pulmonary edema. Additionally, it is important to note that removing MAST/PASG devices is a serious procedure that must be carefully monitored and managed. When the device is removed, blood pressure drastically falls and the body reacts as if it is quickly losing blood, so rescuers should avoid removing the device before the patient is admitted to the hospital, or should be prepared to stabilize the patient once more. The drawbacks of these devices leave them with minimal recommended use, instead favoring quickly transporting patients to a trauma center.

Cervical Collars

Cervical collars wrap around the cervical spine (vertebrae C1 to C7) to reduce or eliminate pain in the head and neck, and maintain neutral alignment down the cervical spine. They originally were used with the intention of immobilizing the spine, but this is actually not physically possible. Even in a cervical collar, the vertebrae of the cervical spine are able to move. However, the presence of the collar does remind patients to avoid large movements of the head and neck. Emergency services have switched to using soft cervical collars over rigid collars in recent decades. Soft cervical collars are flexible and fit specifically to the patient. They are less likely to restrict the airway, and are more comfortable for the patient. Additionally, they may be recommended by medical professionals for chronic or long-term neck issues. Some variations of these collars can even be bought at most pharmacies and drug stores; often people who have a history of neck and back problems will purchase them to manage temporary bouts of pain at home.

Rigid cervical collars are made of an inflexible plastic material. They were commonly used in emergency situations until recently; as of 2015, most emergency medical services prefer the use of a soft cervical collar in cases where the patient needs to limit spinal movement.

Though once considered a universal best practice in emergency contexts, using a rigid cervical collar has many limitations and can often harm patients (which ultimately led to the sharp decrease in their usage). Research showed that most patients experiencing an emergency did not actually face any risk of spinal injury; therefore, using a cervical collar was a waste of resources. In fact, many patients suffered more because the unnecessary cervical collar hindered the patient's ability to receive adequate assisted ventilation, as the hard-plastic material of the rigid cervical collars actually made it more difficult to maintain a patent airway and manage oxygen administration. Additionally, rigid cervical collars often place undue pressure on the cervical spinal cord and the arteries and veins that serve the head and neck. This, in turn, can cause neurological dysfunction and hazardous levels of intracranial blood pressure.

Consequently, it is recommended that the use of a rigid cervical collar is limited to cases of severe trauma, fracture, or dislocation of the head, neck, or spinal cord, rather than as a standard technique for any emergency situation.

Signs of definite spinal injury that would warrant the use of a cervical collar include paralysis; loss of normally voluntary functions (such as bladder control); numbness in the patient's extremities; muscle spasms; severe pain in the head, neck, upper back, or shoulders; uncontrollable movements; or poor neurological functioning.

Rapid Extrication

Rapid extrication refers to a technique where a patient is quickly moved from the scene of the trauma and stabilized onto a stretcher. It is a systematic process that is meant to keep vital areas of the patient's body—such as the head, neck, and pelvis—safe from additional trauma or stress while quickly preparing the patient for transport. It should be used in contexts where the scene is dangerous (such as due to an environmental hazard), the patient needs to be transported immediately (such as when suffering from catastrophic, life-threatening injuries), or the patient is in the way of other patients who need immediate care. It is most commonly used in motor vehicle accidents where the patient has to be removed from the vehicle in a seated position and ends in a supine position. Because this is a relatively fast process with multiple components, it requires a team of multiple EMT personnel to carry it out.

The technique begins by ensuring as much safety for the EMT personnel as possible. Although the scene may be safe, the process must move at a fast pace and precautions should be taken to ensure that neither the EMT personnel nor the patient will be harmed by environmental factors during rapid extrication. EMT personnel should also take the time to administer gloves, goggles, and any other self-protective barriers that should be used when handling a patient. One EMT team member should stand or crouch behind the patient and stabilize the patient's head and neck and maintain neutral alignment of the cervical spine.

If there is time, another EMT team member should perform a quick assessment of the patient's motor and sensory functions, and place a cervical collar, if needed. A third EMT team member should prepare the stretcher (or long board, if the situation warrants it). When it is time to move the patient to the stretcher, the first team member should support the patient's head and neck, the second team member should support the patient's torso and pelvis, and the third team member should support the patient's legs. Together, they should place the patient onto the long board in one motion while preserving the neutral alignment of the spine. All sensory and motor functions should be monitored while the patient is in transport.

Practice Questions

1. Which demographic of patients makes up the majority of multisystem trauma cases?
   a. Adult
   b. Elderly (over age 70)
   c. Pediatric
   d. Immunocompromised

2. What is the primary difference between a Hare traction splint and a Sager traction splint?
   a. A Hare traction splint is a bipolar medical device, while a Sager traction splint is a unipolar traction device.
   b. A Hare traction splint is for adult patients, while a Sager traction splint is for pediatric patients.
   c. A Hare traction splint is for large lower limbs, while a Sager traction splint is for smaller upper bones, such as in the hand.
   d. A Hare traction splint is for rapid splinting, while a Sager traction splint takes more time to properly employ.

3. What is an advantage of modern-day tourniquets?
   a. They are simple, consisting of only sterile gauze.
   b. They can be effectively established by one person and in under one minute.
   c. They contain a built-in antibiotic dispensing unit and can be used for medical situations other than wound care.
   d. They can only be placed in hospital settings, which provide a more sterile environment.

4. An EMT team arrives at a scene where a male patient appears to have been stabbed and is bleeding moderately. As the team walks toward the patient, the patient holds one hand up and yells, slurring his words, "Don't come near me or I will attack!" The patient looks dazed and disoriented, but he glances around, and his eyes fall upon a small metal rod that is nearby. He begins to lunge toward it. What option is available to the EMT team at this point?
   a. The team should immediately leave the scene and let the patient fend for himself.
   b. The team should pull out any available items that could be used as weapons and prepare for self-defense actions.
   c. The team should attempt to restrain the patient, using established guidelines set by their geographic region and medical organization.
   d. The team should estimate the patient's body mass, and the EMT team leader should shoot the patient with an appropriately dosed tranquilizer dart.

5. Which emergency trauma practice has shifted greatly in indications and methodology in recent years?
   a. Spinal immobilization
   b. Extremity splinting
   c. Tourniquet application
   d. On-site amputation

6. An EMT team is called to the scene of an emergency. They see an older female patient lying on the ground, clutching her thigh at a spot from where blood is flowing heavily. She seems confused and pale, and is breathing heavily. Her eyes are fluttering as if they are about to close, and she is unable to respond when a rescuer calls to her. A quick blood pressure assessment shows a reading of 100/65. What condition is this patient exhibiting signs of?
   a. Delusion
   b. Hypovolemic shock
   c. Stroke
   d. Heart failure

7. Which of the following indicate the definite need for spinal immobilization?
   I. Intoxication
   II. A fall during the emergency situation
   III. Tender points along the cervical vertebrae
   IV. Blunt force trauma of the head
   a. Choice I only
   b. Choice II only
   c. Choices II and III
   d. Choices III and IV

8. An EMT team arrives to the scene of an emergency. A gunfire fight occurred, and a teenage female bystander was hit by two bullets. One bullet hit the patient in the chest and exited through her back; bright red blood is spurting from the wound. Another bullet hit her near her hip and does not appear to have exited; it may be lodged in or near the patient's spine. What would be the appropriate first course of action by rescuers?
   a. Stabilize the open chest wound
   b. Immobilize the patient on a long board and check for spinal damage
   c. Ask the patient her medical history and any details she can remember about the suspects
   d. Immobilize the patient using a Kendrick extrication device

9. What is the best order of operations to stop severe skin wound bleeding in an injured patient?
   a. Sterilize the area, place a one-inch tourniquet directly over the wound, and tighten until it cannot be dislodged.
   b. Find the largest bandage available and tightly tie it over the wound; place the limb in a sling.
   c. Clean away debris, place a sterile cloth or bandage over the wound, apply a tourniquet near the wound, and immobilize the area.
   d. Transport the patient immediately and deal with the bleeding during transport.

10. Which of these conditions is characterized by fluid buildup around the heart muscle, which ultimately limits the heart's ability to pump?
   a. Hypovolemic shock syndrome
   b. Pulmonary edema
   c. Lung tumors
   d. Pericardial tamponade

This material is provided for exam preparation purposes only and does not indicate an endorsement of any specific scientific, political, or religious point of view. © TPB Publishing. You have been licensed one copy of this document for personal use only. Any other reproduction or redistribution is strictly prohibited. All rights

11. An EMT team is called to the scene of a serious motor vehicle accident. The 19-year-old driver of the vehicle is alive, but was thrown against the steering wheel and was also caught in the torso by his improperly positioned lap belt. Once extricated from the vehicle, he gets up and tries to walk. What onset of symptoms should EMT personnel continuously monitor for?
    a. Abdominal distention and tenderness, internal hemorrhage, and abnormal stomach tension
    b. Pelvic and leg fractures
    c. Chest and arm pain, indicative of a cardiac event triggered by stress
    d. Neck pain

12. A patient appears to have a broken tibia; the piece of bone below the break point is diagonal and is at a sharp angle to the patellofemoral joint. What type of fracture is this?
    a. Oblique
    b. Open
    c. Transverse
    d. Closed

13. Which layer of the skin is affected by third-degree burns?
    a. The hypodermis
    b. The epidermis
    c. The dermis
    d. All layers of the skin

14. A magnitude-8 earthquake hits a small city in the middle of the night, and many buildings collapse onto the people inside of them. EMT personnel are dispatched as soon as it is safe to drive, and they find a number of patients inside their homes that are showing signs of compressed limbs, shock, and edema in the limbs. What condition are these residents suffering from?
    a. Kidney disease
    b. Vascular disease
    c. Crush syndrome
    d. Cushing's syndrome

15. What are the Five P's that should be monitored for in a patient afflicted by compartment syndrome?
    a. Pain, Pallor, Paresthesia, Pulse, Paralysis
    b. Pain, Posture, Pallor, Pericardia, Pulse
    c. Pain, Pulse, Posture, Pulmonary, Pediatric surgery
    d. Posture, Pallor, Pulse, Paralysis, Paraplegia

16. What are the three aspects that the Glasgow Coma Scale measures to provide an overall patient assessment?
    a. Eye movement, hand movement, pulse
    b. Eye opening, verbal response, motor response
    c. Brain scan, heart scan, verbal response
    d. Sensory awareness, musculoskeletal response, sound assessment

17. A patient with blunt force trauma to the back of the skull has been transported to the hospital and has had brain imaging performed. Imaging shows a severe traumatic injury to the frontal lobe. This injury can be classified as which of the following?
    a. Coup injury
    b. Contrecoup injury
    c. Temporal injury
    d. Stroke

18. Which of these conditions is characterized by pooled blood between the skull and the outer layer of the brain?
    a. A coup injury
    b. A neurological edema
    c. Meningitis
    d. Epidural hematoma

Answer Explanations

1. C: Pediatric patients are most susceptible to multisystem trauma, because their brains and bodies are still developing. A blow to the head or chest often results in the failure of other systems. While elderly and immunocompromised patients can suffer greatly in the event of multisystem trauma injuries, they do not make up the majority of cases.

2. A: A Hare traction splint utilizes two rods to support a broken limb, while a Sager traction splint utilizes a single rod. The other options are not accurate.

3. B: Modern tourniquets can be quickly administered in under a minute and by a single rescuer. Sterile gauze tourniquets are very antiquated. Modern tourniquets do not have built-in antibiotic dispensing and can be used in a wide variety of settings.

4. C: In this case, the EMT rescuers are allowed to restrain the patient due to the verbal and physical threats. They should follow guidelines that are established for them, and be sure to document the situation in its entirety as well. Patients should not be left to fend for themselves, fought, or tranquilized. In these cases, rescuers will need to work together to provide care to the best of their ability.

5. A: Spinal immobilization techniques have shifted from being accepted as a universal practice in most emergency cases, to requiring stringent indications before immobilizing a patient. This is due to many cases of spinal immobilization causing more patient harm than benefit. The other options do not apply.

6. B: Confusion, pale skin, shortness of breath, loss of consciousness, and low blood pressure are all indicators of hypovolemic shock. The detail about the patient's leg bleeding indicates a possible femoral artery blow, which would lead to a large amount of blood loss. This is a common precursor to hypovolemic shock. Some of the symptoms could apply to the other options provided, but all of the symptoms listed apply to hypovolemic shock.

7. D: Direct pain and trauma to the head, neck, or spine indicate the need for spinal immobilization. Intoxication or a fall alone are not enough to indicate the need for immobilization, and doing so in these cases may cause more harm than benefit.

8. A: The chest wound is the most critical injury in this case. Because the site is spurting bright red blood, the bullet likely hit a vital artery. The patient could bleed out within minutes. Gunshot patients should never be immobilized, and patient history can be collected at a later time, when the patient is in a stable condition.

9. C: All debris should be cleared from the site, but large objects may need to remain intact. Removing them may cause further bleeding. Tourniquets should be applied near the wound, but never directly over it. Bandages should never be tied over wounds by emergency responders; this is an extremely antiquated method. Patient bleeding should be stabilized before transport.

10. D: This describes pericardial or cardiac tamponade. This situation can be caused by acute factors, such as cardiac arrest or infection in the area, or chronic conditions such as kidney disease. The other options listed can sometimes contribute to the incidence of pericardial tamponade, but are not characterized by the symptom described in the question.

11. A: These are symptoms of abdominal trauma, which is indicated from the manner in which the patient was thrown against the steering wheel and lap belt. Abdominal trauma can be overlooked, especially in the presence of other injuries. Injuries can also take some time to worsen. However, these injuries can quickly turn fatal if internal bleeding or organ damage remains undetected. Because the patient is walking, leg and pelvic fractures are unlikely. In a young adult patient, a cardiac event is unlikely, and neck pain is likely to have presented immediately, rather than later on.

12. A: Oblique fractures occur diagonally across the bone, and are common in tibia breaks. A closed fracture is where the bone is broken, but the pieces are still aligned. A transverse fracture takes place horizontally across the bone. An open fracture is one where the bone moves out of alignment and may break through the skin.

13. D: Third-degree burns are the most serious type of burns and affect all three layers of the skin: the epidermis, which is the thinnest and most superficial layer; the dermis, which is much thicker and lies underneath the epidermis; and the hypodermis, which consists of fat and connective tissues. First-degree burns affect only the epidermis, while second-degree burns affect the epidermis and dermis only.

14. C: Crush syndrome is a common affliction in earthquake-related traumas, and is caused by severe compression to an area of muscles and bone. It causes shock, renal failure, and tissue necrosis. The other options listed are chronic issues not brought on by the sudden compression of tissues.

15. A: Compartment syndrome refers to nerve and blood vessel compression in a body compartment (typically a limb) that occurs as a result of trauma or overuse. Rescuers should monitor for the Five P's: the level of *p*ain the patient feels, whether the skin turns pale (*p*allor, indicative of decreased blood flow), whether the patient feels numb or tingling in the area (*p*aresthesia), whether there is a faint or lack of *p*ulse in the area, and the inability to move the area (*p*aralysis). The other options do not apply.

16. B: The Glasgow Coma Scale scores each of these areas to assess brain functioning in patients who experienced a head or brain injury. The final score will fall between 3 and 15. A score between 3 and 8 indicates severe brain injury. A score between 9 and 12 indicates moderate brain injury. A score between 13 and 15 indicates a mild brain injury. Mild brain injuries can often go undetected, while moderate and severe scores correlate with long-term disability. The other options are fictional.

17. B: A contrecoup injury refers to any brain injury that occurs on the opposite side of where an impact took place. A coup injury refers to any brain injury that occurs on the side where an impact took place. A temporal injury normally affects the side of the head. A stroke is an internal brain injury that is caused by a blockage in the blood vessels that serve it.

18. D: These symptoms are indicative of an epidural hematoma, which is brain bleeding as a result of head trauma. A coup injury refers to damage directly on the brain at the site of impact. A neurological edema is not a real condition. Meningitis is an infectious disease that causes brain swelling.

Medical, Obstetrics, and Gynecology

Standard Assessment: Adult and Pediatric Patients

The primary goal of an Emergency Medical Technician (EMT) is to provide emergency on-site medical assistance and to transport a patient to a medical facility. Regardless of the emergency situation, all events require a standard assessment of the scene and patient before making any evaluations, attempted diagnoses, or treatments.

Upon arriving at the site of an emergency call, an EMT should do the following for both children and adults:

- Assess the situation, ensuring the scene is safe before proceeding.

- Maintain and support the patient's ABCs.

- Take the patient's vital signs: pulse, respiration rates, blood pressure, pulse oxygenation, pain level, and any other relevant measurements.

- Administer high-concentration oxygen via a non-rebreathing mask or a bag mask, if necessary.

- Determine appropriate interventions where local protocols allow, such as spinal stabilization, minimization of bleeding, epinephrine shots, CPR, etc.

- Obtain the patient's history regarding the current emergency by using the mnemonic *OPQRST*, either directly from the patient or, in the case of children, the patient's caretaker:

- *O*nset: Did the pain start gradually or suddenly? What was the patient doing when the pain started?

- *P*rovokes: What makes the pain better or worse?

- *Q*uality: Ask the patient to describe the pain; for example, sharp or dull?

- *R*adiates: Ask the patient to identify the area containing the most pain; then ask if the pain radiates to any other part of the body.

- *S*everity: Describe the pain on a scale from 1 to 10.

- *T*ime: When did the pain start?

- Obtain a SAMPLE history, either directly from the patient or, in the case of children, the patient's caretaker. SAMPLE is an acronym that stands for: *s*igns and symptoms, *a*llergies, *m*edications, *p*ast medical history, *l*ast oral intake, *e*vents leading up to the incident.

- If the situation is non-life-threatening, assess and evaluate the patient to determine the cause of the pain or illness.

- Prepare the patient for immediate transport to an appropriate medical facility.

Neurological Emergencies

There are several neurological conditions that are considered medical emergencies. In adults, the most severe are strokes and seizures. For children, seizures and headaches are of the utmost concern. Almost all neurological events result in an **altered mental status (AMS)**, or a change in behavior caused by a loss or interruption in brain function. AMS patients require immediate attention. Using the AVPU scale, the patient's level of consciousness should be the first thing assessed. The following list is a popular mnemonic (TIPS AEIOU) that describes the most common causes of AMS: *T*rauma, *I*nfection, *P*sychogenic causes, *S*eizure/syncope, *A*lcohol, *E*lectrolyte imbalance, *I*nsulin, *O*piates, *U*remia (kidney disease). Since AMS is a common symptom in diabetic emergencies, it's important to always check blood glucose levels when a patient is experiencing AMS.

Stroke

A **stroke** is caused by a blockage of blood to the brain that results in a loss of brain function. An **ischemic** stroke is caused by clots in the blood vessels within the brain, resulting in a restriction of blood flow and tissue death. A **hemorrhagic** stroke occurs when a blood vessel ruptures, causing a decrease in blood volume and flow as well as blood leakage into brain tissues. Strokes are most prevalent in adults, but they may occur in children who have certain diseases, such as sickle cell disease or congenital heart problems, which can cause strokes.

Symptoms of a stroke include: weakness or numbness in the face and limbs, particularly on one side of the body; difficulty speaking, understanding speech, or loss of speech (adults); loss of vision or dimming in one or both eyes; loss of balance or walking instability; and an intense headache with a sudden onset. Strokes can affect bodily functions including swallowing, making it important to check the airway in patients who are unresponsive. An oropharyngeal or nasopharyngeal airway may be needed as well as suctioning. If there's danger of secretions getting into the airway, the patient should be placed in the recovery position. Immediate transport of stroke patients to a hospital is necessary.

Seizures

A **seizure** is an electrical dysfunction of the neurological system that causes uncontrollable muscle movements and abnormal consciousness. Upon responding to a call involving a seizure, an EMT must determine in which part of the body the seizure began. The EMT must also make certain not to place anything in the patient's mouth to avoid both a biting and choking hazard. In adults, the most common type of seizure is a **generalized tonic-clonic seizure**. Symptoms include loss of consciousness followed by muscle rigidity and convulsion. It may also be accompanied by **tachycardia** (rapid heartbeat), sweating, and hyperventilation. In children, a **febrile seizure** is the most common type, caused by a high fever and resulting in a loss of consciousness followed by convulsions and muscle rigidity.

Headaches

A headache may be a sign of an underlying, life-threatening illness, so it's imperative to check for signs of stroke, meningitis, or a gaseous poisoning, such as from carbon monoxide. Severe headaches that occur suddenly, sometimes along with other symptoms such as a stiff neck, seizures, fever, vomiting, or altered mental status, could be life-threatening. It's also important to ensure the patient is comfortable and placed in a quiet environment with minimal lighting, and to transport the patient to the hospital.

Abdominal Disorders

Most abdominal pain isn't the result of a life-threatening condition. It's important to be aware of what conditions could be life-threatening, however, especially in children. Upon first responding, an EMT is required to take patient vitals, support and maintain ABCs, assess body position and mental status, as well as identify the chief complaint and type of abdominal pain. Identifying the type of pain can help with a future diagnosis.

There are three primary types of abdominal pain. **Visceral pain**, or stimulation of an organ's nerve fibers caused by stretching of the organ's wall, is not localized and is often felt as a generalized dull ache. **Parietal** *(somatic)* **pain** is caused by irritation to the parietal peritoneal wall. The **peritoneum** is a serous membrane rich in nerves that lines the abdominal wall and protects the organs. Parietal pain is felt more locally and often described as sharp or stabbing. Finally, **referred pain** is a radiating pain felt somewhere other than the area that actually hurts. For example, a person experiencing irritation of the spleen may feel discomfort in their right shoulder.

In order to assess and identify the cause of abdominal pain, EMTs should have a basic understanding of abdominal anatomy.

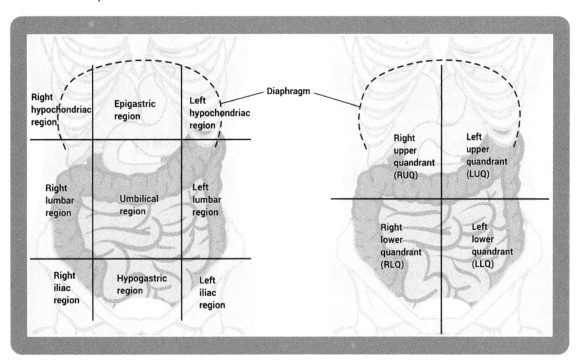

The abdomen is divided into four basic quadrants. Pain in any of these regions may originate in the organs associated with the respective quadrant.

Quadrant	Associated Organs
Right upper quadrant (RUQ)	Liver, gallbladder, and parts of the large intestine
Left upper quadrant (LUQ)	Stomach, spleen, pancreas, and part of the large intestine
Right lower quadrant (RLQ)	Appendix, small intestine, and (in women) fallopian tube and ovary
Left lower quadrant (LLQ)	Part of the small and large intestines, and (in women) the fallopian tube and ovary

Causes of Abdominal Pain

Abdominal pain is generally caused by irritation, stretching, or inflammation of an organ, as well as a decreased blood supply or a ruptured vessel.

The most common causes for abdominal pain in adults include:

- Abdominal aortic aneurysm: rupture of the aorta due to weakened arterial wall
- Appendicitis: inflammation of the appendix
- Bowel obstruction: blockage in the intestine
- Cholecystitis: inflammation of the gallbladder
- Constipation: decreased peristalsis leading to difficulty having bowel movements
- Cystitis: bladder infection
- Ectopic pregnancy: fetal implantation outside of uterus
- Esophagitis: inflammation of the esophagus
- Food poisoning
- Gas or air swallowing (most common in children)
- Kidney stones
- Pancreatitis: inflammation of the pancreas
- Peptic ulcer: erosion of the lining of the stomach
- Peritonitis: inflammation of the peritoneum
- Urinary tract infection

Assessing Abdominal Pain

Upon first responding to a call, it's imperative to determine whether the patient will need immediate medical attention; that is, determine if the patient is "sick" or "not sick." The patient is sick if they show signs of: **decreased perfusion**, i.e., decreased blood pressure, cold extremities, restlessness, confusion; **ischemic chest pain**, or complaints of crushing pressure in middle of chest; **pleuritic (respiratory) issues**, which present as shortness of breath, hyperventilation, etc.; and **signs of panic**, which must be present with other critical signs.

If the patient shows signs of illness, treatment should include supporting and maintaining ABCs, administering high-flow oxygen, placing the patient in supine position, monitoring vital signs, and

100

preparing for immediate transport to a medical facility. If the patient doesn't seem to be in any immediate danger, an EMT should perform an abdominal exam.

Performing an Abdominal Exam

To help determine the location and cause of pain, an EMT should perform an abdominal exam as outlined in the following procedure:

- Lay the patient in a supine position, facing up.

- Ask the patient to identify the location of the pain.

- Palpate the abdomen by pressing on the unaffected areas first. If the patient seems to be guarding, palpate the affected area *gently* after examining other areas. Palpation that is too hard or deep may result in organ rupture or perforation.

- Inspect the abdomen for distension, swelling, surgical scars, or changes in skin color.

If the cause of pain doesn't appear to be serious, treatment may consist of the following:

1. Placing the patient into a position of comfort
2. Administering a low-to-moderate flow of oxygen
3. Monitoring vital signs
4. Preparing the patient for transport, if necessary

Immunology (Allergic Reactions)

Immunology is the study of the immune system, which controls the physiological response to foreign invaders such as viruses, organisms, and bacteria. Immunologic emergencies consist of allergic reactions and **anaphylaxis**—an extreme and life-threatening allergic reaction. At least 1,000 Americans die each year due to such emergencies.

An **allergic reaction** is an exaggerated immune response to an external stimulus, which can present in the form of a bite, sting, or ingested or airborne particles. This stimulus then signals the immune system to release chemicals to combat the foreign invader, known as **histamines** and **leukotrienes**, both of which contribute to the allergic response. Allergic reactions may be mild, resulting in sneezing, watery eyes and nose, or hives, or the reactions may be severe, resulting in anaphylactic shock and respiratory failure.

Allergic reactions have five primary causes: medications, foods, insect stings or bites that inject venom (envenomation), chemicals (such as those in makeup or latex), and plants/animals (poison ivy, cat dander, pollen, dust, etc.).

Anaphylaxis affects multiple organs and, if left untreated, can cause rapid death. Signs and symptoms of anaphylaxis include: coughing and/or wheezing (high-pitched whistling); pain; itching; tightness in the chest; shortness of breath; difficulty breathing; and trouble swallowing. The patient may show neurological symptoms such as confusion, weakness, fainting, and dizziness. The patient's integumentary system may show symptoms such as hives or urticaria; rash; itchiness; pale skin; and swollen, itchy, or red skin, lips, eyes, and tongue. The patient may present with cardiological symptoms

such as rapid heartbeat, a weak pulse, and low blood pressure. The patient may experience gastrointestinal symptoms such as nausea, vomiting, cramps, or diarrhea.

Epinephrine

Epinephrine reverses the effects of severe allergic reactions by causing vasoconstriction and hypertension. Application of epinephrine is necessary in severe and life-threatening allergic reactions, but it's essential for an EMT to know if local protocols allow an EMT to administer an epinephrine injection. The appropriate dosage of epinephrine is 0.15 milligrams for children under 66 pounds and 0.30 milligrams for adults.

Assessing an Immunologic Emergency

To properly assess and treat an immunological emergency, an EMT should follow these procedures:

- Assess the scene and environment to ensure it is safe (e.g., no bees are present) and take notice of the surroundings to determine the allergen (e.g., a giant beehive, food that may have triggered an allergy, etc.).

- Make a quick and primary assessment of the patient. Assess whether the patient is in danger of anaphylaxis. If a severe allergic reaction seems likely, call for advanced life support (ALS). Take and monitor vital signs.

- Initiate any necessary treatments. If the patient is unconscious, evaluate and treat ABCs. Administer high-flow oxygen and use basic life support or automated external defibrillator (AED) if their blood pressure or pulse is dangerously low. Maintain the normal body temperature of 98 degrees if hypothermia is detected. Place the patient in the supine position if anaphylaxis is suspected. If a stinger is still in place, swipe the stinger away with a hard object, such as a credit card, but do *not* remove the stinger with tweezers. If the patient is conscious, obtain their chief complaint, SAMPLE history, and OPQRST. Determine what, if any, interventions have already been performed, such as allergy medicine or epinephrine shots. In severe cases, an epinephrine injection is necessary to prevent anaphylactic shock. Depending on training, some EMTs may not be permitted to directly administer epinephrine, but they may be permitted to assist the patient in doing so. Patients who have a history of the allergy may already have a kit in their possession.

- Prepare the patient for transport, if necessary.

Infectious Disease

An **infectious disease** is a pathology caused by harmful organisms, such as bacteria, fungi, parasites, and viruses. Many infectious diseases are **communicable**, which means they can be transferred through touch, breathing, saliva, blood, and other bodily substances. The goal of an EMT is to properly care for and transport a patient with an infectious disease while keeping the disease contained via decontamination and other sterile practices. Infectious diseases that cannot be contained often lead to widespread infections of the population known as **epidemics** and **pandemics**. It's imperative that an EMT recognize the signs, symptoms, and mode of transmission of many infectious diseases in order to

properly treat, contain, and protect themselves from it. The table below contains information on the most common infectious diseases.

Disease	Signs and Symptoms	Mode of Transmission
Meningitis (Inflammation of the meninges)	Fever Headache Severely stiff neck Kernig's sign (inability to extend leg) Brudzinski sign (hips and knees flex when neck is flexed)	Saliva (kissing, coughing, sneezing, etc.). Contaminated hands
Tuberculosis (Bacterial infection of the lungs)	Persistent cough Night sweats Fatigue Hemoptysis (coughing blood) Hoarseness of voice	Breathing airborne particles (coughing, sneezing, etc.).
Pneumonia (Inflammation of the lungs)	High fever Chills Pain in chest Expectorant cough Trouble breathing	Breathing airborne droplets (coughing, sneezing, etc.) Contaminated hands
Mononucleosis (Abnormal white blood cell count)	Sore throat Swollen lymph nodes Headache Muscle aches General malaise	Direct contact with saliva
Influenza (Viral infection of the lungs)	Fever Muscle aches Chills Respiratory problems	Breathing airborne droplets (coughing, sneezing, etc.) Contaminated hands
Hepatitis B (Inflammation of the liver)	Loss of appetite Jaundice Yellowing of the eyes Abdominal pain	Sharing needles
Hepatitis C (Inflammation of the liver)	Loss of appetite Jaundice Yellowing of the eyes Abdominal Pain	Blood-to-blood contact Sexual contact Blood transfusion Unsafe medical practices Mother to child

Disease	Signs and Symptoms	Mode of Transmission
Human Immunodeficiency Virus (HIV) (Destruction of the immune system)	Fever Fatigue Loss of appetite Recurrent infections Flu-like symptoms	Blood-to-blood contact Sexual contact Bodily fluids
Norovirus (Viral inflammation of stomach and intestines)	Diarrhea (watery) Nausea and vomiting Stomach pain Fever Weakness Body aches	Eating contaminated food Touching contaminated surfaces

Per the Occupational Health and Safety Administration (OHSA) and the Center for Disease Control and Prevention (CDC), EMTs are responsible for three primary concerns: to protect the health of the public, to manage outbreaks, and to prevent epidemics. These concerns are maintained by practicing proper hygiene, obtaining proper immunizations, wearing appropriate protective equipment, sterilizing the ambulance and medical equipment after use, and possibly undergoing quarantine. Each infectious disease has guidelines for managing it and caring for a patient. These guidelines are the same for both adults and children.

In order to comply with the above concerns, an EMT must be familiar with the cleaning routines associated with infectious diseases. To keep an ambulance and its equipment disinfected, a paramedic is required to appropriately dispose of medical waste, remove and appropriately discard used linens, wash and scrub any contaminated areas or surfaces, appropriately disinfect any equipment that cannot be discarded, and clean the stretcher (and any spills) with a germicidal-viricidal solution.

Assessing and Responding to an Infectious Emergency

When treating a patient with an infectious disease, EMTs must ensure they are wearing the appropriate personal protective equipment, generally in the form of disposable gloves and a protective mask. Other equipment, such as gowns, may be necessary depending on the illness. Once protective equipment has been applied, the patient's signs and symptoms must be assessed to determine the kind of illness. Protective equipment for the patient—usually a surgical mask—should be administered depending on the disease's mode of transmission. Having contained the disease as much as possible, an EMT may then maintain and support ABCs, take the patient's vital signs, assess the patient's mental status, and obtain SAMPLE and OPQRST histories. The patient should then be placed in a position of comfort, treated for dehydration, and prepared for transportation to a hospital. After the patient has been successfully delivered, the ambulance and equipment must be disinfected. All infectious disease incidents must be reported to the appropriate personnel.

Endocrine Disorders

The **endocrine system** is a collection of glands that secrete hormones. These hormones regulate countless physiological processes, including growth, metabolism, sexual reproduction, sleep, mood, and tissue development. Its primary function is to maintain **homeostasis**, which means keeping the body's internal condition stable. The endocrine system consists of the hypothalamus, pituitary gland, adrenal

glands, thyroid and parathyroid glands, pancreas, and the ovaries in females and the testicles in males. Hormones secreted from these glands are released into the bloodstream and carried to the intended tissues and organs. Although the endocrine system and the nervous system are closely linked, while the nervous system acts rapidly, the endocrine system acts very slowly.

Major Endocrine Glands

Hypothalamus: A part of the brain, the hypothalamus connects the nervous system to the endocrine system via the pituitary gland. Although it is considered part of the nervous system, it plays a dual role in regulating endocrine organs.

Pituitary Gland: A pea-sized gland found at the bottom of the hypothalamus. It has two lobes, called the anterior and posterior lobes. It plays an important role in regulating the function of other endocrine glands. The hormones released control growth, blood pressure, certain functions of the sex organs, salt concentration of the kidneys, internal temperature regulation, and pain relief.

Thyroid Gland: This gland releases hormones, such as thyroxine, that are important for metabolism, growth and development, temperature regulation, and brain development during infancy and childhood. Thyroid hormones also monitor the amount of circulating calcium in the body.

Parathyroid Glands: These are four pea-sized glands located on the posterior surface of the thyroid. The main hormone secreted is called parathyroid hormone (PTH) and helps with the thyroid's regulation of calcium in the body.

Thymus Gland: The thymus is located in the chest cavity, embedded in connective tissue. It produces several hormones important for development and maintenance of normal immunological defenses. One hormone promotes the development and maturation of lymphocytes, which strengthens the immune system.

Adrenal Gland: One adrenal gland is attached to the top of each kidney. It produces adrenaline and is responsible for the "fight or flight" reactions in the face of danger or stress. The hormones epinephrine and norepinephrine cooperate to regulate states of arousal.

Pancreas: The pancreas is an organ that has both endocrine and exocrine functions. The endocrine functions are controlled by the pancreatic islets of Langerhans, which are groups of beta cells scattered throughout the gland that secrete insulin to lower blood sugar levels in the body. Neighboring alpha cells secrete glucagon to raise blood sugar.

Pineal Gland: The pineal gland secretes melatonin, a hormone derived from the neurotransmitter serotonin. Melatonin can slow the maturation of sperm, oocytes, and reproductive organs. It also regulates the body's circadian rhythm, which is the natural awake/asleep cycle. It also serves an important role in protecting the CNS tissues from neural toxins.

Testes and Ovaries: These glands secrete testosterone and estrogen, respectively, and are responsible for secondary sex characteristics, as well as reproduction.

Endocrine System Function

The endocrine system works primarily through **negative feedback loops**, meaning that the body senses changes in hormone levels within the bloodstream, and then releases hormones to oppose those changes. For example, when a person eats, their blood glucose rises, signaling the pancreas to release

insulin, which causes glucose uptake in fat and muscle cells and effectively lowers blood glucose to normal levels.

Unlike exocrine glands, endocrine glands are ductless, meaning they secrete hormones directly into the bloodstream instead of through a duct. Exocrine glands include sweat glands, mammary glands, salivary glands, and the stomach and liver. The only endocrine gland that has an exocrine function is the pancreas, which secretes enzymes that break down the molecular components of food as well as secrete insulin and glucagon to control blood glucose levels.

Endocrine disorders are caused by an imbalance in the production of hormones and/or a complication in the body's ability to use the hormones produced. The most common endocrine emergencies, their signs and symptoms, and their treatments are discussed below.

Thyroid Disorders
Hyperthyroidism
Hyperthyroidism is caused by the overproduction of thyroid hormones (free T3 and T4), which causes a hyperactive metabolism. This can cause weight loss, increased appetite, heat intolerance, and weakness, as well as an enlarged thyroid gland, called a goiter. One endocrinological emergency related to hyperthyroidism is **thyrotoxic crisis**—a rare and potentially fatal emergency characterized by extremely high fever (106 °F or above), tachycardia, hypotension, irritability, delirium, coma, and nausea and/or vomiting. Emergency medical services are primarily supportive, so treating a patient with thyrotoxic crisis involves supporting and maintaining the ABCs and expediting patient transport to the hospital.

Hypothyroidism
The opposite of hyperthyroidism is hypothyroidism—the underproduction of thyroid hormone that causes a hypoactive metabolism, which may lead to weight gain or difficulty losing weight, fatigue, and mood swings. A **myxedema coma** is a hypothyroid-related emergency characterized by swelling of the skin and underlying tissues, making the skin appear waxy. Signs and symptoms include fatigue, lethargy, slowed mental function, cold intolerance, hypothermia, hypotension, and bradycardia. If left untreated, these symptoms can ultimately result in a coma. Treatment for a patient with myxedema involves supporting and closely monitoring ABCs (especially cardiac and pulmonary status), administering IV access but limiting fluids, assessing for other possible etiologies, and expediting patient transport to a hospital.

Adrenal Disorders
Addison's Disease
Addison's Disease is the inability of the adrenal cortex to produce **aldosterone** and **cortisol**, the hormones that govern the body's salt and water balance and help to fight stress and infections, respectively. Patients with Addison's Disease will experience **hyperkalemia** (too much potassium), darkening of the skin, **hypoglycemia** (low blood sugar), early-morning nausea, vomiting, and diarrhea, and possibly sudden cardiovascular collapse. Emergency medical services require the support and maintenance of the patient's ABCs, monitoring glucose levels, treating hypoglycemia if necessary, administering an IV for abundant fluids, and immediate transport to the hospital.

Cushing's Syndrome
Cushing's Syndrome occurs when the adrenal gland produces too much cortisol, which stimulates the pituitary gland to produce too much adrenocorticotropic hormone (ACTH). A patient with Cushing's may present with a "moon-faced" appearance, weight gain, and fat accumulation on the upper back (called a

"buffalo hump"), as well as in the shoulders (supraclavicular fat pad) and/or the abdomen. Patients may also experience slow healing of wounds, mood swings, skin changes (such as acne), difficulty concentrating or impaired memory, increased facial hair, and purplish abdominal striae. An EMT responding to a call for a patient with this disease will need to support and maintain the ABCs, obtain SAMPLE and OPQRST histories, prepare the patient for transport, and report any observations of Cushing's to the receiving faculty.

Pancreatic Disorders

Diabetes

Diabetes is characterized by the body's inability to metabolize glucose caused by an insufficient supply or utilization of **insulin**, which enables to body to absorb glucose. If the body cannot efficiently take in glucose in order to perform cellular respiration, the tissues will eventually waste away and become necrotic.

Diabetes is divided into two categories: **Type 1 (insulin-dependent)** and **Type 2 (non-insulin-dependent).** Type 1 diabetes occurs when the body's immune system destroys the pancreas' insulin-producing cells (called beta cells) in the islets of Langerhans. For this reason, it's considered an autoimmune disease. Because the body cannot produce insulin, injections of insulin are required over the patient's lifetime in order to control blood sugar. Also known as juvenile diabetes, patients are typically diagnosed in childhood or adolescence.

Type 2 diabetes is characterized by the body's inability to effectively respond to the insulin that it produces. This disease usually manifests in an adult's middle-age years (although it is occurring more frequently in younger and younger patients) as a result of sedentary lifestyle, a diet high in refined sugar, hereditary factors, and comorbidities such as high blood pressure and obesity. Treatment involves lifestyle changes such as healthy diet and exercise, and sometimes also a regime of medications that regulate the body's ability to produce and use insulin and control blood glucose.

Signs and symptoms of diabetes include frequent, plentiful urination (polyuria), increased thirst and frequent drinking (polydipsia), extreme hunger and excessive eating (polyphagia), bedwetting in children who usually don't urinate in their sleep, blurred vision, and fatigue. Children with diabetes typically experience seizures and dehydration.

Symptomatic hypoglycemia (low blood sugar) and **symptomatic hyperglycemia** (high blood sugar) are common emergencies associated with both types of diabetes. Although both conditions can cause altered mental status, a hypoglycemic patient may appear to be intoxicated since their level of consciousness may be depressed. The hypoglycemic patient's breathing may range from normal to rapid, their pulse rapid but weak, their skin may feel cold and clammy, and their blood pressure will be low. Patients experiencing hyperglycemia could have deep and rapid breathing with a rapid, weak, and thready pulse; dry, warm skin; and normal or low blood pressure. It's important to check the patient's blood glucose level. Patients with symptomatic hypoglycemia will need glucose, while hyperglycemic patients require insulin and fluids—provided by ALS or at the hospital—and rapid transport to the hospital. A serious complication of hyperglycemia is the development of cerebral edema. If there's any confusion about which condition the patient is experiencing, give glucose. Unconsciousness and the inability to swallow are the only contraindications to giving oral glucose.

A diabetic emergency known as **diabetic ketoacidosis (DKA)** or a hyperglycemic crisis is the most common type of endocrinological emergency to which an EMT will respond. DKA is a condition where the body uses fat and other sources for fuel instead of glucose, resulting in waste products that cause

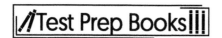
the blood to become acidic. A patient experiencing a hyperglycemic crisis will have fruity-smelling breath, deep and labored breathing (Kussmaul respirations), vomiting, abdominal pain, and even unconsciousness. The patient may have an emergency medical identification symbol on a bracelet that identifies him or her as a diabetic. An EMT responding to a DKA call can provide care by supporting and maintaining the ABCs, obtaining SAMPLE and OPQRST histories (especially diabetic history), and obtaining blood glucose level (and vital signs. The patient will need IV fluids and insulin, so immediate transport to a hospital is imperative for the patient's survival and recovery.

Psychiatric

A **psychiatric emergency** involves any psychiatric event in which the individual may harm themselves or others, including attempted suicide, depression, substance abuse, or violent behaviors. In general, there is very little hands-on treatment an EMT can perform. In most cases, a psychiatric emergency requires an EMT to call law enforcement and to restrain the individual. If restraint is necessary, the EMT should ensure that the police and at least four other people are present for legal purposes.

The following situations may be present in a psychiatric emergency:

- Agitated delirium: the patient is confused, disoriented, and possibly experiencing hallucinations. The patient may also present with restless activity with no known purpose.

- Organic brain syndrome: a temporary or permanent dysfunction of the brain that may be caused by a disruption of physiological activity, such as adequate blood to brain tissue.

- Functional disorder: dysfunction of organs with no known reason.

When analyzing a psychiatric emergency, an EMT should first assess the situation to be certain it is safe. If the patient is conscious, an EMT should also calmly identify themselves to the patient, and then identify any possible mechanisms of injury (MOI), such as head trauma. Finally, the EMT may perform standard emergency procedures, such as supporting and maintaining ABCs, taking vital signs, and SAMPLE and OPQRST histories. An EMT must be certain never to transport a psychiatric patient in the prone (face-down) position, as the patient may go into respiratory distress or cardiac arrest.

Toxicology

Toxicological emergencies are generally the result of poisonings and drug overdoses. EMTs must follow this very specific protocol:

Observe the Scene
Assess the situation, paying close attention to the surroundings to ensure there aren't signs of an airborne toxin (such as multiple unconscious or flailing victims) or any weapons. Identify the nature of illness (NOI), such as open alcohol bottles, syringes, empty containers, or strange odors. Determine if any/all patients are presenting with altered mental statuses, as patients may become unexpectedly violent.

Pre-Hospital Treatment
Maintain and support ABCs and vital signs and identify any life-threatening conditions. Obtain SAMPLE and OPQRST histories from the patient or their family members/friends. Perform a physical examination of the patient, with particular focus on the area of the body in which the toxin was exposed. If the event

was intentional, treat the situation as a psychiatric emergency in addition to a toxicological emergency. If the patient has taken a harmful or lethal dose of a suspected toxin, repeat vital signs every 5 minutes. Pay particular attention to the patient's breathing, as alcohol, opiates, and inhalants can depress the central nervous system and cause respiratory distress. Inhalants may also lead to seizures.

If the patient has ingested any poisons, it may be necessary to administer activated charcoal, bearing in mind that activated charcoal cannot be given to any patients with AMS. If the patient can have activated charcoal, shake the drink well then present it in a covered cup with a straw. The dose should be 12.5 to 20 g for children, and 25 to 50 g for adults. Take all containers, bottles, and labels from the scene to the receiving hospital for documentation and investigation. If the patient is suspected to have food poisoning, take the food to the receiving hospital.

Hematology

Hematology is the study, prevention, and treatment of blood-related disorders. Blood is composed of plasma and red blood cells and it carries countless physiological elements that maintain and protect the body, such as hormones, white blood cells, and platelets. Red blood cells also contain **hemoglobin**, the molecule that carries oxygen to tissues for cellular respiration. **Plasma** functions to suspend and transport these blood constituents and is composed of fluids, proteins, electrolytes, gases, and waste products. An essential hematological organ is the **spleen**, which is primarily responsible for the production and removal of red blood cells and the recycling of iron. It also serves as a blood reserve in cases of severe blood loss.

Emergencies and Pathophysiology

For an EMT, hematologic emergencies are rare and difficult to treat. The following emergencies outline the most common hematological diseases, their signs and symptoms, and treatment that an EMT can perform.

Sickle Cell Disease

Sickle cell disease is a genetic disorder that causes short-living (16 days) red blood cells to be sickle- or oblong-shaped—resulting in a deformation of hemoglobin that causes it to become a very poor carrier for oxygen. It may cause hypoxia, the rupture of blood vessels and spleen, and death. Children with sickle cell disease are most likely to die from infection. They are also at risk for ischemic stroke. It's most common in people of African or Mediterranean descent.

A sickle-cell emergency is caused by a blockage of blood to tissues and organs (**vaso-occlusive crisis**), a deficiency in red blood cell production (**aplastic crisis**), the rapid destruction of red blood cells (**hemolysis**), or an acute and painful enlargement of the spleen (**splenic sequestration crisis**). Signs and symptoms of a sickle-cell crisis include increased respiration, swelling of the digits, jaundice, signs of pneumonia, and priapism in male patients. Emergency medical services consist of supporting and maintaining ABCs, managing respiratory distress, obtaining SAMPLE and OPQRST histories, and preparing the patient for immediate transport. High-flow oxygen should be delivered at a rate of 12 to 15 L/min through a nonrebreathing mask if the patient is having trouble breathing or appears to have an AMS.

Clotting Disorders

A **clotting disorder** is a disease characterized by the body's inability to make sufficient proteins for **thrombosis**—the development of a clot to stop bleeding. There are two primary and opposing disorders;

thrombophilia is the body's tendency to develop random blood clots, and **hemophilia**, most common in males, is the inability to form blood clots when needed. Thrombophilia isn't common in pediatric patients and is treated with blood-thinning medications. **Deep vein thrombosis**, the formation of a blood clot in a deep vein, causes painful swelling and tenderness in one leg (generally the calf), warm skin, a deep ache in the clot area, and redness of the skin, particularly in the back of the leg below the knee.

Patients experiencing a hemophilic emergency may present with spontaneous and acute chronic bleeding, plentiful large and deep bruises, joint swelling and tenderness, and blood in the urine or stool. Emergency medical services consist of supporting and maintaining ABCs while noticing any signs of blood loss, bleeding of an unknown origin, and hypoxia. SAMPLE and OPQRST histories must be obtained and the patient must be transported to a hospital. If the patient has any signs of AMS or is having trouble breathing, administer high-flow oxygen using a nonrebreathing mask at a rate of 12 to 15 L/min.

Genitourinary (GU)/Renal

Genitourinary refers to the organs of the urinary and genital tracts. The renal, or urinary, tract consists of the kidneys, bladder, urethra, and ureters. The genital tract contains the organs of reproduction. For females, these are the vagina, uterus, fallopian tubes, and ovaries. For males, the organs are the testes, epididymis, vas deferens, prostate, penis, and seminal vesicles. The genital and urinary tracts are combined into a singular tract because they share a common origin and use the same pathways, such as the male urethra for sperm and urine excretion.

Comparison of the Female and Male Genitourinary Tracts

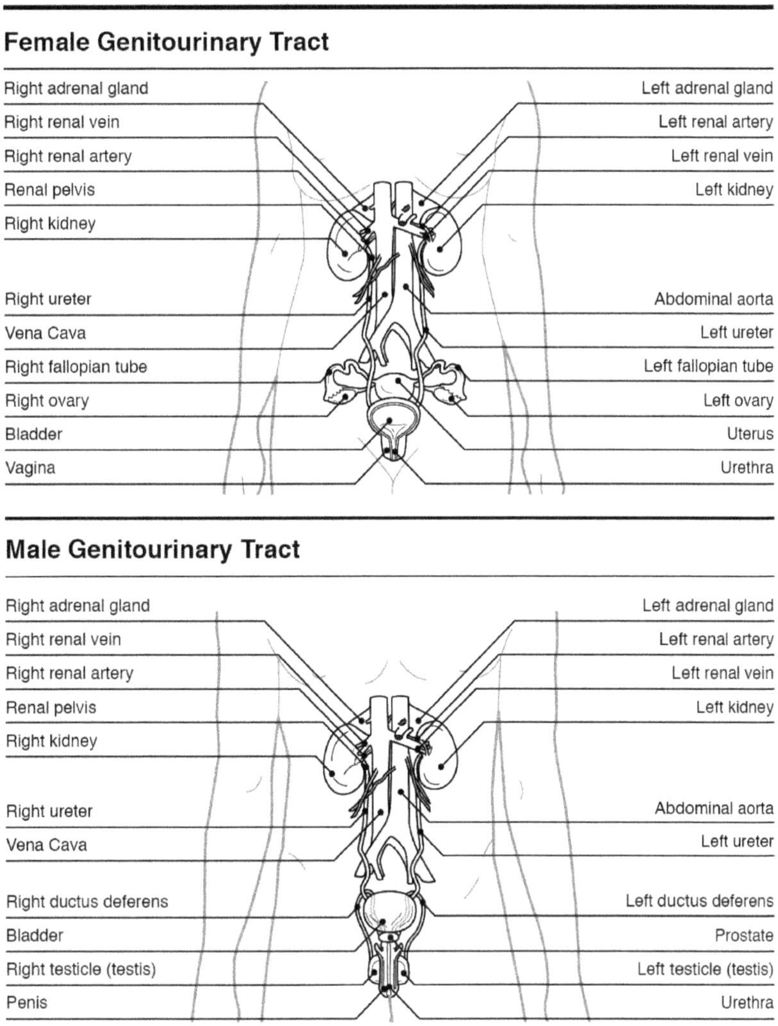
Female Genitourinary Tract
Right adrenal gland
Right renal vein
Right renal artery
Renal pelvis
Right kidney
Right ureter
Vena Cava
Right fallopian tube
Right ovary
Bladder
Vagina
Left adrenal gland
Left renal artery
Left renal vein
Left kidney
Abdominal aorta
Left ureter
Left fallopian tube
Left ovary
Uterus
Urethra
Male Genitourinary Tract
Right adrenal gland
Right renal vein
Right renal artery
Renal pelvis
Right kidney
Right ureter
Vena Cava
Right ductus deferens
Bladder
Right testicle (testis)
Penis
Left adrenal gland
Left renal artery
Left renal vein
Left kidney
Abdominal aorta
Left ureter
Left ductus deferens
Prostate
Left testicle (testis)
Urethra

The function of the urinary system is to balance, filter, and regulate the body's levels of fluids, electrolytes, and metabolites, as well as eliminate waste and regulate blood volume, pressure, and acidity. In order to fully understand the potentially deadly emergencies of the genitourinary system, an EMT should know its anatomy and physiology.

Anatomy, Physiology, and Filtration Process of the Renal Tract

The **kidneys** are bean-shaped organs located on either side of the spinal column in the rear abdominal cavity within the retroperitoneal space. They are the organ involved in balancing electrolytes and water by filtering waste products from blood into urine. The **ureters** transport urine to the bladder. In a healthy individual, the kidneys receive anywhere from 12 to 30 percent of the body's systemic cardiac output.

The **nephrons** are the structural and functional units that act as filters and create urine. Each is composed of the **glomerulus**, the **glomerular (Bowman's) capsule**, the **proximal convoluted tubule**, the **loop of Henle**, and the **distal convoluted tubule**, which are illustrated in the following figure. A

glomerulus is a cluster of capillaries that function as the main filter of blood that enters the kidney. The rate at which blood is filtered through the glomerulus is called the **glomerular filtration rate** (GFR). In the first step of filtration, blood moves from the **afferent arteriole** (the arteriole from the renal artery) into the capillaries of the glomerulus, causing the pressure to increase. As the pressure increases, fluid and solutes are forced from the glomerulus into the Bowman's capsule, a double-layered "cup" containing cells called **podocytes** that serve as filtration slits, allowing the filterable components of the blood to pass through the nephron.

Blood contains filterable and non-filterable components. Filterable components are water, nitrogenous waste, and nutrients. Non-filterable components—blood cells, platelets, and albumins—leave the glomerulus through the **efferent arteriole** (arteriole traveling away from the glomerulus). The filterable components form the glomerular filtrate, which passes through the various components of the nephron to eventually form urine.

After leaving the glomerulus, the filtrate passes through the proximal tubule into the loop of Henle, where water and electrolytes are reabsorbed. Following the loop of Henle, the filtrate enters the distal collecting duct (DCT) through the distal tubule. Antidiuretic hormone (ADH), secreted from the posterior pituitary gland, and aldosterone, secreted from the kidney, control the composition of the urine.

Aldosterone plays a key role in reabsorption of materials, and ADH contributes to water retention. Indeed, 99% of the filtrate is reabsorbed in the body, and the remaining 1% is released as urine.

Structure of a Nephron

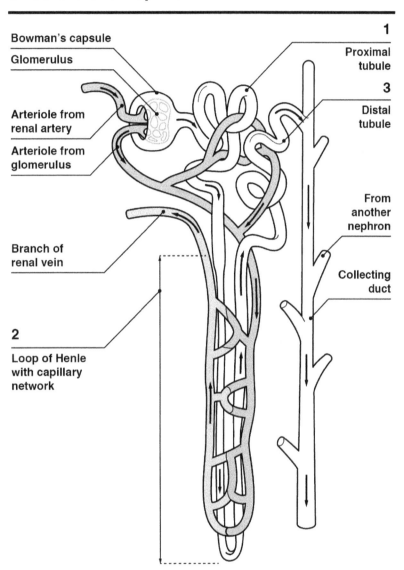

Once urine is formed, it enters the collecting ducts and passes through the calyces before proceeding to the renal pelvises and entering the ureters, which transport the urine to the bladder. The bladder holds urine until it's full. Signals from the brain prevent a person from urinating by contracting the external urinary sphincter until conditions to void are favorable.

Finally, once the external urinary sphincter is voluntarily relaxed, the urine enters the urethra—the final transport pathway for elimination.

113

Genitourinary Emergencies and Disorders

Genitourinary emergencies can be extremely dangerous if left untreated. The following list outlines the most common emergencies, their signs and symptoms, and the treatments an EMT can perform.

Urinary Tract Infections (UTI)

A UTI is an infection, usually within the urethra and bladder, that occurs when normal bacteria on the body's external surfaces, called **flora**, enter the urethra and multiply. Antibiotics are needed to kill the infection. Patients with a UTI may experience painful and frequent urination, or an urge to urinate when not necessary, as well as difficulty urinating. An EMT must support and maintain the patient's ABCs, take SAMPLE and OPQRST histories, and be prepared for the patient to experience nausea and vomiting. All patients should be transported to the hospital in a comfortable position.

Renal Calculi (Kidney Stones)

Kidney stones are solid crystalline masses that form in the renal pelvis of the kidney and become trapped anywhere along the urinary tract. They're created by an excess of insoluble salts and uric acid. A patient with kidney stones may present with severe pain in the side and back. This pain may spread to the lower abdomen and groin, causing a guarding of the abdomen, discolored urine, and symptoms of a UTI.

Acute Renal Failure (ARF)

Acute renal failure is characterized by a sudden decrease in filtration through the glomeruli of the nephron, causing toxins to accumulate in the blood. It occurs suddenly, usually over days or weeks. The condition is extremely dangerous and has a mortality rate of 50-80% in severe cases. If left untreated, it can lead to heart failure and metabolic acidosis. A patient experiencing ARF may present with a urine output of less than 500 mL/day (**oliguria**), complete cessation of urine production (**anuria**), as well as hypertension, tachycardia, pain and distention of the abdomen, altered mental status, and prolonged bleeding. Emergency medical services for ARF involve supporting and maintain ABCs, taking SAMPLE and OPQRST histories, placing the patient in the supine position, and preparing them for immediate transport to the hospital. Advanced life support (ALS) services may be required to provide IV fluids.

Chronic Renal Failure

Chronic renal failure is the progressive and irreversible loss of kidney function due to permanent damage to nephrons. Occurring over a period of months, CRF leads to the development of systemic complications that can cause death, including **uremia** (fluid, hormonal, and electrolyte imbalances), **azotemia** (abnormally high levels of blood nitrogen), pericarditis, and pulmonary edema. Signs and symptoms of CRF include an altered mental status, swelling of the feet and ankles, nausea and vomiting, hypotension, and tachycardia. Emergency medical care is similar to patients with ARF. Advanced life support (ALS) services may be needed to provide IV fluids to correct electrolyte imbalances.

Gynecology and Obstetrics

Gynecology is the study, protection, and maintenance of female reproductive health. **Obstetrics** is the study of birth and delivery. These branches of medicine are confluent and are treated as one study by practicing physicians.

Anatomy of the Female Reproductive System

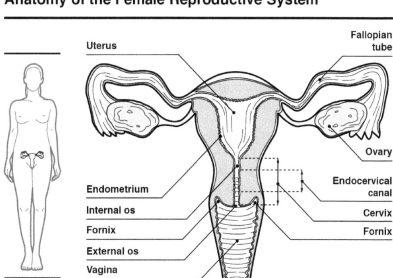

As with all diseases, it's helpful for an EMT to have a general understanding of female anatomy, which is illustrated above. The **vagina**, the canal involved in sexual intercourse and birth, is the opening at the bottom end of the birth canal and contains **Bartholin glands**, which secrete mucus to lubricate the vagina. The uterine opening to the birth canal is called the **cervix**. The **ovaries** are the primary female reproductive organs and are considered glands. They regulate the menstrual cycle and contain **follicles** that produce, at regular intervals, an **ovum** (egg), which, when fertilized by the sperm, eventually develops into a fetus. The **fallopian tubes** are vessels that transport the ovum to the **uterus** (the muscular organ that houses the embryo and contracts during labor), which is where fertilization takes place. There is one fallopian tube per ovary.

Gynecological emergencies can be fatal. If one is suspected, the most important thing an EMT can do is support and maintain the ABCs, and transport the patient to the hospital as quickly as possible. In addition to potential life-threatening diseases, a gynecological emergency call may include rape and sexual assault.

There is a specific protocol an EMT must perform regarding a woman's health, which is described below:

- Assess the scene: Determine if the scene is safe and if assistance is necessary. Identify the type of call (either a medical call or trauma call), the number of patients, and whether standard precautions have been taken. It's also important to note where the patient has been found. Identify the overall appearance of the patient. Note if she is conscious, if there are any obvious life threats, her emotional state, difficulty breathing, any signs of injury, and the position in which she was found.

- Protect and assess the patient: Ask any people not involved in the incident to leave the area to maintain the patient's privacy. Evaluate the patient's overall appearance, especially in the abdomen, noting any bruises, stretch marks, surgical scarring, swollen or distended abdomen, or needle tracks. Palpate the abdomen, starting at the quadrant farther from the pain. Expedite transport if the patient is bleeding, as this may be a sign of shock.

- Obtain medical history and details of the incident, if possible: Determine the MOI (mechanism of injury) or the NOI (nature of illness) and the patient's chief complaint. If the patient is bleeding excessively, be certain to obtain their gynecological history. Ask the patient if there is any possibility that she is pregnant and what kind of contraception she uses, if any. Inquire about the patient's obstetrics gravida, para, and abortion (GPA) history, including the number of times (if any) that the patient has been pregnant, given birth, and had an abortion, respectively.

- Treat the patient: If the patient is bleeding vaginally and there are signs of shock, treat it as shock. The patient may not show signs of shock, so it's important to check for a rapid or a weak pulse and skin that is sweaty, cool, or pale. Use sanitary pads externally to soak up blood, noting the number used. Place the patient in the supine position and administer oxygen. Place the patient on her left side if she is pregnant. Maintain and support ABCs. Prepare the patient for transport to the hospital. While en route, pay attention to the status of the patient by noting any improvement or decline, while consistently checking vitals.

Gynecological Emergencies

Ectopic Pregnancy

An ectopic pregnancy occurs when a fertilized oocyte (egg) is implanted outside of the uterus, typically within one of the fallopian tubes. It's extremely dangerous, as it may lead to rupture of the tube if not caught. Signs and symptoms of an ectopic pregnancy include generalized pain on one side of the abdomen, vaginal bleeding, a distended and swollen abdomen, and signs of shock. Ectopic pregnancy should be suspected if the woman reports a missed menstrual period and these signs are present. EMT care includes treating the patient for shock, supporting and maintaining ABCs, and transporting the patient on their left side (left lateral recumbent). It's also imperative never to give the patient anything by mouth and to keep the patient warm.

Pelvic Inflammatory Disease

Pelvic inflammatory disease (PID) is an inflammation of the fallopian tubes and the surrounding tissues of the pelvis, including the uterus and ovaries. It's the most common reason a woman will call for emergency medical services and is caused by organisms entering the uterus through the cervix. It occurs primarily in sexually active women, but may also be caused by the use of an intrauterine device (IUD). STDs are the main cause of PID, especially untreated chlamydia. PID is a serious condition that can lead to ovarian abscesses and scarring of the fallopian tubes, which can result in ectopic pregnancies. There's

not much care that an EMT can administer for a patient that presents with PID, but an EMT can assess the patient and determine if there's abdominal pain during or after menstruation and if there are signs of peritoneal irritation. The EMT should also obtain SAMPLE and OPQRST histories and transport her comfortably and gently to a hospital.

Ovarian Cysts, Torsion, and Abscesses

An **ovarian** *cyst* is an extraordinarily painful condition caused by fluid-filled sacs on or within the ovary. If the cyst doesn't resolve, it may grow to a significant size and cause ovarian torsion, resulting in extreme lower abdominal pain that may present with nausea and vomiting. A **tubo-ovarian abscess** occurs when the fallopian tubes and ovaries are blocked by a large, infectious mass. Signs and symptoms of ovarian cysts may also include a dull, achy pain in the lower back and legs; breast tenderness; and painful menstruation.

If an ovarian cyst doesn't resolve, it may rupture. Signs and symptoms of a ruptured cyst include sharp pain in the lower abdomen, dizziness, weakness, and loss of consciousness. A patient with a tubo-ovarian abscess may present with severe abdominal pain, guarding of the abdomen, nausea and vomiting, fever, and abdominal distention. EMT care for an ovarian cyst and a tubo-ovarian abscess is the same as an ectopic pregnancy, while patients with ovarian torsion should be given an IV for pain medication and dehydration.

Sexually Transmitted Diseases

A sexually transmitted disease (STD) is a disease or infection transmitted through sexual contact. If a sexually transmitted disease is suspected, EMT treatment requires the administration of oxygen and an IV line, controlling any bleeding, and administering analgesics and antiemetics.

There are many kinds of STDs, the most common of which are listed below:

- **Bacterial vaginosis**: An overgrowth of bacteria in the vagina that may cause itching, burning, and a foul, "fishy" smell. If left untreated, it can lead to premature birth and PID. It's generally treated with metronidazole.

- **Chlamydia**: A disease caused by the **Chlamydia trachomatis** bacterium. Signs and symptoms include pain in the lower abdomen and back pain during intercourse, and/or bleeding between periods. It's also the STD most likely to cause PID.

- **Genital herpes**: An infection of the genitals, buttocks, or anal area characterized by sores and small red bumps that may blister. Herpes is caused by the herpes simplex virus and is divided into two categories based on the location: Type I is found on the lips and mouth, and Type II is found on the genitals.

- **Gonorrhea**: A disease acquired through the *Neisseria gonorrhoeae* bacterium. Signs and symptoms, which occur 2-10 days after exposure, may present as painful urination, burning or itching, and a yellowish or bloody vaginal discharge.

Sexual Assault

Sexual assault is any sexual activity that occurs without the consent of the recipient, the most common of which is rape, or forced sexual intercourse. An EMT should expect police involvement with sexual assault calls. When responding to a call, it's important to ask the patient if she would be more comfortable with a male or female EMT and to be cognizant of the patient's privacy, taking a very brief

survey and history. It is *especially* important to preserve evidence, discouraging the patient from taking any actions that should undermine or destroy evidence. When assessing the patient, a paramedic must make a written observation her emotional state, the condition of her clothes, and any obvious injuries. It's imperative that an EMT remains nonjudgmental and compassionate.

Obstetric Emergencies

An obstetric emergency typically presents itself in the form of a field delivery. A **field delivery** means that an infant is birthed outside of a medical facility. If a field delivery seems inevitable, an EMT should wear the appropriate protective equipment, such as gloves, a gown, and eye protection. When assessing a patient in an obstetric emergency, an EMT will need to determine if the patient is in active labor or if delivery is certain. Signs of trauma or injury and observations of any drug paraphernalia or liquor bottles are necessary to ascertain the possibility of fetal alcohol syndrome.

Once the scene and patient have been assessed, an EMT may proceed to general supportive care, including maintaining and supporting ABCs, taking SAMPLE and OPQRST histories, and remaining alert for any signs of shock.

Labor/Normal Deliveries

Once labor has initiated, it cannot be prevented or slowed. A woman experiencing labor will present with a firm abdomen, a need to push or bear down, or crowning, which is when the head is visible at the opening of the vagina. An EMT should adhere to the following procedure for delivering a baby:

- Inform the patient that she will be giving birth outside of a hospital. Be calm and reassuring, protecting her privacy as much as possible. Someone should be watching the mother during the entire process.

- Place the patient in a comfortable position on a firm, flat surface on top of sterile sheets, supporting her head, neck, and back with pillows or blankets. She can have her feet flat on the surface/floor with her knees spread apart. She may be more comfortable on her side or in another position. Allow this if it is safe and the EMT can deliver the infant with the mother in this position.

- Constantly watch for crowning, as women who have given birth before may experience a speedy labor and delivery and their perineum can tear. Time the frequency and the length of the contractions. Once the head is crowning, put off transporting the patient until the infant is delivered. Transport to the hospital during delivery should only occur if the EMT is not confident in their ability to assist with delivering the baby.

- While wearing sterile gloves, be sure to suction the mouth and nose of the infant with a bulb syringe once it starts to emerge. Ensure that the umbilical cord isn't wrapped around the infant's neck, and guide the head downward to help the shoulders emerge. Be sure to carefully support the infant's body during the delivery; the body will be slippery.

- Once the neonate has fully emerged, dry the infant and keep it warm. Using a warm blanket, wrap the baby, making sure the top of the head is covered with only the face uncovered. Stimulate the newborn to breathe, if it isn't already, by positioning its head above its body, vigorously rubbing its back, buttocks, or feet. If breathing does not begin 15-30 seconds after delivery, or the infant's heart rate doesn't get above 60 beats per minute, administer 100% oxygen with a BVM. CPR must be performed by two EMTs using a 3:1 ratio of compressions to

118

ventilation, with 120 total actions per minute. One EMT will provide ventilation, while the other will perform chest compressions using the hand-encircling technique. If infant death or stillbirth has occurred, do not attempt to resuscitate.

- After the newborn has been warmed, dry, and is breathing, place the infant on the mother's chest. Record the sex and the time of delivery. Obtain height, weight, and head circumference of the infant, if possible, as well as an APGAR score. Once the infant has been delivered, prepare to transport the patient, being alert for a possible need to deliver the placenta.

Labor/Abnormal Deliveries

Occasionally, an EMT may encounter an abnormal delivery. Some of these complications are life-threatening to the mother and the infant, and may result in the inability to deliver the child in the field, so patient transport must be rapid and careful.

If there's a fluid-filled sac instead of an infant's head at crowning, it is considered an unruptured amniotic sac. An EMT must puncture it by pinching and twisting the sac until fluid runs out, suctioning the nose and mouth as soon as the head emerges.

In a **breech delivery**, the buttocks of the baby are shown at crowning instead of the head, putting the infant at great risk of trauma. The EMT should call for advanced life support (ALS) and contact medical control. Breech deliveries are typically slow, allowing time for transport to the hospital. However, the baby must be delivered if the buttocks have already emerged from the vagina. The baby's buttocks and legs should spontaneously deliver, and the body must be supported. In order to keep the infant from suffocating, the EMT can make a "V" with their fingers and insert them into the vagina to create an airway. If a complete delivery doesn't occur, the EMT should transport the patient to the hospital immediately while holding their fingers in the vagina in order to ensure the baby is able to breathe until delivery is possible.

A **nuchal cord** occurs when the umbilical cord is wrapped around the newborn's throat, which can lead to strangling and suffocation. If the cord cannot be slipped over the head and shoulder, the EMT must clamp the cord in two places approximately two inches apart, make a cut between the clamps, unwrap the cord, and continue with delivery as usual.

Both **limb presentation** and **prolapse of the umbilical cord** require immediate transport to a hospital with the mother in a hips-up, head-down position. In the case of a prolapsed umbilical cord, her feet should be raised 6 to 12 inches and a pillow should be placed under her hips. If an arm, leg, or foot presents instead of the head, the EMT must cover the limb with a sterile towel. If the umbilical cord presents itself outside of the vagina before delivery, the umbilical cord should not be pushed back into the vagina, but instead, the infant's head should be gently pushed away from the cord, which should be covered with a sterile towel dampened with saline, and high-flow oxygen must be administered.

A **spontaneous abortion**, also known as a miscarriage, occurs when the fetus dies and is delivered before the 20th week of gestation. The EMT must maintain and support the mother's ABCs and prepare her for immediate transport to the hospital. If the patient is bleeding, treatment for shock may be expected. The EMT will need to cover the vagina with a sterile pad and collect any expulsions from the vagina, without ever pulling the tissue, while constantly monitoring the patient and taking serial vitals.

Practice Questions

1. Difficulty speaking, loss of speech, difficulty understanding speech, and weakness or numbness in the face and limbs, particularly on one side of the body, are signs and symptoms of which of the following emergencies?
   a. Seizures
   b. Hypothyroidism
   c. Stroke
   d. Cushing's syndrome

2. Which of the following procedures must an EMT perform at every emergency call?
   I. Support and maintain ABCs
   II. Attempt to obtain SAMPLE and OPQRST histories
   III. Treat for shock
   IV. Quickly apply a tourniquet
   a. Choice I only
   b. Choices I and II
   c. Choices I, II, and IV
   d. All of the above

3. A type of abdominal pain caused by stimulation of an organ's nerve fibers due to stretching of the organ's wall is referred to as which of the following?
   a. Visceral pain
   b. Parietal pain
   c. Referred pain
   d. Somatic pain

4. A 22-year-old male patient presents with pain in the lower-right quadrant of the abdomen. Which of the following is the likeliest cause of the pain?
   a. Kidney stones
   b. Food poisoning
   c. Appendicitis
   d. Urinary tract infection

5. Which of the following is NOT a step that should be followed when performing an abdominal exam?
   a. Ask the patient to identify the location of the pain.
   b. Lay the patient down in a prone position.
   c. Palpate the abdomen by pressing on the unaffected areas first.
   d. Inspect for changes in skin color.

6. A 40-year-old female patient presents with difficulty breathing, swollen lips and eyes, tightness of chest, and dizziness. The emergency call has come from a restaurant. Which of the following treatments should be given to the patient?
   a. 5 mg of penicillin
   b. 0.15 mg of epinephrine
   c. 0.30 mg of epinephrine
   d. 40 mg of docusate

7. Which of the following infectious diseases is transmitted through airborne particles and presents with a persistent cough, night sweats, and hemoptysis?
   a. Tuberculosis
   b. Meningitis
   c. Pneumonia
   d. Influenza

8. When responding to an infectious emergency, which of the following must an EMT do first?
   a. Support and maintain ABCs.
   b. Obtain SAMPLE and OPQRST histories.
   c. Place the patient in a position of comfort and treat for dehydration.
   d. Put on personal protective equipment.

9. The primary function of the endocrine system is to maintain which of the following?
   a. Heartbeat
   b. Respiration
   c. Electrolyte and water balance
   d. Homeostasis

10. Which of the following organs functions as both an endocrine and exocrine gland?
   a. The kidney
   b. The spleen
   c. The pancreas
   d. The stomach

11. A 55-year-old female patient presents with a waxy and swollen appearance, fatigue, cold intolerance, hypothermia, hypotension, and bradycardia. Which of the following diseases might the patient have?
   a. Hyperthyroidism
   b. Hypothyroidism
   c. Diabetes
   d. Addison's disease

12. A patient experiencing a hyperglycemic crisis, or diabetic ketoacidosis (DKA), will have which prominent sign?
   a. Fruity-smelling breath
   b. Swollen legs and feet
   c. A buffalo hump
   d. Shallow breathing

13. A situation in which a patient may harm themselves or others—including attempted suicide, depression, and substance abuse—is called which of the following?
   a. A toxicological emergency
   b. A psychiatric emergency
   c. A hematological emergency
   d. An immunological emergency

121

14. Upon arriving to the scene of a call, an EMT notices a strong odor and several unconscious people on the ground. Which of the following emergencies has most likely occurred?
    a. A toxicological emergency
    b. A psychiatric emergency
    c. A hematological emergency
    d. An immunological emergency

15. A young African American male presents with jaundice, signs of pneumonia, and priapism. Which of the following conditions might this patient have?
    a. Hemophilia
    b. Thrombophilia
    c. Sickle cell disease
    d. A urinary tract infection

16. What is the name for the structural and functional units that create and transport urine, located in the cortex of the kidney?
    a. Glomeruli
    b. Nephrons
    c. Loops of Henle
    d. Distal tubules

17. Podocytes, located in the Bowman's capsule of the nephron, allow which of the following components to pass into the proximal tubule?
    a. Albumins
    b. Platelets
    c. Blood cells
    d. Nitrogenous waste

18. A 60-year-old male patient presents with hypertension, tachycardia, and pain and distention in his abdomen. He seems confused and disoriented. When the EMT obtains his SAMPLE and OPQRST histories, the man reports that he hasn't urinated in two days, despite drinking lots of water, and doesn't have a history of kidney function loss. Which of the following diseases is the patient most likely experiencing?
    a. Chronic renal failure
    b. Kidney stones
    c. A urinary tract infection
    d. Acute renal failure

19. The muscular tube that connects the outer surface to the cervix in a woman's birth canal is referred to as which of the following?
    a. The uterus
    b. The bladder
    c. The vagina
    d. The ovaries

20. A 23-year-old female patient presents with extreme lower abdominal pain and fever. She is guarding her abdomen, which appears to be bloated. Which of the following conditions is the patient most likely experiencing?
    a. A tubo-ovarian abscess
    b. A ruptured ovarian cyst
    c. Ovarian torsion
    d. An ectopic pregnancy

21. An EMT receives a call to respond to a pregnant woman complaining of contractions. Upon arriving at the scene, the EMT discovers the baby is crowning. Which of the following must the EMT NOT do during delivery?
    a. Watch and monitor the mother.
    b. Place sterile sheets under the mother.
    c. Suction the baby's mouth and nose.
    d. Ensure that the umbilical cord is not wrapped around the baby's throat.

22. A woman appears to be having a breech delivery. Which of the following should an EMT do to protect the baby from trauma?
    a. Cover the exposed limb with a sterile towel.
    b. Make a "V" with their fingers and insert them into the vagina.
    c. Cover the vagina with a sterile pad and collect any vaginal expulsions.
    d. Puncture the amniotic sac by pinching and twisting it.

23. Which of the following conditions is caused by the body's immune system attacking its own insulin-producing pancreatic cells?
    a. Type 1 diabetes
    b. Type 2 diabetes
    c. Hyperglycemic crisis
    d. Myxedema coma

24. Which of the following diabetic conditions typically presents itself in early childhood?
    a. Type 1 diabetes
    b. Type 2 diabetes
    c. Gestational diabetes
    d. Non-insulin-dependent diabetes

25. While taking a stroll in the park, an EMT hears a loud yelp. A young boy yells that he's been stung. He shows signs of anaphylaxis and indicates the area where he was stung. The EMT inspects the area and finds a small but evident stinger lodged in his skin. Which of the following should the EMT NOT do?
    a. Inquire if the boy has any epinephrine.
    b. Place the patient in supine position.
    c. Remove the stinger with tweezers.
    d. Swipe away the stinger with a credit card.

Books

26. A 40-year-old female patient presents with jaundice, yellowing of her eyes, and abdominal pain. After the EMT supports and maintains her ABCs and obtains her SAMPLE and OPQRST histories, she confesses to the EMT that she's an IV heroin user. Which of the following diseases does the patient most likely have?
a. Hepatitis A
b. Hepatitis B
c. Hepatitis D
d. Hepatitis E

27. Which of the following hormones is primarily responsible for regulating metabolism?
a. Insulin
b. Testosterone
c. Adrenaline
d. Thyroid hormone

28. Which of the following signs and symptoms are characteristic of Cushing's syndrome?
a. Moon-shaped face, weight gain, and fat accumulation in the back and shoulders
b. Extremely high fever (106 °F or above), hypotension, and goiter
c. Hyperkalemia, darkening of the skin, and hypoglycemia
d. Deep and labored breathing, vomiting, abdominal pain, and unconsciousness

29. A cluster of capillaries that functions as the main filter of the blood entering the kidney is known as which of the following?
a. The Bowman's capsule
b. The loop of Henle
c. The glomerulus
d. The nephron

30. Which of the following STDs, if left untreated, is the most common cause of pelvic inflammatory disease (PID)?
a. Bacterial vaginosis
b. Genital herpes
c. Gonorrhea
d. Chlamydia

Answer Explanations

1. C: Stroke is caused by a loss of brain function, leading to difficulty speaking, loss of speech, difficulty understanding speech, and weakness or numbness in the face and limbs, particularly on one side of the body. Signs and symptoms of seizures include convulsions and muscle rigidity, so Choice *A* is false. Hypothyroidism is characterized by fatigue, lethargy, slow mental function, and waxy appearance, making Choice *B* incorrect. Cushing's syndrome is associated with weight gain and fat accumulation; therefore, Choice *D* is false.

2. B: An EMT must always check, support, and maintain a patient's airway, breathing, and circulation, as well as inquire about medical history and events leading to the emergency, making Choice *B* the correct answer. Not all emergency medical situations will result in shock, nor will a tourniquet always be necessary.

3. A: Visceral pain is caused by stimulation to an organ's nerve fibers due to stretching of the organ's wall, so Choice *A* is the correct answer. Parietal pain is caused by irritation to the parietal peritoneal wall, making Choice *B* false. Referred pain occurs when a radiating pain is felt elsewhere than the point of origin, so Choice *C* is also false. Somatic pain is caused by injury to the bones, muscles, skin, and connective tissues, making *D* incorrect as well.

4. C: The organs found in the lower-right quadrant of the abdomen are the appendix, small intestine, and female reproductive organs. Kidney stones are felt more in the back and side, as the kidneys are located in the retroperitoneal space, making Choice *A* false. Food poisoning is usually felt in the stomach and intestinal area and usually presents with nausea, vomiting, and diarrhea; therefore, Choice *B* is incorrect. The urinary bladder isn't found in the lower-right quadrant of the abdomen, so Choice *D* is incorrect. A key symptom of appendicitis is pain in the lower-right quadrant, making Choice *C* the correct answer.

5. B: The only way that an EMT can perform an abdominal exam is with the patient lying face up, known as supine position. Having the patient lie prone, or face down, makes an abdominal exam impossible, so Choice *B* is the correct answer. Every other choice is correct for the appropriate way to perform an abdominal exam.

6. C: Based on the description of the signs and symptoms, one can conclude that the patient is suffering from anaphylaxis, meaning that she will require a shot of epinephrine, making Choices *A* and *D* both incorrect. Because the patient is 40 years old, she will need 0.30 mg of epinephrine, the correct adult dose; therefore, Choice *C* is the correct answer. Choice *B* is incorrect, because 0.15 mg is the dose for a pediatric patient.

7. A: Tuberculosis is an infection of the lungs that causes a persistent cough, night sweats, and hemoptysis, or coughing blood. It's transmitted via coughing, making Choice A the correct answer. Meningitis is transmitted through saliva and contaminated hands and presents with none of the stated symptoms, so Choice *B* is incorrect. Choice *C* is false because coughing blood isn't a common sign or symptom of pneumonia, and Choice *D* is incorrect because influenza presents with fever, muscle aches, chills, and respiratory problems.

125

8. D: Choices *A*, *B*, and *C* are procedures that an EMT must perform during an infectious emergency response; however, the EMT must always protect themselves *first* with protective equipment in order to prevent the disease from spreading, making Choice *D* the correct answer.

9. D: The primary function of the endocrine system is to maintain homeostasis, which means it makes constant adjustments to the body's systemic physiology to maintain a stable internal environment. Homeostasis requires an adequate heart rate, respirations, and water and electrolyte balance, as well as many other physiological processes; therefore, Choice *D* is the correct answer. The other answers are false because they represent only one aspect of homeostasis.

10. C: The pancreas functions as an exocrine gland because it secretes enzymes that break down food components. It also functions as an endocrine gland because it secretes hormones that regulate blood sugar levels. The kidney isn't a gland; it is an organ located directly below the adrenal glands. The stomach is an organ that contains exocrine glands that secrete hydrochloric acid. Like the kidney and the stomach, the spleen is an organ, not a gland. Therefore, the only correct answer is *C*.

11. B: Hypothyroidism is caused by too little thyroid hormone, which regulates metabolism, causing a hypoactive metabolism and leading to a waxy and swollen appearance, cold intolerance, hypothermia, hypotension, and bradycardia. Hyperthyroidism is caused by an excess of thyroid hormone and causes a hyperactive metabolism, resulting in weight loss and loss of appetite, so Choice *A* is incorrect. Diabetes is caused by an issue with insulin production or utilization and blood glucose imbalance, and the signs and symptoms are frequent urination, increased thirst, and excessive hunger, so Choice *C* is false. Choice *D* is incorrect because Addison's disease is caused by too little cortisol and aldosterone production, leading to hyperkalemia, darkening of the skin, and hypoglycemia.

12. A: A hyperglycemic crisis is characterized by too much blood sugar, which can lead to a patient's breath smelling fruity because of blood that passes through the lungs. Choice *B* is false because DKA doesn't cause edema, so there would be no swollen legs and feet. Choice *C* is false, as buffalo hump is a symptom of Cushing's disease. Choice *D* is incorrect, as a patient with DKA would present with deep and labored breathing, as opposed to shallow breathing.

13. B: A situation in which a patient may harm themselves or others—including attempted suicide, depression, and substance abuse—is classified as a psychiatric emergency, so Choice *B* is correct. Toxicology deals with poisons, toxins, and substance abuse, so a toxicological emergency involving drugs and alcohol may also be categorized as a psychiatric emergency, but not always. Hematology involves blood-related emergencies, and immunology involves allergic reactions, so Choices *A*, *C*, and *D* are incorrect.

14. A: An emergency involving a strange odor and several unconscious people is indicative of an airborne poisoning, making this a toxicological emergency. Psychiatric emergencies involve mentally unstable patients, hematological emergencies are blood-related emergencies, and immunological emergencies involve allergic reactions. Nothing within the question indicates mental instability or bleeding, and it is unlikely that multiple patients have the same allergy, hood that multiple patients have the same allergy is unlikely, so Choices *B*, *C*, and *D* are incorrect.

15. C: Sickle cell disease is most common in African Americans, and due to the abnormal shape and size of the blood cells, the liver cannot properly filter them, causing jaundice and yellowing of the eyes. Priapism results from the blood's inability to exit the erection chambers, becoming trapped and causing a prolonged erection. Choice *C* is the correct answer. Hemophilia is the body's inability to stop bleeding,

and thrombophilia is the body's inability to stop clotting. A urinary tract infection presents with different signs and symptoms than those described, such as painful urination and a frequent urge to urinate.

16. B: The nephron is the structural and functional unit that creates and transports urine. The glomerulus, loop of Henle, and distal tubules are parts of the nephron involved in creating and transporting urine depending on their respective functions, so Choices *A*, *C*, and *D* are incorrect, as they represent only a part of the unit.

17. D: Podocytes are slits that allow filterable components of the filtrate to pass through to the proximal tubule to become urine. Filterable components are water, nutrients, and nitrogenous waste. Non-filterable components are blood cells, platelets, and albumins. Choices *A*, *B*, and *C* are all non-filterable components, making Choice *D* the correct answer.

18. D: The most telling aspect of this man's condition is that he hasn't urinated in two days, indicative of some sort of renal condition, and that he doesn't have a previous history of kidney function loss. Hypertension, tachycardia, and distention of the abdomen imply that urine cannot be formed, increasing blood pressure and causing edema. Acute renal failure is characterized by a sudden decrease in filtration through the glomeruli of the nephron, which causes all of these symptoms, as well as anuria (the complete cessation of urine production), to occur over a period of days or weeks, making Choice *D* the correct answer. Chronic renal failure, Choice *A*, is incorrect because the patient doesn't have a history of renal disease and has none of the signs and symptoms. Kidney stones are crystallized salts that form in the kidney and become trapped in the urinary tract, but they don't stop urine production, so Choice *B* is false. A urinary tract infection doesn't cease urine production, so Choice *C* is also incorrect.

19. C: The uterus and ovaries aren't part of the birth canal, so Choices *A* and *D* are false. The cervix is the uppermost portion of the birth canal, so Choice *B* is incorrect, making Choice *C* the correct answer. The vagina is the muscular tube on the lowermost portion of the birth canal that connects the exterior environment to the cervix.

20. A: A patient with a tubo-ovarian abscess may present with severe abdominal pain, guarding of the abdomen, nausea and vomiting, fever, and abdominal distention. Although abdominal pain is also typical of ruptured ovarian cysts, ovarian torsion, and ectopic pregnancies, those conditions have other signs and symptoms that are different, so Choices *B*, *C*, and *D* are incorrect.

21. A: Because an EMT needs to be completely present and ready for the delivery, an EMT shouldn't monitor the mother (unless there are plenty of EMTs on site); someone else should be stationed at the head of the mother to report any concerning changes. All other answer choices are procedures an EMT must perform in order to ensure a successful delivery, so Choices *B*, *C*, and *D* are incorrect.

22. B: A breech delivery means that the baby is crowning buttocks-first, which can lead to suffocation, so an EMT will need to make a "V" with their fingers and insert them into the vagina in order to keep the airway open for the baby. An exposed limb indicates a limb presentation delivery, not a breech delivery, so Choice *A* is false. An EMT should cover the vagina with a sterile pad and collect expulsions only in the event of a spontaneous abortion, so Choice *C* is also false. If an EMT needs to rupture a sac, it indicates an unruptured amniotic sac, not a breech delivery, so Choice *D* is also incorrect.

23. A: Type 1 diabetes is characterized by the body's immune system attacking its own insulin-producing pancreatic cells, so Choice *A* is the correct answer. Type 2 diabetes is when the pancreas produces

insulin but the body can't effectively utilize it, and it isn't an autoimmune disease like Type 1 diabetes. A hyperglycemic crisis can be caused by either Type 1 or Type 2, and a myxedema coma has nothing to do with diabetes.

24. A: Type 1 diabetes, or insulin-dependent diabetes, is an autoimmune disease that presents itself in early childhood. Type 2 diabetes and non-insulin-dependent diabetes are both names for the same condition, so Choices *B* and *D* are false. Gestational diabetes occurs during pregnancy, not childhood, so Choice *C* is incorrect.

25. C: An EMT should never attempt to remove the stinger with tweezers, as tweezers will squeeze the remaining venom into the skin. Instead, an EMT should remove it with a credit card, so Choice *D* is incorrect. Patients experiencing anaphylaxis will generally need epinephrine, so it's important to ask the patient if they have epinephrine on them, as many EMTs aren't permitted to administer epinephrine, making Choice *A* incorrect. Further, anaphylaxis can cause shock, so the patient should be placed in supine position, making Choice *B* also false.

26. B: All the signs and symptoms are characteristic of hepatitis; however, hepatitis B is specifically caused by sharing needles. As the patient is an IV heroin user, the correct answer is Choice *B*. Hepatitis A, D, and E have different modes of transmission.

27. D: Thyroid hormone is responsible for regulating metabolism, so Choice *D* is the correct answer. Insulin is involved in glucose uptake into tissues, testosterone is for sperm production and secondary male sexual characteristics, and adrenaline is responsible for mechanisms in the fight-or-flight response, making Choices *A*, *B*, and *C* incorrect.

28. A: Cushing's syndrome occurs when the adrenal gland has been too active, producing too much cortisol, which stimulates the pituitary gland to produce too much adrenocorticotropic hormone (ACTH). A patient with Cushing's may present with a "moon-faced" appearance, weight gain, and fat accumulation on the upper back (called a "buffalo hump") as well as in the shoulders and/or the abdomen (called a supraclavicular fat pad). Extremely high fever (106 °F or above), hypotension, and goiter are symptoms of hyperthyroidism, so Choice *B* is incorrect. Hyperkalemia, darkening of the skin, and hypoglycemia are signs of Addison's disease, so *C* is incorrect. Deep and labored breathing, vomiting, abdominal pain, and unconsciousness indicate diabetes.

29. C: A cluster of capillaries that functions as the main filter of the blood entering the kidney is known as the glomerulus, so Choice *C* is correct. The Bowman's capsule surrounds the glomerulus and receives fluid and solutes from it; therefore, Choice *A* is incorrect. The loop of Henle is a part of the kidney tubule where water and nutrients are reabsorbed, so Choice *B* is false. The nephron is the unit containing all of these anatomical features, making Choice *D* incorrect as well.

30. D: While bacterial vaginosis and gonorrhea may lead to PID, chlamydia causes the most cases of PID, making Choice *D* the correct answer. Genital herpes doesn't involve the cervix or uterus, where PID occurs, so Choices *A*, *B*, and *C* are incorrect.

Operations

Maintain Vehicle and Equipment Readiness

EMTs use a variety of vehicles to respond to an emergency, including fire engines, ambulances, and air transport. Some volunteer EMTs even utilize their personal vehicles. No matter the type, the vehicles must be fully functional and able to respond at a moment's notice. This readiness requires consistent and ongoing maintenance.

Communications Readiness

Radio equipment readiness is vital to the safety and operations of EMTs, so that they can communicate with each other and with the dispatching unit.

Equipment Readiness

Preparation entails ensuring that each vehicle is fully equipped with the designated proper inventory. Organizations use a daily ambulance inspection checklist to verify that the appropriate equipment, medications, and supplies are present. The checklist highlights items under the following categories:

- Airway management
- Suction
- Personal protection
- Patient assessment/diagnostic measurements
- Immobilization
- Cardiac management/care
- Obstetrics and gynecology
- Bleeding control and wound management
- Vehicle and receiving facility communication
- Medications
- Transport

The table below provides an example of the types of equipment and supplies needed for services. This list is not all inclusive and is only intended to provide a sample inventory of items.

Category	Equipment or Supply Examples
Airway Management	Pocket masks, bag valve masks, oxygen units, portable oxygen tanks
Suction	Wide bore tubing, bulb suction for infants with saline drops, suction aspirator
Personal Protection	Eye and face protection, disposable gloves, fluid resistant gowns or overalls, disposable biohazard bags for non-sharp waste bags
Patient Assessment/Diagnostic Measurements	Pulse oximeters for pediatric and adult patients, blood pressure cuffs in all sizes, patient care flashlights, scissors to cut clothing
Cardiac Management/Care	Defibrillator with age-appropriate pads
Obstetrics and Gynecology	Sterile obstetrical kit that includes towels, 4x4 dressings, bulb suction, sterile gloves, cord clamps and ties, blanket, thermal absorbent blanket and head cover, heat-reflective material to cover infant
Bleeding Control and Wound Management	Sterile gauze in multiple sizes, gauze rolls, occlusive dressings, sterile water, hypoallergenic and regular adhesive tape
Vehicle and Receiving Facility Communication	Two-way radio frequency communication equipment
Medications	Approved medications such as activated charcoal, Acetaminophen, Albuterol, Aspirin, Diazepam, Epinephrine HCL, Fentanyl, Glucagon, IV electrolyte solutions, Nitroglycerin, Nitrous oxide, Oxytocin, and Sodium bicarbonate
Transport	Pillows, towels, sheets, blankets, stretchers, gurneys, stabilizing instruments
Immobilization	Backboards, cervical collars, head immobilizers, splints
Other Equipment	Continuous positive airway pressure (CPAP) equipment, nebulizer, advanced airways, intravenous (IV) solutions, fluid bag pole or roof hook

Standards and Guidelines

The **Occupational Safety and Health Administration (OSHA)** provides input for ambulance standards, and protects workers by ensuring their work environments are safe. Thus, along with the **National Institute for Occupational Safety and Health (NIOSH)**, they have equipment inventories that identify items such as those listed in the table above.

The **Commission on Accreditation of Ambulance Services (CAAS)** supports efforts to enhance the quality of patient care within the medical transportation system. This committee set many standards for the ambulance industry. Agencies with accreditation by CAAS meet a "gold standard" set by the ambulance service industry.

The agency or organization for which an EMT works will have a protocol that must be followed to ensure proper vehicle and equipment readiness. Additional guidelines may also exist for the city, county, or ambulance district regarding the medications, equipment, and supplies that an ambulance carries. Many of these guidelines require that vehicles remain ready for service and able to respond to the scene of an emergency at any given time.

Vehicle Maintenance

Vehicles should undergo regular cleaning to reduce the growth or spread of contaminants or communicable diseases. EMTs should utilize only approved solutions and practices to clean vehicle surfaces, such as floors and walls.

Next, all vehicles must have a vehicle safety and mechanical inspection. The table below provides a list of common areas that appear on the checklists for a ground ambulance vehicle inspection and mechanical inspection. A failure in any of these items could create problems in transporting patients and EMT staff during emergencies.

Item	Description
Engine	Ensure that it will start
Battery	Review the battery's charge status, fluid level, and connections
Sirens	Ensure that sirens are audible and functional
Transmission Fluid	Review the fluid level and condition
Power Steering Fluid	Review the fluid level, hose condition, and connections
Brakes	Individually assess the parking and vehicle brake systems to provide a review of fluid levels, condition, and any instance of leaks or wear
Tail Lights	Ensure both tail lights are operational
Headlights	Ensure all headlights are operational
Clearance Lights	Ensure all clearance lights are operational
Emergency Lights	Ensure emergency lights are functional and rotational
Horn	Ensure the vehicle and air horn are functioning correctly
Tires	Ensure all tires have even wear, adequate tread, and are properly inflated
Wheel Bearings	Ensure wheel bearings are properly adjusted and lubricated
Chassis Frame	Ensure vehicle components are secured to chassis frame, wiring is correctly installed, and all interfaces follow established regulatory guidelines for the style of vehicle in use
Suspension System	Check the shocks, springs, and stabilizer bars

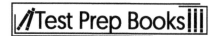

Item	Description
Heating System	Ensure the heating system is functioning, particularly in cold climates
Air Conditioning System	Ensure the cooling system is functioning, especially in hot climates
Fuel Level	Ensure there is an adequate fuel supply
Drive	Ensure the vehicle is able to safely and adequately handle and travel roadways

Operating Emergency Vehicles

The emergency medical technician is responsible for operating emergency vehicles in response to emergency situations, as well as for assisting with non-emergency calls, including those calls seeking transport of patients from hospitals to their home. Non-emergency transportation may also include movement of patients from a local facility to a larger medical center or to a long-term rehab facility.

Emergency vehicles are at an increased risk for being involved in accidents. Common roadway distractions (i.e., cell phones, loud radios, other technology) directly impact how engaged other drivers are on the road and affect how other drivers respond to emergency vehicles. Additionally, many newer vehicles diminish roadway noise, including sirens, which also contributes to the risk that emergency vehicles face. Intersection collisions are among the most common types of crashes that ambulance drivers encounter. Accidents frequently occur when there are multiple-vehicle responses, as non-EMT drivers are not expecting a second or third emergency vehicle.

The inherent function of an emergency vehicle, which often involves traveling at high speeds along an unfamiliar route in a heavy vehicle, poses significant risks in itself. Establishing strategic routes, noting heavy traffic areas and heavy traffic times, and identifying the best route before departure can effectively reduce confusion or anxiety during travel. Driving makes up one component of teamwork among EMTs. The driver's focus should be on the road, while the team member riding in the passenger seat utilizes various forms of technology to assist with travel (i.e., GPS, phones, radio communication, or laptops). The passenger team member can use travel time to gain additional information about the emergency call from dispatch personnel. Drivers must follow the laws of the road to reduce the risk of creating another dangerous scenario. This effort includes maintaining a safe distance between the vehicle and other vehicles on the road and appropriately utilizing the vehicle's lights and sirens. This compliance also includes ensuring that the driver and passengers in the front and back of the vehicle always wear seatbelts.

Providing Scene Leadership

Scene safety is imperative during an emergency. Often, the EMT leader plays a crucial role in determining scene safety and how to proceed in safe and unsafe environments. Therefore, it is important to identify who will serve as lead EMT before arriving at the scene of an emergency. This essential step promotes efficiency and reduces the danger of miscommunication and errors.

The Lead EMT
The lead EMT will give direction at the scene, ensuring safety for the patient and the EMT team. Monitoring progress of multiple teams of emergency personnel may fall to the leader to manage. This

also serves to organize and streamline vital actions that the EMT team takes when assisting the patient. When operating in a small team, the lead EMT may also be responsible for necessary procedures, such as conducting the patient assessment or interviewing witnesses. However, he or she may need to encourage collaboration and exchange of ideas at the scene while also carrying out life-sustaining operations, such as assisting with airway management.

Team Members

Team members should follow the direction of their leader, knowing that each member has a designated role in reducing further risk to the patient. Not only must each member perform their role with proficiency and efficiency, but each member must understand the importance of collaboration and coordination of their efforts with others who are responding to the scene.

During emergency calls, EMTs not only function as a member of a small team or a group of multiple EMT teams, but EMTs can also participate as team members who are supporting other emergency service responders.

EMTs must have an understanding of the roles of each responder at the scene. Other response agencies, including the police and fire departments, may arrive on the site in the case of an emergency. Collaboration is key during these instances.

Assessing the Scene

Upon arrival at the scene, EMTs must quickly assess the environment around them to determine if hazards exist that may create additional challenges for the patient or responders. Examples of hazards include:

- Downed power lines
- Fuel spills
- Chemical spills
- Individual(s) carrying weapons
- Traffic volume
- Signs of fighting
- Aggressive animals
- Darkness or unusual silence in a home

If a scene is not safe, EMTs do not have to initiate rescue actions on behalf of the patient until the environment is safe enough for them to enter. Next, the EMTs should look for indicators of what caused the emergency situation. For example, a patient next to a downed power line may indicate that the patient was electrocuted.

Scene Management

Scene management includes having the capacity to address multiple emergencies as they are unfolding in adverse conditions. EMTs must demonstrate organization and proactivity in swiftly establishing and sustaining scene safety, for rapid stabilization and transport of the patient. Upon arrival at the scene, after assessing their surroundings for any security risks that might impact both the patient and EMT staff, as noted above, EMTs must assess the number of patients requiring attention. Once additional help arrives, EMTs should not leave the scene until the lead EMT gives approval to exit. Leaving a scene before confirming a departure has been permitted can create risk for negligence or abandonment.

Positioning the Vehicle

The positioning of the vehicle at the scene has a significant role in how well EMTs can deliver patient care. Also, the positioning of the vehicle directly impacts the safety of the scene. Positioning vehicles in the emergency lane or on a blocked road supports scene safety. This practice allows for traffic to continue moving in other lanes at a slower pace and may allow for other emergency vehicles to easily arrive on the scene or exit the scene. The goal is to not hamper rescue or treatment efforts.

Sometimes, it may be necessary to utilize a vehicle as a barricade to protect EMT and other emergency personnel on the scene. Barricading is ideal if one is driving a larger vehicle, rather than a smaller one such as a van. The wheels of a vehicle should be in a position that allow for it to roll away from EMT personnel during a rescue event, should the vehicle be struck by traffic.

Emergency vehicles should always be visible to others approaching. Therefore, operators of emergency vehicles should select a convenient place to park—one that presents the least amount of danger or risk to others. Vehicles may require movement to another area. If the movement of a vehicle is required, it is necessary that the operator ensures the occupants are safe inside the vehicle. Once again, passengers must wear seatbelts.

Lighting

Caution is a must for EMT personnel when using headlights after sunset. Headlights facing oncoming traffic can blind the driver coming in the opposite direction and pose a risk for further injury. Also, some studies indicate that red revolving beacons may inadvertently attract intoxicated or exhausted drivers. It is recommended that headlights be shut off, and the amber rear-sealed beam blinkers be used to alert drivers that the vehicle is stopped.

Engaging Bystanders

During an emergency event, family, friends, witnesses, and other bystanders are often present. EMTs should show empathy, but also be careful to not break a patient's confidentiality or privacy while rendering care. EMTs may provide an explanation of what is happening, but must be mindful to not create privacy issues.

Violent Activity at Unsecured Scenes

Violence is a challenging problem that EMTs and other **emergency medical service (EMS)** personnel will likely encounter at some point. It is highly possible that an EMT may arrive at an active crime scene that the telecommunicator did not initially detect or identify. EMTs must report an active crime scene to the telecommunications center upon identification of this situation. EMTs should not remain at an active crime scene if the offender is still present, as this can pose a threat to their safety. Instead, EMTs should retreat from an unsafe scene until it is safe. Often, this requires collaboration with law enforcement teams. When possible and safe to do so, the EMT team should take the patient with them.

Crime Scenes and Preserving Evidence

EMTs should exercise caution and limit their disturbance of a crime scene, as their actions could compromise an active investigation by law enforcement. Adhering to this practice may mean a brief

discussion with EMT personnel to determine how they will enter the crime scene and how many workers at a given time will assist in treating or removing the victim(s).

Hazardous Materials

EMTs will confront incidents in which a single hazardous substance or multiple hazardous materials are present. **The Institute of Hazardous Materials Management (IHMM)** defines **hazardous materials** as any biological, chemical, radiological, or physical agent that can potentially harm animals, humans, and the environment alone or in combination with another substance. OSHA generalizes this definition, identifying that a hazardous material consists of a chemical or substance that presents itself as a physical or health hazard. These substances are detrimental to an individual's health if released (e.g., as a result of spillage, leakage, pouring, emission, disposal, dumping, etc.).

EMTs' Involvement in Hazardous Events

Hazmat (hazardous material) events are dangerous and can impact both the victim and the EMTs arriving on the scene. There are instances in which the EMT will not know that there are hazardous materials in the area. An abundance of alertness and caution should be exercised in scenes where details of what caused the emergency are limited or unknown.

Motor Vehicle Accidents
Materials may be released before the arrival of EMTs, just as they are approaching the scene, or as care is taking place. An example of this is a response to a motor vehicle accident in which one of the vehicles involved is transporting hazardous materials.

Sick Person or Inexplicable Collapse
Initial reports may be vague, such as reporting that someone is sick or collapsed, without providing further details.

Suicide Attempts
EMTs may be at risk of exposure to hazardous materials during suicide attempts when carbon monoxide or gas asphyxiation may have been used by the victim.

Civil Disturbance
EMTs may have to respond to a civil disturbance in which hazardous materials were used, such as drugs or other chemicals. Signs of hazardous materials may not be obvious, or there may be a delay in reactions, or a secondary release.

Although some events will only impact a small group of people, other events will be widespread in nature, leading to a loss of multiple lives. Upon arrival at the scene, hazardous materials signs and vehicles should serve as a warning of the presence of a hazmat team.

EMTs are not necessarily expected to "manage" the hazardous event. They may, however, have an active role in notifying other people of the event and assisting in the overall control of the scene itself. EMS agencies have a responsibility to ensure staff has adequate training and can effectively engage other agencies that may arrive on the scene.

Role of the EMT at a Hazmat Event

First responders to a hazardous scene must complete basic, vital steps. The role of the EMT at a hazmat event is to complete the following tasks:

- Assess for environmental activities and the potential effect on patient care
- Assess the adequacy of available resources
- Notify the proper authorities

If the EMT is the only one on the scene upon discovering a hazardous material, proper notification of various authorities is essential. Necessary notifications include:

- Law enforcement
- Fire department
- Hazardous materials response personnel
- Public works
- Water and sewer department (for runoff)

Ideally, EMTs should park uphill from leaking hazards and one-hundred feet from wreckage. They should set the parking brake to reduce the risk for rollaway accidents involving the emergency vehicle.

Collaborative Operations with the Hazardous Materials Team

EMTs will process personnel who wear protective chemical clothing through medical evaluation before and after decontamination duties. Decontamination must occur to prevent the contamination of others beyond the scene. It is important to note that EMTs should not transport a patient without first ensuring decontamination has taken place. Isolation of the victim is critical until he or she undergoes an evaluation and is eligible for transport or release.

Zones of Operation for EMTs

EMTs operate within what is known as the **cold zone**—the space in which there is no contact with hazardous materials. The **warm zone** duties fall to those specialists capable of performing the decontamination procedure. Meanwhile, hazmat officials function within the actual **hot zone**.

An EMT's Role in a Hazardous Materials Emergency

Conditions that EMTs will commonly treat at the scene of a hazardous materials emergency include:

- Airway injuries related to thermal or chemical burns
- Poison ingestion
- Chemical and biological exposure
- Lacerations or punctures associated with projectiles
- Frostbite

EMT leadership means being able to react at a moment's notice, should the safety of the scene suddenly decline. The lead EMT's concern is not only for the safety of the patient, but also for the safety of other EMTs.

Standard Precautions

EMTs should follow standard patient precautions once the scene is secure. When working with patients, wearing gloves is essential, as doing so reduces the risk of spreading communicable diseases. Handwashing protocol also remains in place.

Protective eyewear may be necessary in cases where blood or other bodily fluids are present. A **high-efficiency particulate air filter (HEPA) mask** may also be an option if an EMT confronts a patient who is coughing, which can spread an airborne illness such as tuberculosis.

Finally, EMTs should maintain their personal immunization records and routine health examinations. This self-care contributes to the EMT's ability to remain healthy and able to work during emergency situations, and prevents patients from contracting disease from the responder.

Air Medical Service

Air medical service utilization takes place for medical, operational, and rescue reasons. If an EMT participates in supporting air medical transport, he or she should be familiar with the local protocol. For example, helicopter transports require the availability of a 100 × 100 foot area free of wires, trees, people, and other loose objects in order to land. This clearance must also be free of slopes with angles greater than eight degrees. Helicopters have very specific areas where it is safe to approach them, and therefore, EMTs should familiarize themselves with the danger areas of a helicopter, for instance, the tail rotor. The helicopter crew will direct patient loading, and EMT staff should follow the guidance of the helicopter crew during this operation.

Helicopter Danger and Approach Areas

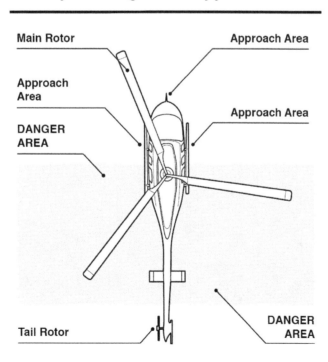

137

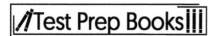
The following shows the proper way to approach a helicopter:

Approach to a Helicopter

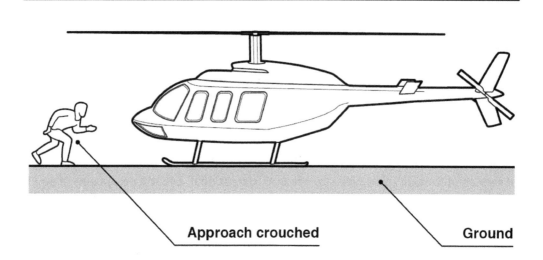

Approach crouched   Ground

Approach to a Helicopter on a Hillside

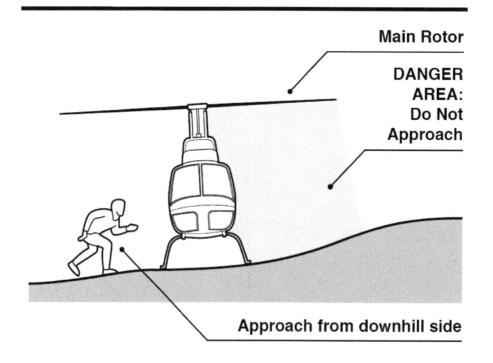

Main Rotor

DANGER AREA: Do Not Approach

Approach from downhill side

Communication at Scene of an Emergency

Emergency scenes can be chaotic in nature. Emergency responders must remain composed during an emergency so that they can effectively communicate with their team and the patient; they must also be able to carry out their tasks in an objective manner. There may also be bystanders, such as the victim's family, who might require emotional support from EMTs. Witnessing an accident or collapse can be a traumatizing experience for some people; therefore, EMTs should be prepared to wear many hats in these situations.

Rural Areas

Rural areas may present a challenge for EMS for a variety of reasons. For example, rural crews may encounter the difficulties of working with equipment that is old, may be unable to quickly reach the scene, or may be unable to gather adequate information about the scene before arrival. Communication may be further hampered due to dead spots along the route, which impact radio transmission, cell service, and other methods of gathering information. Each of these are challenges that EMTs must consider when supporting rural communities.

Resolving an Emergency Incident

The **National Association of Emergency Medical Technicians (NAEMT)** states that it is important to immediately report incidents as they occur, so as to reduce the risk of repetition in the future. Also, reporting mistakes as they happen can improve patient safety. Finally, communication about an incident reduces the risk for legal action by the affected party.

The Patient Safety Act

The **Patient Safety Act** provides EMS organizations and staff with the ability to gather information about safety events. The Patient Safety Act also allows and encourages EMS practitioners to voluntarily report safety incidents.

Providing Emotional Support

During the interview process following an emergency, it may be necessary for EMT staff to provide emotional support to family, friends, witnesses, or coworkers. In these instances, EMTs will have to demonstrate a level of empathy. EMTs should remember to take care of themselves as well, keeping an eye out for signs of stress and burnout. Everyone copes differently with stressful work environments. A physically, emotionally, and mentally healthy EMT is able to provide the best level of care for a patient in need.

Maintaining Medical/Legal Standards

It is expected that EMTs will adhere to guidelines of practice associated with their license and certifications, which mandate their scope of practice. Responders are expected to adhere to their state's standards (note that standards vary by state) to ensure adequate protection of the patient and the EMT. The **Medical Practice Act** permits medical directors or physicians to delegate certain procedures to EMS personnel. EMTs are held to a standard of care that dictates how someone with their training should perform, given a situation or circumstance, using similar equipment.

There are multiple organizations that contribute to establishing these standards of care, including:

- The American Heart Association (AHA)
- American Ambulance Association (AAA)
- National Association of Emergency Medical Technicians (NAEMT)
- State Department of Health
- Department of Transportation

Also, regional systems may dictate standards of care.

Avoiding Negligence

Negligence is the failure to demonstrate the care that a reasonably sensible individual would exhibit in a given situation. Failure of an EMT to adequately perform their duty may leave the responder open to a lawsuit. The table below provides a summary of types of negligence and descriptions of each.

Type of Negligence	Description
Simple (Ordinary) Negligence	Simple or ordinary negligence is not gross nor is it malicious in nature, but does define a failure to follow the ordinary care protocol
Gross Negligence	Gross negligence occurs when there is a complete disregard or concern for others' safety
Comparative Negligence	Comparative negligence occurs when the plaintiff is partially responsible for injuries to himself or herself
Criminal Negligence	Criminal negligence takes place when the deviation from the standard of care is so great that it leads to detrimental, often preventable, risk or death

To prove negligence, a patient must have evidence that demonstrates the obligation to care exists, a breach of duty regarding the standard of care occurred, an injury was the consequence, and that the breach of duty led to the injury:

- Duty to Act on Behalf of the Patient: Patients must establish that a necessary duty existed to provide care to the patient in a reasonable capacity.

- Breach in the Standard of Care: Patients must be able to show that there was a failure to act on their behalf at a reasonable level by the EMT; a standard of care was not met.

- An Injury Occurred: There must be evidence or a demonstration that there was an injury or tangible harm to the patient.

- The Breach Caused the Injury: Patients must demonstrate that the breach of duty was a direct cause of their injury. EMTs are at risk for accusations of abandonment or negligence if they terminate care without a patient's consent or without the establishment of continuing care from another resource.

Abandonment

Abandonment occurs when EMT professionals terminate patient engagement and services without an adequate reason. Transferring a patient's care to someone with fewer skills than the EMT, for example, is abandonment. Examples of abandonment include failure to transport a patient or transferring care to a less capable professional.

Libel

Libel is the defamation of someone's reputation—through written or other media forms—using false statements. During the documentation process, EMTs must ensure that their documentation remains objective in nature—that is, not subjective. Patient history and assessment findings are examples of objective findings. For example, documenting that someone "looks under the influence" could be categorized as subjective information and thus, as libel. The table below provides additional examples of libel.

Libelous Statements
Documentation of the following in a patient's chart, with libelous statements in boldface:
"The patient continues to slur his words and **appears to be drunk.**"
"**The patient appears to be schizophrenic.** He kept yelling at EMT Jones each time he tried to apply a dressing to the right forearm."
"Patient reported feeling dizzy and light-headed. **It was clear that she was faking these symptoms to get attention from her family.**"

Slander

Slander is the verbal defamation of someone's name or character in which a false statement is made that may prove harmful to the individual's reputation or that of their family. It is rife with malicious intent and disregard for the damage that the false statements might cause. Slander qualifies as a tort or civil wrong, which can form the basis for a lawsuit.

Consent

EMTs must obtain **consent** from a competent adult or emancipated minor who is not classified by the courts as being medically incompetent to deliver care or to transport a patient to the hospital. Competent patients are lucid, able to understand instructions, follow commands, answer questions, and understand treatment recommendations. Also, a competent patient understands the consequences of their actions. Consent enables patients to formally make decisions about the care they are about to receive, as detailed in the table below.

Consent
Patients who grant consent understand:
The presence of injury and illness
Treatment recommendations
Potential benefits, risks, and dangers of treatment
Treatment alternatives
The potential adverse outcomes of refusing treatment or transport

Transporting a competent patient against their will to the hospital could lead to assault and battery charges against EMTs. **Assault** occurs when a person experiences fear of bodily harm without giving consent. **Battery** occurs with the unlawful touching of a person.

Implied Consent

Consent can be *implied* in those instances in which patients are not able to express their wants, such as when they are in an unconscious state. Failure to obtain consent prior to transport of a patient can create a liability, leaving an EMT at risk for accusations of kidnapping, false imprisonment, or bodily harm. Thus, EMTs must ensure and document that the patient is physically, emotionally, or mentally incapable of granting consent.

Reasonable Force

EMTs may use *reasonable force* to manage or control a disorderly or violent patient to prevent injury or harm to the patient, other EMT staff, or others on the scene. Excessive force creates the risk for lawsuits, therefore EMT staff must tread lightly when using force or restraints on combative patients.

Actual Consent (Informed or Expressed)

Actual consent, also known as *informed* or **expressed consent**, is consent that is given by an individual who is legally and mentally capable of making decisions pertaining to their health and well-being prior to treatment. The patient understands the extent of the care they are to receive, including the risks and benefits of the procedure. Patients do have the right to revoke their consent at any time during treatment or transport.

Involuntary Consent

Involuntary consent is the treatment of an adult against that patient's will and may take place only under the following conditions:

- A magistrate orders treatment
- A peace officer or corrections officer orders treatment for a patient under arrest or in custody

142

It is important to note that a competent adult who is under the custody of police does not lose the right to give consent or make their own decisions about medical treatment. Involuntary consent should only occur in the case of an emergency to save a life or limb.

Minors' Consent

Individuals under the age of 18 years of age are **minors**. They are not an **emancipated minor** (an adult) per the court. Parents, guardians, or other adults who have a close relation to the child may provide actual consent. Implied consent applies in those instances in which there is a life or limb threat, or any parental refusal of treatment. As with adults, mentally competent parents and guardians have the right to refuse care for their child. They, too, should receive information about the risks, benefits, treatments, and alternatives for care. If the parent or guardian still refuses care, EMTs must attempt to obtain their signature, or that of a witness, prior to leaving the scene.

Consent for Emancipated Minors

As noted above, emancipated minors are adults. Emancipated minors are persons under the age of 18 who are legally independent of any biological or non-biological guardians, therefore they can declare decisions about their health care without the input of another person. They may be married, pregnant, or a member of the armed forces who live independently without adult supervision. It is this qualification as an adult that gives them the right to give informed consent.

Withdrawing Consent

Competent adults may choose to **withdraw consent** for transport or treatment after care is underway. Their refusal of care, however, must be an informed refusal.

Refusal of Care or Transport

There is a chance that the patient may refuse care or transport. The EMT should assess if the individual refusing care is mentally and physically competent to make this decision and understands the possible significance of refusing care. It is within the rights of mentally competent adults to refuse treatment. The EMT must inform the patient of the risks, benefits, potential treatments, or alternatives. Finally, if the patient still refuses care, the EMT must document the refusal and obtain a signature from the patient or witness that validates the patient's refusal of care. If the patient refuses to sign the form, the EMT must also document this refusal. Should a patient refuse transport or care, EMTs may say one of the following statements (or something similar) to the patient:

- "You can call 911 at any time for assistance, should you change your mind."

- "If your symptoms worsen or you do not feel better, you can contact 911 for help. An ambulance will come to pick you up and take you to an emergency room."

Some patients may decide to accept only a portion of the treatment recommendation and refuse the remainder of the treatment plan. It is up to the EMT to discuss the risks that may accompany partial treatments, document the patient's refusal of the treatment, and obtain the signature of the patient or a witness. Witnesses can include law enforcement or other emergency service professionals who are present on the scene.

Good Samaritan Laws

Good Samaritan laws provide protection for those who perform an act in good faith to achieve a standard of care. This protection includes tending to those who are suffering from injury, illness, or who are in need of rescue. The intention of this law is to reduce the degree of fear of would-be rescuers who fear legal retaliation for unintentional injury or wrongful death that might result from a mistake while rendering care. The ideal candidates for these laws are those who do not have a duty to act on behalf of someone suffering from injury or at risk of death (such as a bystander or passerby).

However, many states do have similar laws to provide legal protection for EMTs as well. Some states, like California, provide legal protection to all EMS providers who are acting under the scope of healthcare employment. Other states, like Virginia, provide additional legal protection to government, non-profit, and volunteer EMS personnel only. A number of states distinctly mention that this immunity is provided to responders who are acting without compensation, but are ambiguous regarding off-duty EMTs. Therefore, knowing the specific immunity laws (and noting the exact wording) for the state in which an EMT is licensed is important.

Confidentiality

Patient confidentiality promotes the security of a patient's medical and personal health information. The practice of **confidentiality** means that there is a protection in place that prevents the sharing or distribution of a patient's medical history, assessment findings, or treatment. **The Health Insurance Portability and Accountability Act (HIPAA)** requires medical professionals to protect the privacy of patients as it pertains to their medical treatment and other personal health information. Information exchange is limited strictly to those involved with the patient's care. HIPAA violations incur risk of civil and criminal penalties.

Patient confidentiality is vital. Confidentiality guarantees patient privacy and gives testimony to an EMT's professionalism. The release of patient information should only take place under the following conditions:

- To support continuity of care efforts
- To support law enforcement operations
- To fulfill a third-party billing requirement
- When under subpoena
- When patient consents to release information (patient signs consent)

EMTs are at risk for accusations of invasion of privacy if they release confidential information about a patient without legal justification.

Patients may review their records or request copies of their records. They also have the right to restrict who has access to their health records, thus requiring providers to communicate with them only (excluding the instances listed above).

Reporting Requirements

There are a few circumstances where a medical professional may share a patient's confidential information. Events that require reporting include the birth of a child, child abuse, elder abuse, sexual assault, injury due to felony, injuries that occur because of drugs, or death. Finally, EMTs may share

144

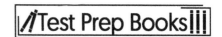

patient information with emergency room staff such as nurses and doctors. EMTs must be careful to avoid accusations, by presenting information in an objective manner.

The table below provides a brief overview of the reporting requirements for different scenarios:

Situation	Actions
Crime Scene	EMTs should survey the scene, document what they observe, be careful to not disturb the scene, and report findings to law enforcement
Child Abuse	EMTs must report child abuse observations to law enforcement, treating physicians, and child protective services
Sexual Assaults	EMTs must report the assault to law enforcement, with the permission of the patient, and retain evidence
Death	EMTs should document their findings and contact the coroner and law enforcement without disturbing the scene

Inappropriate release of a patient's medical information can lead to a lawsuit against the EMT, under the category of libel or slander. EMTs found guilty must pay financial damages to the patient.

Professional Development

EMTs may participate in refresher courses to reinforce or update their skillset. Also, EMTs may pursue continuing education opportunities in a variety of settings, including online classrooms, local colleges, or universities. Continuing education courses are a wonderful way to build knowledge and keep up with the evolution of healthcare.

Practice Questions

1. Which level of consent takes place if a patient is unconscious during delivery of care?
    a. Implied consent
    b. Expressed consent
    c. Actual consent
    d. Informed consent

2. When can a minor give consent for their own care?
    a. All minors under the age of 18 can give consent for their own care.
    b. Only emancipated minors can give consent for their own care.
    c. Only minors between the ages of 16 and 18 can give consent for their own care.
    d. Minors can only give consent for care in the presence of a guardian or parent.

3. An EMT who hands off care to someone with a lesser skillset or licensure level may be accused of which of the following?
    a. Assault
    b. Abandonment
    c. Exposure
    d. Desertion

4. If a competent patient refuses transport to the hospital and the EMT takes the injured party to the hospital against that person's will, the EMT is at risk for which of the following legal charges?
    I. Assault
    II. Battery
    III. Kidnapping
    a. Choice I only
    b. Choices I and III
    c. Choices II and III
    d. All of the above

5. Who can give consent for minors not emancipated by the court?
    I. Parents
    II. Guardians
    III. Adults who are close to the minor in relationship
    a. Choice I only
    b. Choice II only
    c. Choices I and II
    d. All of the above

6. Which of the following is an example of when involuntary consent MIGHT take place?
    a. The parent of a minor gives consent for care.
    b. A magistrate orders treatment for a prisoner.
    c. A patient is unconscious.
    d. A prisoner previously gave expressed consent for treatment two months ago following injury and is still being treated.

7. When should EMTs decide who will be the leader on the scene of an emergency?
   a. There does not need to be a leader at the scene.
   b. Whoever drives to the scene is automatically the leader.
   c. The leader should be determined prior to arrival at the scene.
   d. The passenger EMT is always the designated leader at a scene.

8. How might an EMT offer support to a witness of an emergency?
   a. Offer empathy
   b. Avoid any show of emotion
   c. Remain objective
   d. Share subjective advice

9. Which of the following terms refers to subjective documentation in a patient's chart that may prove harmful to a patient's reputation?
   a. Slander
   b. Libel
   c. Negligence
   d. Informed confidentiality

10. What type of force may an EMT use to prevent a patient from harming themselves?
    a. Lawful force
    b. Reserved force
    c. Reasonable force
    d. Force with justification

11. During an air medical transport, what should EMT staff do?
    a. Take the lead in giving directions at the scene
    b. Approach the helicopter from the rear of the aircraft
    c. Follow the lead of the air transport crew
    d. Disregard local protocol for air transports

12. On the way to or from a scene, ambulances are involved in which types of crashes most often?
    a. Rear-end crashes
    b. Intersection collisions
    c. Ambulance rollover crashes
    d. Crashes resulting from brake failures

13. What should EMTs do if a scene is not safe?
    a. EMTs should render care even if they suspect a scene is not safe for entry.
    b. EMTs should render care once they notify local law enforcement.
    c. EMTs should render care once they activate additional emergency services from surrounding towns.
    d. EMTs have the right to not enter a scene that appears to be unsafe.

14. How frequently should EMTs assess vehicle readiness?
  I. Daily
  II. After emergency care is provided
  III. Only as needed
  a. Choice I only
  b. Choice II only
  c. Choice III only
  d. Choices I and II

15. When can patients be transported during a hazardous event?
  a. Before decontamination
  b. After decontamination
  c. During decontamination
  d. Decontamination is not a necessity for transport to a medical facility

Answer Explanations

1. A: Implied consent is an acceptable form of consent for someone who is unconscious and unable to speak, or to sign a form granting consent to receive care or transport to a facility. Actual consent, which is also known as informed or expressed consent, is attainable from a patient who is alert, awake, knowledgeable, and mentally capable of making decisions.

2. B: An adult must be present to make decisions regarding a child's medical care unless the child is an emancipated minor. Emancipated minors are individuals under the age of 18 who are legally independent of any biological or non-biological guardians. Because of this, they can declare decisions about their health care without the input of another person.

3. B: EMTs should not release a patient to a lower level of care or to someone who is less skilled than they are because it may create risk for the patient and opens the EMT up to legal risks. The term for such an activity is abandonment because the EMT is leaving the patient with someone who more than likely will not be able to provide the same quality of care.

4. D: EMTs must be careful in transporting a patient to a medical treatment facility against their will or ignoring their refusal to receive care. This action is the equivalent of kidnapping, assault, and battery in the eyes of the law. Thus, all of these choices are correct.

5. D: Consent for minors should be given by a close adult relation, parent, or legal guardian of a minor. Minors or children under the age of 18 are not considered to be legally competent or capable of making decisions about their health care, and they need the guidance or influence of a capable adult who can make decisions on their behalf.

6. B: Involuntary consent occurs when care is given to an adult against their will. In other words, the patient did not agree to accept care from the EMT. However, a legal entity does have the power to make decisions regarding the patient's health care. The remaining options are not valid descriptions of involuntary consent.

7. C: The leader should be determined prior to arrival at the scene to minimize confusion or chaos while allowing for efficiency and effective management of an emergency. Organizations may have rules or policies in place for determining leaders, but the person driving or riding in the passenger seat is not necessarily the leader at the scene.

8. A: Witnesses of an emergency event may require comfort or help understanding what they saw. EMTs may need to offer empathy or compassion to bystanders who participate in the interview process. While EMTs must remain objective in their assessment of a patient, they are permitted to be compassionate. The remaining options listed present a less-than-caring approach to supporting those affected by an emotionally painful or traumatic event.

9. B: EMTs should document only objective findings in their assessment of a patient, withholding subjective assessments. Written information that proves to be damaging to a patient's reputation could leave an EMT liable, as could slander—a verbal defamation of a person's reputation. EMTs should avoid writing words or saying things that could prove harmful to the patient or the patient's family in the public eye.

10. C: There may be a time when patients require some degree of reasonable force to prevent them from unintentional harm to themselves and others. The remaining choices are not terms associated with the removal of a patient with the intention of reducing risk of harm to self or others.

11. C: EMTs should follow the lead of the air transport crew to reduce the risk of errors or further injury to the patient. Approaching an aircraft from the wrong angle or direction can lead to injury or death. A crew member can point out the safer routes of loading the patient into the aircraft. EMTs should familiarize themselves with the local protocol to ensure that the aircraft crew does not receive guidance to land in a dangerous space that could cause further injury to the patient, or injury to the EMTs and transport crew.

12. B: Ambulances may be involved in any of the listed types of crashes, but they are most often involved in collision crashes that take place in intersections. The dangers of intersections include traffic lights, confused drivers, drivers who may not hear the sirens, or multiple vehicles en route to the scene of the emergency crossing paths or running into each other.

13. D: EMTs have the right to not enter a scene that is unsafe for them or the patient, or a scene that might cause harm to others. For example, a scene in which a contaminant is leaking and posing risk to the patient and surrounding area could prove dangerous to the EMTs and create additional risk for a receiving hospital or medical treatment facility.

14. D: EMTs should ensure their vehicles are able and ready to respond to an emergency and transport an ill or injured patient. This ability to sustain a state of readiness requires a consistent schedule. Many organizations use an inventory checklist to ensure that consistent assessment takes place.

15. B: EMTs should not transport patients from the hazardous materials site until decontamination is complete. The goal in following this rule is to reduce the risk for spreading a dangerous contaminant beyond the scene to others.

Index

Long Boards, 84
Loop of Henle, 109, 121, 123, 125
Mechanical Patient Restraint, 85
Mechanism of Injury (MOI), 80
Medical Practice Act, 136
Melanin, 69
Melena, 63
Metabolic Acidosis, 71, 111
Military Anti-Shock Trousers (MAST)/Pneumatic Anti-Shock Garments (PASG), 86
Minors, 140, 143, 146
Mitral Valve, 42, 52
Moderate Diffuse Axonal Injury, 74
Multisystem Trauma, 58, 59, 89, 93
Musculoskeletal Injuries, 68
Mydriasis, 79
Myocardial Contusion, 65
Myocardial Rupture, 65
Myxedema Coma, 104, 120, 124
Nasal Cannulas, 28, 30
Nasotracheal and Nasopharyngeal Suctioning, 30
National Association of Emergency Medical Technicians (NAEMT), 136, 137
National Institute for Occupational Safety and Health (NIOSH), 127
Natural Disasters, 60
Neck, 14, 19, 25, 29, 30, 51, 58, 59, 61, 63, 72, 77, 78, 80, 83, 84, 87, 88, 91, 93, 94, 101, 115
Negative Feedback Loops, 103
Negligence, 130, 137, 144
Nephrons, 109, 111, 119
Neural Processes (Axons), 73
Non-Rebreather Masks, 28
Nuchal Cord, 116
Oblique Fractures, 67, 94
Obstetrics, 95, 112, 113, 126, 127
Occupational Safety and Health Administration (OSHA), 127
Oliguria, 111
One-Way Tricuspid Valve, 42
Open Fracture, 67, 84, 94
Open Pneumothorax, 65
Open Vault Fractures, 75
Open Wounds, 70
Oropharyngeal Suctioning, 30
Orthostatic Hypotension, 49, 63

Osteoblasts, 68
Outer Epidermis, 68
Ovarian, 113, 114, 120, 124
Ovaries, 102, 108, 112, 113, 114, 119, 124
Ovum, 112
Pancreas, 66, 97, 98, 102, 103, 104, 105, 118, 123, 124
Pandemics, 100
Parathyroid Glands, 102, 103
Parietal, 97, 117, 122
Patient Safety Act, 136
Pediatric Patients, 11, 13, 14, 16, 17, 21, 22, 23, 25, 27, 29, 32, 37, 39, 41, 43, 46, 49, 50, 52, 53, 56, 57, 58, 59, 61, 65, 67, 85, 86, 89, 93, 107
Pelvic Inflammatory Disease, 113, 121
Penetrating Trauma, 63, 81, 82
Pericardial Tamponade, 65, 90, 93
Peritoneum, 63, 66, 97, 98
Peritonitis, 62, 66, 98
Phalangeal, 68
Pineal Gland, 103
Pituitary Gland, 102, 103, 104, 109, 125
Plasma, 69, 107
Platelet Plug, 69
Platelets, 69, 107, 109, 119, 124
Pleuritic (Respiratory) Issues, 98
Pneumatic Antishock Garment (PASG), 68
Pneumothorax, 32, 65
Podocytes, 109, 119, 124
Preeclampsia, 49, 55, 57
Pressure Points, 63
Primary Brain Injury, 75
Prolapse of the Umbilical Cord, 116
Proximal Convoluted Tubule, 109
Psychiatric Emergency, 106, 118, 119, 123
Pulmonary Embolism, 18, 27
Pulmonary Loop, 41
Puncture Wounds, 70
Radial Artery, 63
Rapid Extrication, 87, 88
Referred Pain, 97, 117, 122
Reperfusion, 71
Respiratory Syncytial Virus, 27
Retrograde Amnesia, 74
Retroperitoneal Space, 66, 109, 122
Rhonchi, 64

Dear EMT Test Taker,

We would like to start by thanking you for purchasing this study guide for your EMT exam. We hope that we exceeded your expectations.

Our goal in creating this study guide was to cover all of the topics that you will see on the test. We also strove to make our practice questions as similar as possible to what you will encounter on test day. With that being said, if you found something that you feel was not up to your standards, please send us an email and let us know.

We would also like to let you know about other books in our catalog that may interest you.

ATI TEAS

This can be found on Amazon: amazon.com/dp/1637757964

HESI

amazon.com/dp/1637756372

We have study guides in a wide variety of fields. If the one you are looking for isn't listed above, then try searching for it on Amazon or send us an email.

Thanks Again and Happy Testing!
Product Development Team
info@studyguideteam.com

FREE Test Taking Tips DVD Offer

To help us better serve you, we have developed a Test Taking Tips DVD that we would like to give you for FREE. **This DVD covers world-class test taking tips that you can use to be even more successful when you are taking your test.**

All that we ask is that you email us your feedback about your study guide. Please let us know what you thought about it – whether that is good, bad or indifferent.

To get your **FREE Test Taking Tips DVD**, email freedvd@studyguideteam.com with "FREE DVD" in the subject line and the following information in the body of the email:

      a. The title of your study guide.

      b. Your product rating on a scale of 1-5, with 5 being the highest rating.

      c. Your feedback about the study guide. What did you think of it?

      d. Your full name and shipping address to send your free DVD.

If you have any questions or concerns, please don't hesitate to contact us at freedvd@studyguideteam.com.

Thanks again!